BARONESS OF HOBCAW

BARONESS
OF HOBCAW

The Life of Belle W. Baruch

MARY E. MILLER

The University of South Carolina Press

© 2006 University of South Carolina

Cloth edition published by the University of South Carolina Press, 2006
Paperback edition published in Columbia, South Carolina,
by the University of South Carolina Press, 2010

www.sc.edu/uscpress

Manufactured in the United States of America

21 20 19 18 17 16 15 14 13 12   10 9 8 7 6 5 4 3 2

The Library of Congress has cataloged the cloth edition as follows:

Miller, Mary E., 1936–
    Baroness of Hobcaw : the life of Belle W. Baruch / Mary E. Miller.
        p. cm.
    Includes bibliographical references and index.
    ISBN-13: 978-1-57003-655-2 (cloth : alk. paper)
    ISBN-10: 1-57003-655-1 (cloth : alk. paper)
        1. Baruch, Belle Wilcox, 1899–1964. 2. Environmentalists—South Carolina—Biography.
    3. Feminists—United States—Biography. 4. Pacifists—United States—Biography.
    5. Horsemanship—South Carolina. 6. Hobcaw Barony (S.C.)—Biography. 7. South
    Carolina—Biography. I. Title.
    CT275.B47694M55 2006
    975.7'89—dc22
    [B]   2006016885

ISBN: 978-1-57003-959-1 (pbk)

CONTENTS

CONTENTS

ILLUSTRATIONS

ACKNOWLEDGMENTS

No biography is written without a great deal of help and cooperation, and I owe a great debt to many people who shared their memories of Belle Baruch.

Without Ella Severin, resident trustee and director of long-range planning for the Belle W. Baruch Foundation, this book could not have been written. Miss Severin shared her memories, letters, and memorabilia of her fifteen years as Belle's companion and opened the archives of the foundation as well as the doors of Bellefield Plantation and Hobcaw House.

Belle's younger sister, Renee Baruch Samstag, declined to be interviewed as such but shared her memories and admiration of her older sister, answered questions, verified facts, and did meet with me briefly in her New York apartment.

The staff of the Belle W. Baruch Foundation were invaluable in sharing information and suggesting avenues of exploration. George Chastain, executive director of the foundation, and Lee Brockington, historian for the property, were especially generous in exchanging information and resources.

Varvara Hasselbalch Heyd was endlessly patient and generous, speaking openly of her lifelong friendship with Belle Baruch, sharing letters, memorabilia, and invaluable insights. A professional photographer, Varvara also shared photographs of Belle, her family, and friends.

My thanks to Robert Darthez, Christiane Daoudi, and Yvette Bozigian, the children of Jean Darthez, Belle's French groom and dear friend, for their recollections of life at Bellefield Plantation.

Lois Massey, now deceased, shared her diaries and letters and twenty-five years of memories, as did Nolan and Cynthia Taylor, Francena McCants, Prince Jenkins, and Elizabeth Navarro.

James Bessinger Jr. helped me to see the lands and waters of Hobcaw Barony through the eyes of Belle Baruch and introduced me to his father, James Bessinger Sr., who spun tales of Belle and Hobcaw as it was many years ago.

Thanks also owed to Paul Dollfus, Abe Fogle, Anne Johnston, Barbara Donohoe Jostes, Minnie Kennedy, Bill Landsman, Louise Milam, and Inez Alford Villafranca.

1

Paternal Pride and Future Hope

Belle Baruch could outride, outshoot, outhunt, and outsail most of the young men of her acquaintance—not the most desirable attributes for a young lady in the polite society of 1918. For most of her growing years, Belle had been admonished to "act like a lady" and reminded that men did not like to be bested in competition by women. Belle, on the other hand, liked to win and to compete against the best, male or female.

Energetic and restless, she craved adventure and excitement. Not for Belle a sedate trot on a bridle path, but a thundering gallop through the moonlit woods in pursuit of a fox. Not for Belle stately dressage, but the thrill of jumping and the rigors of the steeplechase.

Today her slender height and athletic prowess would merit envy and admiration, but when Belle was introduced to society, her six-foot, two-inch height towered over most of her contemporaries. She moved with the elegance and grace of a perfectly disciplined body, but her solemn brown eyes acknowledged that society's feminine ideal was petite, gentle, curly haired, and flatteringly in need of male assistance and guidance.

Nearly every aspect of heredity and environment created an insurmountable dichotomy in the life of Belle Wilcox Baruch. Her Jewish-Christian, North-South heritage dictated conflicting ethical and social values. Privileges of great wealth were tempered by strict admonitions of social responsibility. Even the era into which she was born in 1899 fostered a duality of spirit in its young women, who were expected to sublimate their independence and talents to the needs of men. For proud, independent Belle, society's expectations were burdensome and frustrating.

Born out of her time, Belle would constantly challenge the strictures of a society that did not allow women to vote, to compete against male athletes, to govern their own destinies, or to live according to their own moral code. She would struggle with the duality of her nature, forging a place in society where she lived according to her own rules.

Independence and determination were the norm for her Baruch ancestors. *Baruch* is the Hebrew word for blessed, and certainly Belle's father, Bernard Mannes Baruch, was blessed with more than his share of worldly goods, charm, and stunning good looks. Bernhard Baruch, Belle's great-grandfather, claimed descent from Baruch the Scribe, secretary to the prophet Jeremiah, and author of the book of Baruch, one of the prophetic books of the Hebrew Bible.

The first Baruch to reach American shores was Belle's grandfather, Simon, a Jewish immigrant who became one of the most respected physicians of his time. Simon Baruch was born in Schwersenz (present-day Swarzêdz) near Poland in East Prussia. Immigrating to the United States in 1855, fifteen-year-old Simon went to the only person he knew there, Mannes Baum, who was from Simon's home village.

The Baum family welcomed Simon, employing him as a bookkeeper in their small general store in Camden, South Carolina. So impressed were the Baums with the personable, industrious young man that they sent him to the South Carolina Medical College in Charleston and thence to Richmond to the Medical College of Virginia. Young Baruch graduated from medical college just after the Civil War began. Though he abhorred slavery, he was loyal to his adopted state, where the first shots of the Civil War were fired. Simon was quickly accepted by the Confederacy as an assistant surgeon, and Mannes Baum presented the young officer with his Confederate uniform and sword.

Baruch was captured twice by the Union army, the first time at the battle of Antietam and again at Gettysburg. Treated with respect as an officer and physician, he was exchanged both times after brief periods of internment. His appreciation for the courtesies of his Union captors no doubt influenced his decision to move north years later. However, he would never lose his intense love and loyalty for the South. Ordinarily a quiet, reserved man, Simon Baruch would leap to his feet with a distinctive, piercing rebel yell whenever he heard the strains of "Dixie." To the embarrassment of his wife, he was even known to do so on one occasion at New York's staid Metropolitan Opera House.

As the circumstances of war permitted, Simon courted the lovely young Isabelle Wolfe, oldest daughter of Sarah Cohen and Saling Wolfe. The Wolfes were a respected Jewish family, well established in South Carolina society. A native of Prussia like Baruch, Saling Wolfe owned several plantations near Winnsboro in Fairfield County. Sarah Cohen's ancestors had come to American shores generations earlier. One of them, Isaac Marks, served in the Continental army. Undaunted by Isabelle's wealth and social position, young Baruch pressed his suit. By war's end, of course, the fabulous wealth of Saling Wolfe had vanished in flames.

Known as Belle to family and friends, Isabelle admired the young doctor and had even painted his portrait. And it was his own image that nearly cost Simon Baruch his bride. When Yankees attacked her father's plantation, Belle tried to hide Simon's portrait, but a Union soldier tore it from her hands and ripped it with his bayonet. When Belle protested, he slapped the defiant southern girl. Belle was rescued by a dashing Yankee captain named Cantine who did not tolerate such behavior from his troops. Cantine captured young Belle's romantic imagination, and after he left, they corresponded.

When Simon Baruch came home from the war, having lost nearly everything, he was determined that he would not lose his love. He quickly reestablished himself in Belle's affections and swept her into marriage.

Now a full surgeon, Baruch returned to Camden and established his medical practice. Though raised in luxury, Belle worked at his side and bore him four sons: Hartwig (1868), Bernard (1870), Herman (1872), and Sailing (1874). She encouraged Simon to leave the Reconstruction South in 1880 and move the family to New York, where he established a medical reputation as a pioneer in hydrotherapy and as the surgeon who first diagnosed and successfully operated upon a case of appendicitis.[1] He was also intensely dedicated to the health needs of the poor, agitating successfully for the establishment of free public baths in large cities. Simon Baruch devoted much of his career to the poor and underprivileged of his adopted country. Late in his life, Baruch declared: "If I did not stand ready to consecrate heart and soul and all that I possess to the defense of my adopted country, I would despise myself as a scoundrel and a perjurer and regard myself as an ingrate to the government which has, for 60 years, enhanced and protected my life, my honor and my happiness." Dr. Baruch bequeathed to his sons and his granddaughter Belle his qualities of intense patriotism and dedication to public service.

Not that Bernard Mannes Baruch, Simon's second son and Belle's father, was thinking of public service when Belle was born on August 16, 1899. One day he would be known as the Wolf of Wall Street and adviser to U.S. presidents from Woodrow Wilson to Dwight D. Eisenhower, but in 1899, one

3

month after Belle's birth, he bought a seat on the New York Stock Exchange for forty thousand dollars, intent on parlaying the million dollars he had already made as an investor into an even greater fortune.

Baruch had started on "the Street" as a runner at age nineteen. By twenty-five he was a partner in a Wall Street firm, but his personal fortune fluctuated wildly as he learned his trade. He had a reputation as a "plunger," and no doubt some of that was due to his intense desire to earn a large enough fortune to wed Annie Griffen. Called Anne by family and friends, the tall, elegant daughter of Benjamin and Renee Wilcox Griffen did not expect such wealth from her handsome suitor, but Baruch had his own expectations.

Anne would wait seven long years to marry Bernard, who struggled in the meantime against two major impediments to the marriage, his fluctuating fortunes and Anne's father. Benjamin Griffen, the grandson of an Episcopalian minister, was part owner of Van Horne, Griffen & Company, glass importers. While he thought highly of young Baruch, he opposed the courtship because Baruch was a Jew. He believed that their religious differences would present an insurmountable barrier to a successful marriage. Fortunately for Baruch, Anne's mother was charmed by the tall, handsome young man, and she both encouraged and helped to conceal their long relationship.

Finally, Baruch made a sixty-thousand-dollar profit—a veritable fortune in the last decade of the nineteenth century—speculating in shares of American Sugar Refining. Gleefully, he telephoned Anne with the exciting news that now they could be married. Somewhat skeptically, Anne replied, "You'll lose it as quickly as you made it." Baruch insisted on speaking to her father that night. Politely but firmly, Benjamin Griffen refused Baruch's suit, stating that the young couple's religious differences were irreconcilable. But Anne was of age and, with her mother's support, she married Bernard Baruch at a quiet ceremony at her family home on October 20, 1897. Her father did not attend.

It was Belle's good fortune to be the first child born of Bernard and Anne's union. Her father had only begun his journey to international renown and financial success. The intoxicating lure of power soon would draw him farther and farther from the family orbit, but when Belle was born, it was still a close-knit circle.

A few days after Belle's birth, Baruch penned a sentimental, rather bad poem to his new daughter, officially christened Isabel:

> Oh Isabel, Oh Isabel,
> The day you first were visible,
> Paternal pride and future hope
> Were centered all in thee.

Oh Isabel, Oh Isabel
We're one and indivisible.
We constitute a family now,
Where there was two, there's three.

By the Poet of the Bourse[2]

Baby Isabel was showered with gifts, including sterling-silver cups, spoons, plates, comb and brush sets, and even gold-and-silver rattles inlaid with mother-of-pearl and ornamented with tiny silver bells. Pearl and diamond pins adorned her silk coats and lace dresses. Included in Belle's baby book is a clipping from the *New York Times* stating that Bernard M. Baruch had been elected to membership in the stock exchange on September 7, 1899.

Although there were nurses and nannies in attendance, Anne Baruch nursed her infant daughter for the first few months, and the baby was the delight of the happy couple and indulgent grandparents. Even Grandfather Griffen mellowed somewhat with the birth of a new granddaughter. On November 1, 1900, at the age of one year, two months, and two weeks, tiny Isabel became the youngest person yet admitted as a member of the Children of the American Revolution.

That Christmas (her second), she was again showered with gifts of money, silver, jewelry, an ermine muff and trimmings for her coat, twenty dollars in gold from Grandfather Griffen, and all the toys and books a child could wish for. Her first word was "papa," and she adored the tall, handsome man. Belle would tell friends how she and her sister and brother would descend upon "papa" in his big bed to roll and tumble and giggle as he arched his long legs into a "bridge" for them to crawl beneath.

Family was important to Bernard Baruch. He revered his parents and loved his brothers. What money he made he shared with them, contributing millions of dollars to universities and hospitals in honor of his father. He was a benevolent, loving, indulgent, and increasingly absent father. As power, prestige, and wealth increased, family time decreased. Days, sometimes weeks and months would pass when the children would not see their father. Knowing that when he thought about them, he did so with love, and he certainly provided abundantly for them, Baruch did not perceive nor really understand the ever-widening emotional gap between himself and his children.

When Belle was three, Bernard Jr. was born. Belle was confused and hurt and did not see what was so marvelous about the so-called heir to the Baruch name. After all, she was a Baruch. What was so wonderful about a boy? And they had even named him after papa! She determined that she could do anything

5

a stupid boy could do, yet do it even better! A sibling rivalry was born that would never end.

Renee was born in 1905, but a new sister did not present much of a problem in Belle's mind. The three Baruch children were not particularly close because each had his or her own nanny and the age gap between the two girls was six years. They had few interests in common until they were grown. They were raised with every luxury. Since they had both a French and German governess, they were trilingual. They had lessons in music, dance, horseback riding, sailing, and tennis. They were also inculcated with stringent rules of behavior. Courtesy and respect for elders were drilled into them. Hair, dress, and fingernails were inspected before dining or going out. Punctuality was expected and the child who was late for dinner did not dine.

With all his millions, however, Baruch could not protect his children from the virulent anti-Semitism of the times. Although Belle and Renee were raised as Episcopalians (Bernard Jr. was to be given his choice of religious faith as he matured), both were denied admission to the exclusive Chapin School that their mother attended. Jews were banned from some of the more exclusive hotels and resorts. They could not join the country clubs of the elite, nor could their children join the Greek fraternities and sororities at the universities. Jews were prohibited from purchasing homes or apartments in certain residential areas and often were ostracized by the wealthy leaders of society.

The Baruch children were blissfully unaware of such bigotry in their early years. Like most children of their social and economic status, the young Baruchs spent most of their time under the protective supervision of a governess and a nanny. Certainly there were large family gatherings, especially among the Baruch relatives, and exciting family vacations. But even on holiday, the Baruch children were attended by governesses and tutors. Their father believed passionately in a classical education, and even extended vacations were not to interfere with the schooling of his children.

Belle was confused, hurt, and bewildered by the gradual diminution of her parents' attention. Anne Baruch, although a reserved and shy woman, was increasingly engaged in the social and charitable events befitting a woman of her elevated social position. Both parents traveled abroad frequently, leaving the children in the care of staff.

Anne Baruch was torn at times between wanting to be with her husband and at home with her children. She was away on Belle's birthday and wrote to her daughter from the Hotel Colorado in Glenwood Springs:

My darling daughter,

You must not think that because I have not written you that I have not thought of you very often. We all mention your name every day, and grandpa is mailing you a book filled with little donkey pictures. . . . We are all very sorry not to be home on your second birthday but tell Auntie Leonora to have Kurrus make you a big cake with 3 candles on it, and the day of the 16th you must cut it yourself. Goodbye, my sweet baby. I hope you will in the future be as much comfort to me as you have been in the past.

With fondest love,
Your devoted mother[3]

Grandfather Baruch composed a special poem for his granddaughter:

ACROSTIC
Written for Belle's birthday
by her Grandfather

Bright as the days you are spending now
E'er may your life with gladness glow.
Love true its woof may around you weave,
Love your dear heart may never leave.

Escape may you from sorrow's sting,
Banish all cares that sadness bring.
And deep within your soul, dear Belle,
Replete with peace, content may dwell.

Until your pure life's waning days,
Crowned are by golden sunset rays.
Heaven's blessings be yours always.

Simon Baruch, M.D.[4]

Margaret Coit, in her biography *Mr. Baruch,* could just as well have been writing about Belle as Renee when she wrote: "Baruch seemed a fabulous and faraway figure, at once the most lovable and the most awe-inspiring of parents. He was always sympathetic toward her small problems . . . and yet somehow, he was a remote and godlike figure who could do no wrong. . . . As a little girl, she would have fleeting memories of her father and mother, fairylike figures sweeping in to say good night, tall and beautiful and glittering with jewels. She could remember the smell of perfume and the sense of excitement, scored by the echo of hasty footsteps, off for a concert or a first night."[5]

Anne Baruch was the disciplinarian and always the bearer of unpopular tidings for the children. If Bernard decided to withdraw some special privilege or refuse a request, mother informed the children. When the children would then plead their case before father, he often would restore the privilege or grant their wishes. "It was a game he played well," Renee recalled, which reflected his almost obsessive need to be universally loved and admired, even by his offspring.

As Belle became aware of her father's wealth and power, she grew intensely private about him, "almost secretive," friends would say. She refused to discuss him and abhorred being sought out because she was Bernard Baruch's daughter. To the young Belle, her parents were now simply "father and mother." As her sister, Renee, expressed it: "They [Bernard and Annie Baruch] were not the kind of people you called mom and dad."

Belle was a busy, inquisitive child, forever exploring and looking for something to do. Energetic, with that fearlessness of physical danger often possessed by young children, she often tried the patience of her nannies and family. There were times of loneliness when she longed for her parents, but her situation was not much different from that of her peers who depended on servants for comfort and affection. Full of curiosity and a zest for living life to its fullest, Belle was generally a happy child. She loved animals and childish adventures, but even her vivid imagination could not have dreamed of the sheer joy and ecstasy that her father's purchase of Hobcaw Barony in 1905 would bring to Belle's life.

2

The Only Real Place on Earth

Though only in his midthirties, Bernard Baruch was a multimillionaire who had always believed that a man needed periods of quiet contemplation. After a major endeavor, he liked to isolate himself and reflect on events to determine what led to their success or failure. He searched for a getaway.

Baruch had always maintained his southern ties, and in 1904, the year his daughter Renee was born, he was invited to visit Sidney and Harold Donaldson at Friendfield Plantation on the Waccamaw Neck in Georgetown County, South Carolina. Baruch was an avid hunter, and the shooting at Friendfield was unparalleled in his experience. He was fascinated with the stories of the original barony and dreamed of recreating the original land grant.

Hobcaw, as the Indians called the area, means "between the waters." The barony was bounded on the east by the Atlantic Ocean, on the west by the Waccamaw River, and on the south by Winyah Bay, wherein empty the waters of the Sampit, Black, Waccamaw, and Great and Little Pee Dee Rivers. The Indians used it as their hunting and fishing grounds. Some historians believe that Hobcaw may be the site of the first ill-fated Spanish settlement in 1526. Until the eighteenth century, the Indians maintained dominion. Then came the English.

John Locke's famous "Grand Model" divided the Carolina colony among the eight lords proprietors in deference to their service to the crown.[1] In 1718 King George I of England granted a barony to John, Lord Carteret, later Earl of Granville. The original property of over twelve thousand acres consisted of maritime and upland forests, cypress swamps, freshwater ponds, oceanfront, and five thousand acres of salt marsh.

Looking at a map of his holdings, Lord Carteret was not impressed, thinking that too much of the land was under water and not tillable. Unaware of the possibilities of rice culture, he sold the barony to John Roberts in 1730. Subsequently, the property was divided, subdivided, sold, and resold several times until eventually rice plantations were established under fourteen different names: Clifton, Forlorn Hope, Rose Hill, Alderly, Annandale, Youngville, Bellefield, Marietta, Friendfield, Strawberry Hill (or Belle Voir), Calais, and Michau. (At one point, William Algernon Alston [1782–1860] split off the seashore tracts of Annandale and Youngville and renamed them Crab Hall. The balance of Annandale became Oryzantia.)

Between 1785 and 1900 the plantations of Hobcaw Barony shared in the era of the great "Rice Princes," when the rice produced in Georgetown County supplied much of Europe and the new colonies of America. William Algernon Alston owned and cultivated several of the plantations that made up the original barony and at one point produced 1.8 million pounds of rice. For over one hundred years the rice plantations flourished, and Georgetown County was one of the wealthiest regions in America.

Then came the Civil War and Reconstruction, plus competition from other newly settled states where rice could be grown without the expensive and labor-intensive system of floodgates and canals required in South Carolina's low-country. Hard times fell on the people of the Waccamaw Neck, and by the beginning of the twentieth century, little but memories remained of the days when the rice culture reigned in the lowcountry.

Enter Bernard Baruch, who shocked his hosts with an offer to buy Friendfield. The property of Friendfield Plantation that the Donaldsons owned incorporated the former plantations of Marietta, the original Friendfield, Strawberry Hill, Calais, Michau, and Cogdell. All of it had been renamed Friendfield Plantation.

Friendfield House, the primary residence, was near the southern tip of the barony on a bluff overlooking Winyah Bay. It was sited on the only piece of property that appears not to have been part of the original barony. In 1711 Alexander Widdicom purchased two hundred acres in what was then Craven County from William Rhett, receiver general of the lords proprietors. Because of its location, it logically would have been part of the barony awarded to Lord Carteret in 1718 had it not already been sold.[2]

What eventually became Cogdell Plantation was near the tip of Waccamaw Neck where an old Indian path reached Winyah Bay. Historians and researchers speculate that Widdicom and/or Rhett chose the isolated tract to trade with either the Indians or the pirates who plied the nearby waters.[3]

After some consideration, the Donaldsons agreed to accept Baruch's offer. Between 1905 and 1907 Baruch bought all but three of the tracts comprising the original grant. Rose Hill, Clifton, and Forlorn Hope had already been purchased by Dr. Isaac Emerson, a pharmacist from Baltimore who developed Bromo-Seltzer, a well-known remedy. He incorporated them into the seven plantations comprising Arcadia Plantation. Baruch named his 17,500-acre retreat Hobcaw Barony.

Baruch was part of what southerners referred to as the "second northern invasion." He and other wealthy Yankees bought extensive properties, mostly for winter hunting and fishing lodges. The advent of the northerners was greeted with ambivalence by native Carolinians. The Yankees provided much-needed jobs and a stronger tax base, but it was difficult to see old and historic properties fall into northern hands. In time, however, Yankee money and civic generosity ensured that many of the vast properties were preserved as private estates or set aside as nature preserves, state parks, recreational areas, and so forth.

Brookgreen Plantation, purchased by Archer M. and Anna Hyatt Huntington, became Huntington Beach State Park and the renowned Brookgreen Gardens. W. H. Yawkey, owner of the Boston Red Sox, purchased White Marsh, South Island, and part of Cat Island. Thomas A. Yawkey, his son, donated most of the property to the South Carolina Heritage Trust to establish the Tom Yawkey Wildlife Center.

Although parts of Arcadia Plantation, especially the beachfront property, have been developed, some of the land remains intact. The plantation house, Prospect Hill, is currently occupied by Lucille Vanderbilt Pate, great-grand-daughter of the Dr. Isaac Emerson mentioned above.

Baruch used Hobcaw Barony primarily as a winter hunting retreat, although some farming was done for his personal use and that of resident staff. He also experimented with rice culture in the 1920s, putting two thousand acres under cultivation. No records remain as to how long he attempted to grow rice or how successful he was. The rice was intended to attract migrating birds. It was never his intent to farm commercially, and most of his crops were either experimental or for personal use.

Friendfield House, affectionately dubbed the "Old Relick," was opened in November around Thanksgiving and usually closed in late April. It was a simple Victorian wood house with a big fireplace in the living room and another in the sunroom that burned logs up to eight feet in length, rag rugs on the floors, red wicker furniture with cushions and pillows gaily printed with flowers and birds, and organdy curtains at the windows. There were Ping-Pong and card tables for after-dinner entertainment. The upstairs bedrooms were spacious and bright with papered walls, ruffled curtains, rag rugs, white painted furniture, and iron beds. There were hot blast stoves in each room and big potbellied stoves warmed the up- and downstairs hallways. Like the surrounding plantations, the front of the house faced the water, overlooking Winyah Bay. In the days when the plantation homes were first built, there were few passable roads; the rivers were the "roads" for the people of the Waccamaw Neck, and the docks served as the reception area for visitors. The stables housed a dozen horses, a mule named By Damn that the children loved to ride, and a goat that pulled a little cart.

To young Belle it was paradise. The thousands of acres contained treasures and wildlife to exceed even her wildest imaginings. With ever-growing enchantment, her child's eyes saw, in their natural setting, white-tailed deer, feral hogs, bobcats, panthers, cougars, raccoons, opossums, squirrels, fearsome alligators, bears, and foxes. There were fascinating, fearsome reptiles: black water moccasins, rattlesnakes, and deadly copperheads.

The trees and swamps housed an endless variety of birds: bald eagles, ospreys, hawks, songbirds, rare species of woodpecker, turkeys, jacksnipe, quail, exotic egrets, ibis, heron, and, of course, the ducks that made Hobcaw one of the most famous hunting retreats in the world. Those privileged to shoot at Hobcaw would say that the sky turned black as the ducks took to the air, "blotting out the sun." Thousands upon thousands took wing and "hundred-duck days" were common, there being no bag limits in those days.

"Captain Jim" Powell, a tall, lanky, tobacco-chewing Carolinian who liked to start the day with a glass of whiskey "to clear the catarrh" before breakfast, was hired by Baruch to help superintend Hobcaw Barony. Though he lacked formal education, he was wise in the ways of men and the land. The Baruch children were like his own to the lowcountry woodsman, and he taught them to shoot and ride, took them fishing and crabbing, and introduced them to the incomparable flavor of shrimp, clams, and oysters fresh from the inlets. A special bond between Belle and the woodsman developed that would remain throughout their lives. She called him "Uncle Sadie," but no one remembers why.

Each day brought new wonders—a spotted fawn crossing the road, turkeys roosting in the trees at dusk, mischievous raccoons hunting for handouts, a mother opossum with babies clinging to her tail. It was Belle who loved the land the most, calling the forests of Hobcaw "the friendliest woods in the world."

Hobcaw for Belle was a magical place, a time out of time. Nothing could have contrasted more sharply with her sophisticated life in New York and along the bustling shores of Long Island and New Jersey where she spent her summers. The streets of New York seemed gray and bare compared to the woods of Hobcaw, with its flowering yellow jessamine, brilliant azaleas, daffodils, water lilies, magnolias, rhododendron, and wondrous array of wildflowers.

Just getting there was a great adventure. The Baruchs traveled by train in their private car from New York to Lanes, South Carolina, where Belle and Junior tussled to see who would be first off the train. Then they jockeyed for position to see who got to sit up front with the driver as they went by horse and carriage nearly twenty miles to Georgetown, where they took a boat to the docks of Hobcaw Barony. There were no telephones at Hobcaw until the mid-1950s. Baruch wanted complete peace and quiet with nothing to disturb the tranquility of the barony. Telegrams and mail were delivered twice a day by boat from Georgetown. If he wanted to call New York or Washington, Baruch went to Georgetown by boat to use a public telephone. Since he was hard-of-hearing, he spoke loudly, and locals recall that people would hang around eavesdropping, hoping to pick up a stock tip or two.

The grounds of Hobcaw were a living history lesson for the eager Baruch children to explore. They traveled the roads of Hobcaw on horseback, buckboard, sulky, carriage, or wagon. Belle could not decide which mode she liked best. The historic King's Highway passed through the heart of the barony. Georgetown was the second oldest settlement in South Carolina, and it was at nearby North Island that Lafayette first stepped ashore in America. Right on the plantation were the remnants of great houses and battlefields. With childish awe Belle poked among the ruins of what was thought to be a British fort. She gazed solemnly at headstones that were rumored to mark the graves of British soldiers killed in Revolutionary War battles with the great Francis Marion, the legendary Swamp Fox. Later, historians identified the site as Confederate earthworks, an unfinished battery from the Civil War era.

At Hobcaw, Belle awoke each day to birdsong. Enchanted, she would lie in her bed listening. Then, needing to act immediately on her thoughts, Belle would dash to the window to gaze out among the trees, curious brown eyes seeking the song makers. She learned to identify the melodies of the thrush, warblers, and marvelous mockingbirds, to know the "peep" of the redbirds and the harsh cries of the quarrelsome blue jays as they squabbled among themselves or with their neighbors. She heard the thrum of the woodpeckers as they signaled their territories and delighted in the tiny Carolina wrens with their yellow breasts. Hummingbirds were everywhere in seemingly perpetual motion.

Jim Powell, for all his responsibilities on the vast estate with its many workers, always found time for Belle's eager questions. Belle would tuck her slender fingers into the big Carolinian's rough, callused hand and listen to the lore of this marvelous land of Hobcaw.

She learned that yellow flies seldom flew before midmorning because they had to wait for the sun to dry the heavy dew from their fragile wings. Hunkering down beside the inquisitive child, Powell would point out the tracks of the deer and the feral hogs, explaining how the hogs always toed in. He could read the fascinating patterns in the sand and dirt, indicating where a rattlesnake had undulated across the sandy road, identifying the sounds that constantly emanated from the woods and swamps, until the symphony of Hobcaw became dear and familiar.

As the years passed, Belle would record her feelings about Hobcaw in the guest book: "Home again!" "The only real place on earth for me . . . a more egoistic feeling than altruistic."[4] Hobcaw was never far from her mind, no matter where she was. The winds across the marshes whispered ancient secrets and implanted the seeds of a passion for this "land between the waters."

Inextricably tied to her dreams of Hobcaw was Jim Powell, who had time and undemanding affection for the tall, gangling girl, something no other adult male in her life offered. Powell taught Belle patience. She learned that if she wanted to see the more elusive, rare birds, she must sit quietly and wait for them to come to her. The woodsman would take Belle into the silent Reserve Swamp where the water was black and deep and the cypress towered overhead, their myriad knobby "knees" breaking the surface to draw oxygen and nourishment. In the spring the swamp glowed with butterweed and blue iris and the magnificent waterbirds that peopled its branches. Ibis, blue and white heron, egrets, and scores of other exotic birds fed in the dark waters and nested in the cypress trees. Water moccasins glided over its still surface, and alligators splashed from the banks into the quiet waters as the adventurers poled their boat through the water. The swamp was silent and mysterious and almost unbearably beautiful.

In bright contrast were the acres and acres of abandoned rice fields, divided by ditches thirty feet wide and twelve to fifteen feet deep, all hand-dug by field slaves in the days of the rice plantations. Belle marveled at the brilliant blue of the indigo buntings as they darted over the fields. The song of the red-winged blackbirds echoed joyously, and she learned that the melody changed with the seasons and that they almost always flew in a fixed triangle with their nests at its center.

Powell would point out the green swards in the midst of the tan fields, explaining that the feral hogs had been rooting there and would have created small pools of water where "puddle ducks" like mallards and pintails would land. "You'd never know as they were there, hidden in the reeds like that, unless you heard them calling," he said. Canvasbacks, on the other hand, liked the open water and hundreds, sometimes thousands, would dot the wide waters of Winyah Bay, feeding on the nearby rice fields. Puddle ducks, Powell opined, were the "best eatin.'"

Belle shuddered in awe at the huge alligator nests set along the shores of the marsh. The 'gators would thrash their huge tails back and forth until they had built a nest of reeds and brush four to six feet high. Then, in its center, they would burrow a deep depression and lay their eggs. The mother didn't lie on the nest but rather beside it, poised to frighten away intruders and predators until the eggs hatched under the warm Carolina sun. Unable to crawl out of the deep nest, the hatchlings would issue frantic little cries, urging the mother to enter the mound and release them into the marsh. Once, a mother 'gator charged from the reeds into the marsh as Belle and Powell passed in their boat. It nearly frightened Belle to death, but Powell laughed and reassured her. "She's just tryin' to scare you off. She won't hurt you none."

Belle would giggle at the antics of the anhinga, or snakebird, a species of waterfowl that swam below the water to hunt for its food. Locals had so named them, seeing only their snakelike black heads darting through the water's surface as they emerged from a hunting dive.

The best fishermen and aerialists, Belle decided, were the ospreys who would drift on the currents of air above Winyah Bay, suddenly folding their wings in a plummeting dive, talons extended to snare their prey. Spreading their powerful wings like a parachute just before hitting the surface, they would rise into the sky, a helpless fish secure in their talons, and fly off to their nests harbored in the tall cypress trees or atop the channel markers in the rivers and bays.

The children loved to go to Clambank, where the oysters and clams were abundant. Asked why they called it Clambank, the old hands would say, "'Cuz it's always been called that" or "'Cuz thas where the clams grow," but others say it's because that was the spot where the fresh oysters, clams, shrimp, and other seafood were stored or "banked" until the folks at the "big house" wanted them.

Sometimes the Baruchs would take the horse and buggy and go up to the main road and cut down the side of Arcadia (owned by the Vanderbilts) to reach North Inlet, Baruch's seafront property. Huge white dunes stretched for miles and were divided from the rest of Hobcaw Barony by the great North Inlet marsh. Here the birds were different—gulls, sandpipers, terns, and comical brown pelicans. There were shells to hunt and sand dollars banked in the sand. Sea oats swayed in the ocean breeze. The children would swim and wade and, when they were hungry, tuck into the great hampers of food packed by the kitchen help. If they were very lucky, they might spot dolphins frolicking off-shore in the wintertime.

Baruch's property included many islands—small patches of land that had been developed as rice fields—teeming with ducks and other wildlife. There were Rabbit and Hare Islands, Ranger Island, and Pumpkin Seed Island, where the snowy egrets, ibis, and blue heron made their rookery. The terns often nested at Bowson's Point, laying their eggs in a shallow depression in the sand. So well disguised were the small speckled eggs that Belle would have stepped on them had Powell not pointed them out.

Belle learned the names and sounds of all the birds—the oystercatchers, skimmers, plovers, curlews, marsh hens—an endless variety. She knew which ducks stayed all year and which migrated. If she came late in the spring, she would see the Canada geese, cranes, and storks winging their way back north.

To Belle, all of nature was a delight—the little fox squirrels scampering amid the trees, anoles inflating their scarlet throats. Powell would laugh and say that the tiny lizards were "showing their money."

Baruch built an elaborate playhouse with a living room, dining room, pantry, and kitchen where the children played and even helped prepare meals and enter-tain guests. Furnished in Victorian style, it was the site of many happy gather-ings. Christmas Eve was often celebrated there, with the children helping to cook and serve dinner for the Hobcaw guests.

Adjacent to the playhouse was a tennis court where Renee, Belle's younger sister, would reign supreme. Like her mother, Renee was more attracted to music and the arts and gentler pastimes than her competitive brother and sis-ter. Although she was an accomplished rider and excellent shot, she let Belle and Junior vie for riding, hunting, and shooting honors. Junior had a reputa-tion as a superior duck caller and at the tender age of eight years was consid-ered a "natural shot," once having killed forty-five ducks with sixty-odd shells.

Belle and Junior organized competing baseball teams among the workers' children, and even as an adult, Belle still insisted that her teams usually won. Brother and sister bickered constantly over whose turn it was to ride the goat cart. Belle howled with laughter when the stubborn goat took off with Junior and ran directly under the house which, in lowcountry style, was raised off the ground. Junior just howled.

As Belle grew older, her explorations broadened until she knew every acre of Hobcaw. She was fascinated by the ruins of the old plantation homes with romantic names like Armourdale, Strawberry, and, especially, Bellefield, whose empty rooms were said to be haunted by the ghost of a young planter and populated with evil spirits and plat-eyes, terrifying creatures who could transform themselves before your very eyes. The more superstitious residents of Georgetown County called Bellefield the White Owl House because, they said, the chief, resident plat-eye most often appeared in the guise of a huge white owl with fiery red eyes. Scorning the ghost stories, Belle was endlessly intrigued by the partially built structure and delighted in climbing about, balancing precariously on the rafters.

It was easy to believe in ghosts at Hobcaw with its silent cemeteries, soughing pine forests, mysterious black swamps, and the ghostly, spreading arms of the huge live oaks garbed in swaying Spanish moss. The roar of bull alligators and shrill cries of exotic birds blended in the night with the gentle murmur of cicadas and the strange croaking of frogs and other swamp creatures. The warning buzz of the huge timber rattlers, the soundless glide of deadly water moccasins, and the slither of unknown reptiles added a thrill of danger.

3

Life Lessons
at Hobcaw

Belle's relationship with the plantation blacks was ambivalent. It was incredible to her that most of the inhabitants of the old slave villages—Friendfield, Strawberry, Alderly, and Barnyard—had never left the plantation. They were born, married, reared families, and died without ever having left the boundaries of the property.

In her youthful arrogance and lack of understanding, it did not occur to Belle that even though slavery had been abolished, the black families of Hobcaw enjoyed little more freedom than had their ancestors. In the American South of 1905, blacks had neither social nor economic power. Technically free, they were still enslaved by lack of education and opportunity as well as economic deprivation. They had no experience of freedom on which to draw. Rather than sympathizing with their plight, Belle was disdainful at what she viewed as timidity and lack of ambition.

When Bernard Baruch bought the plantations, there was grave concern among the black population. By southern tradition, he was expected to provide employment to any black that lived there and wanted to work. But he was, after all, a Yankee and not bound by southern custom, even though he had been born in South Carolina. The people might no longer be slaves, but they were at Baruch's mercy. There was no place for them to go, no work available in the poverty-stricken South. It suited Baruch to have the black villagers remain. He would need their labor for the vast acreage, and he also viewed himself as a humanitarian. Perhaps for his day in the South, he was. Certainly he was no different than most white property owners and better than others.

Baruch provided lumber and materials to double the size of the miserable two-room huts where whole families resided—the parents in a tiny bedroom no bigger than a closet, and grandparents and children in the other common-purpose room that served as living area, kitchen (they cooked over a fireplace), and sleeping quarters. For the first time in memory, the blacks of Hobcaw Barony enjoyed a separate bedroom for their children and kitchens with wood-burning stoves. If it occurred to some that Baruch was also enhancing the value of his property since, in fact, he owned both their homes and the land on which they stood, no one had the audacity to say so. Most were just grateful for the added living space.

Even with the increase in size from two to four rooms, there was great disparity between the living accommodations of workers and owners. The children's playhouse was bigger than the tiny shacks that housed entire families. Minnie Kennedy, a black woman born at Hobcaw, remembers her disbelief when she first saw the "doll house." A child herself at the time, she said, "I was so envious that kids could have a whole house that they just played in. It seemed so unfair."

Baruch renovated Friendfield Village church and even found a preacher, the Reverend Moses Jenkins, to take up residence in Friendfield Village. The children called the preacher Pa Moses and followed him about the dusty roads of Friendfield, hoping for one of the peppermint sticks that were always stuffed in his pockets. The reverend's grandson, Prince (pronounced "Princie"), was the last black person to leave Friendfield Village and worked at Hobcaw until his retirement at age seventy-nine.

Much of what Baruch did was innovative in its day. It would be unfair to accuse him of making a profit from the labor of the black workers because Hobcaw Barony was never a working plantation under Baruch. He made no profit from its operation. He did, however, avail himself of labor at bargain rates. Belle would sometimes visit the villages, especially Friendfield, inhaling the mingled scents of wood smoke and grease as the inhabitants cooked their meals. Chickens, ducks, and pigs added their pungent aroma to this microcosm of southern rural life where inhabitants planted "giant reed" or "gate minder" plants near the doors to ward off evil spirits.

Few people bring such joy or drama to worship as southern blacks, and Belle would sometimes join her father and Hobcaw guests, slipping quietly into the back pew of the barony's little church to listen to the Negro spirituals, chants, prayers, and hand-clapping. It did not occur to the Baruchs that the black parishioners might resent their viewing the prayer services as entertainment.

They were quite sure the Negroes were honored by their presence and would have been shocked had anyone had the temerity to express the smoldering resentment that burned in the hearts of some of the black population.

Baruch also organized barn dances, emptying out the huge garage and hosing down the concrete floor. He fondly recalled these galas as festive occasions where prizes were given for the most colorful costumes and best dancers in various categories. Many enjoyed the dances, prizes, and refreshments, but others resented being ordered to perform for the white folks, hated being put on display as "Mr. Bernie's Negroes."

"It was humiliating," said Minnie Kennedy. "The Baruchs and their guests would sit and watch as if they were at a basketball game. If someone didn't want to dance, the Baruchs insisted. They and their guests would throw pennies, and sometimes nickels and dimes, onto the concrete floor and laugh as the people picked them up. I was just a little girl, but I knew it was demeaning. I refused to pick up the pennies, but my mother insisted. She hated it too but didn't want to jeopardize her job." Baruch would not have discharged a black for refusing to dance, but he had the power to do so, and therein lay the humiliation. He seemed totally unaware that any of his black employees resented the command performances.

Baruch built and equipped a small dispensary and arranged for a doctor to visit each week to treat any medical problems among the workers. He believed passionately in education and built a school for blacks and employed a teacher for them as well as a private teacher for the children of his white employees. As the number of white children grew, Baruch built a small school for them as well and included the white children from Arcadia Plantation. Baruch had no intention of upsetting the social structure of early-twentieth-century America by integrating the school.

Critics today say that Baruch had a moral obligation to do all he did and more, but at the turn of the century, there were still southern states with laws that prohibited teaching blacks to read. Georgetown was unique in that it had opened the Howard School for black children as early as 1906. Admittedly, this inspired Baruch to do the same since he did not want the blacks to leave Hobcaw Barony in order to educate their children.

Cynics might say that Baruch was simply assuring himself a steady supply of cheap labor. At one point, he paid his black laborers the munificent sum of fifty cents a day, and they could also count on a pair of warm long johns as well as hams and turkeys at Christmas. But one must consider the times and Baruch's southern heritage. The South had never recovered from the Civil War and Reconstruction, especially this land of the former rice plantations. Unemployment was rampant among blacks and whites alike. Baruch's maternal grandparents had owned plantations, and his mother had inculcated in her four sons many of her southern values and traditions. She often urged them not to forget their southern ancestry, and when Bernard announced his intention to buy a winter home in his native state, his mother insisted that he not only help the destitute South economically but also "do something for the Negro."

It was an almost feudal lifestyle, one of noblesse oblige, and Belle was absorbing her first lessons in social responsibility according to her father. Baruch was paternalistic in his attitudes, often referring to "my Negroes," and he delighted in being called Baron by his friends and associates. He was delighted when Edith Bolling Wilson (Mrs. Woodrow Wilson) addressed him as "Baron" in their letters and conversations. In later years Bernard Baruch never publicly supported the civil rights movement and, in fact, was suspicious of it. He lamented the exodus of blacks from Hobcaw Barony in the years following World War II but, publicly at least, acknowledged it as part of the social progress of African Americans. Privately, he deplored the rank ingratitude of some of "his people."

He did, however, build a hospital in his hometown of Camden, South Carolina, only after receiving assurances that blacks would be treated there as well as whites. He built a playground for black children in nearby Georgetown and provided college scholarships for white and black students alike. He was quite annoyed, however, to be brought to task by a young black woman for failing to keep his promise to her father to pay for her college education.

William Kennedy was employed by the Baruchs as a general handyman and overseer on the plantation. His wife, Daisy, worked as a housekeeper for the family, and all the children were employed as soon as they were big enough to carry a hoe. Baruch had always told Kennedy that he would pay for any of his children who wanted to go to college. Relying on that promise, Minnie Kennedy applied to South Carolina State College in 1935. Although Kennedy told Baruch that Minnie was attending college, Baruch made no move to pay her expenses. The Kennedys scraped and saved to get Minnie through her four years of school.

After graduation, Minnie again urged her father to ask Baruch for the money the family so desperately needed. Her father shook his head and said no, he wouldn't bother Mr. Baruch. Defiantly, Minnie wrote to Baruch reminding him of his promise and enclosed a detailed statement of her college expenses, including the cost of her class ring. "Tuition was thirty dollars a semester," Minnie Kennedy recalled, "and room and board was twelve dollars a month. The whole bill for the four years was less than five hundred dollars."

Baruch was irritated by the letter and informed Kennedy that Minnie was a very rude young woman, but "a promise is a promise." He sent Kennedy a check for the entire amount. "I have to say," Minnie Kennedy said, "that without Baruch I wouldn't have gone to college or been on the faculty of New York University. I went to college based on his promise to my father."

Minnie Kennedy has been an activist all her life and hated the humiliation of plantation life. "The worst feeling in the world," she said, "is to be powerless. Some people grew up to become adults with that same feeling of powerlessness. Mr. Baruch," she said reflectively, "was no different that any other white man in America at that time. I considered him mean and sometimes thought Belle was just like him, but Mrs. Baruch and Renee and Junior were very kind, humane people. They were our favorites in the family. Of course, none of them were ever in a position of real authority. No one ever said, 'consult Mr. Junior or Miss Renee.' Mr. Baruch and Miss Belle were the authority figures. Mrs. Baruch was just a very kind lady. But plantation life was demeaning to black people, and I can't stand for people to write books saying how happy we all were. There was no reason for people not to treat each other with respect and in a human way."

Minnie Kennedy freely admits that her father would not share her opinion of Bernard Baruch. He considered Baruch a friend, never failing to write to him if he heard he was ill, always sending a Christmas or birthday card. There are letters to Kennedy from Baruch indicating Baruch's warm regard for Kennedy as well. Junior Baruch always made it a point to visit the Kennedy home when he was in the Georgetown area.

Belle shared her father's racial attitudes, and it was not until she lived full-time on the plantation that her attitudes changed. While absorbing her parents' social values, Belle was also taking the first tentative steps toward her evolution as an ecologist and conservationist. In the winter of her thirteenth year, Belle's father asked her to join the annual deer drive at Hobcaw. Belle was thrilled to be included, seeing it as a sign of her father's approval and her own maturity. Proud and excited, she joined the adults, Jim Powell at her side.

Powell led her to a stand in the woods, where they waited quietly and patiently as the servants began the drive that would direct the startled deer toward the waiting hunters. Trembling with excitement, Belle shifted restlessly.

"Quiet, youngun," Powell whispered, "you'll scare 'em off. They gonna be movin' fast. You'll only get one shot."

Nodding, Belle readied her gun. Suddenly they heard the sound of running hooves, and a young buck burst through the trees. Instinctively, Belle swung the gun and fired, dropping the deer with a clean shot through the heart.

"Yeehaw!" Powell shouted. "You did it, girl! Right through the heart!" Laughing, he dipped his hands in the warm blood of the animal and smeared it on Belle's cheeks. "Your first bloodin', child."

Belle stumbled backward, the smell of blood and death heavy in her nostrils. Gazing at the beautiful animal, its eyes glazed in death, she tried vainly to choke back the tears that rushed into her eyes.

"Ah, too much excitement," Powell said gruffly, ruffling her hair and patting her shoulder awkwardly.

Belle's father boasted proudly of his daughter's prowess, and the South Carolina and New York newspapers heralded the feats of the young huntress. The *Georgetown Daily Item* announced that "the deer drive took place on the game preserves of Mr. B. M. Baruch. . . . There were 40 deer jumped and eighteen shots fired, which resulted in only one deer being brought down and that was killed by Miss Baruch, the 13 year old daughter of Mr. Baruch."[1]

The newspaper described her as a "young Diana," saying that she was also the only one of a later hunting party to have any success shooting wild turkeys, having bagged one the day before Christmas and another shortly thereafter.

Belle was disgruntled and jealous when the same newspapers wrote of her brother: "The shooting ability seems to run in the family, for Bernard M. Baruch, Jr., who is only nine years old, killed twenty-eight wild ducks today. . . . The boy slipped out to a stand in the marshes all unknown to his family and his father was much pleased when he returned with a bag full of ducks."[2] Angry at being left behind while his older sister joined the adult hunting party, Junior made sure he got his share of attention.

Belle basked in the warmth of her father's pride and approval, but at heart she was sick over the death of the beautiful animal. She continued to hunt birds, wild pigs, alligators, and other game, but Belle never killed another deer and, as an adult, seldom allowed anyone to hunt them on her property. As the years passed, she saw the number and variety of birds dwindle at Hobcaw, not only from hunting but also because of the destruction of surrounding wetlands. A keen awareness of man's relationship to nature grew within her.

4

A Study in Determination

As Belle entered her teens, she had two great passions—sailing and horses. By age seventeen, she had already won over fifty sailing trophies and in 1916 became the first woman to win the coveted Queen of the Bay Cup sponsored by the Yacht Racing Association of Great South Bay, Long Island.

Skippering her Bellport Bay one-design yacht, *Miladi,* Belle won the race by a corrected time of twenty-two seconds. Flushed and triumphant, the young teen was heralded as one of the "best women skippers on Great South Bay." Despite the irksome gender limitation, Belle posed proudly for family and newspaper photos. She was, however, about to learn just how much men hate losing to women.

The skipper of the second-place yacht, *Invader,* protested *Miladi*'s measurements. The official measurer, R. S. Haight, spent an entire morning measuring Belle's craft. After he had "gathered enough data to sink a ship," as the *Brooklyn Daily Eagle* described it, he announced that *Miladi* exceeded the accepted measurements by eighteen inches, as did all the Bellport Bay one-design boats. Notified of the decision, Belle showed her mettle, earning the admiration of the press. With a smile and a toss of her head, Belle announced: "I am sorry that I did not win the cup. Now I must go out and win the championship." Luck was not with her that year, but she came back later to win again.

When Belle died in 1964, her childhood friend Langdon Post wrote to her father:

> When I received your telegram, addressed to Mary [his sister, Mary Post Howe] and carrying the sad news about Belle, I was standing in the living room of our house watching the sailboat races on the Bay [San Francisco Bay].

Then I was back on the Great South Bay in *Miladi* and Belle was sitting in the stern sheets, hand on the tiller, eyes glued to the luff of the sail, her face a study in concentration and determination as her sensitive hands responded to the minutest shift of the wind. Then we crossed the finish line and the gun went off. We had won again, and again and again, until, finally, the Queen of the Bay.

I had spanned three thousand miles and almost fifty years to what were, perhaps, the happiest summers of my life.[1]

Unfortunately Belle could not spend all her time sailing and riding or exploring at Hobcaw. She had a quick, intelligent mind, but academics did not interest her greatly. Enrolled at the Rayson School on West Seventy-fifth Street in New York, Belle was a somewhat indifferent scholar, although she scored high marks in her religious studies. Well-liked by her fellow students, she was elected class president in both her sophomore and junior years.

Just before her sixteenth birthday, Belle was more thrilled than horrified to be involved in a genuine stagecoach holdup while on holiday in Yellowstone National Park. She and her friend Mary Post were traveling with the Baruch family, and the two girls had wheedled permission to sit up top with the driver, a man named Harris. After considerable coaxing and encouragement from the two girls, Harris was regaling them with tales of the West when the subject of bandits and holdups arose. As Belle later described it:

> We were thrilled with Harris' stories of previous holdups and we longed to have just such an incident happen to us. . . .
>
> It was about twenty minutes to ten in the morning, and the sky was still gray and clouded. . . . We were winding our way up a narrow and long road. As we reached the top of a small hill and had turned the corner, we noticed a coach and surrey ahead of us were stopped. . . . A man with a piece of blue flannel covering his face was standing on the side of the road. He had a Winchester repeater in his hand.[2]

Mary Post shouted a warning to those inside the coach, a warning they first thought of as a joke. A glance out the window assured Bernard Baruch that it was no joke. A quick thinker, he tossed most of his money under the front seat, his wife adding her pearls to the cache. The robber's meager booty was a thick roll of mostly small bills.

To Belle's great delight, a detachment of U.S. cavalrymen soon appeared in hot pursuit of the bandit. More entertained than frightened, the Baruchs even began to wonder if the holdup might be staged theatrics, but it was all very real. The bandit escaped to Belle's confessed delight.

25

The family enjoyed a good laugh the following day when James N. Wallace, then president of the Central Trust Company, telegraphed to Belle's father: "I hear you have been held up. How much did the robber lose?"

Belle's 1917 graduation yearbook, *The Raysonian,* emphasized Belle's love of horses over academics. The legend next to Belle's portrait reads: "My Kingdom for a horse." The stanza of the class poem devoted to Belle states:

There is a young lady named Belle,
Who can ride a fine horse very well;
If studies were horses
She'd lead in all courses,
This much-liked maiden, our Belle!

Belle was collecting riding trophies to match her sailing cups but was increasingly frustrated by the limits of competition. She was a strong, vital young woman of enormous energy, who was very physical, loved sports and dancing, and even liked to wrestle, which sometimes shocked her gentler female friends. Others merrily joined in the rough and tumble, delighted to join in such unladylike behavior. Like most teens, Belle wondered what she might want to do with her life.

5

From Debutante to the World Stage

When Belle graduated from Rayson in 1917, the United States was at war against the kaiser, and there's no doubt that, had she been a man, Belle would have enlisted immediately.

Bernard Baruch had abandoned Wall Street for a life of public service. Woodrow Wilson, whom Baruch admired and respected, had appointed Baruch to the Advisory Commission of the Council of National Defense in 1916 in preparation for greater responsibilities. In 1917, in order to be completely independent of any special-interest groups or conflicts of interest, Baruch sold his seat on the New York Stock Exchange, along with all stocks in war-related industries. In February of that year he was appointed chairman of the Committee on Raw Materials and in 1918 became head of the powerful War Industries Board. Some said he was one of the most powerful men in the country, second only to the president. If he had been busy and absent from home before, it was nothing compared to the absences demanded by the war effort.

In the normal course of events, Belle would have made her debut in December 1917, but as the *New York Sun* then headlined, it was "Relief Work Instead of Receptions for Debutantes." There was no grand "coming out" for Belle, but since she never liked large, glittering social events, she was more relieved than disappointed. Certainly the young women of her social strata were properly introduced to society but in a more subdued, less ostentatious manner in keeping with a country at war. Articles in the *New York Sun* and *New York Herald* on February 24, 1918, indicate that Belle had been introduced to Washington society via an afternoon reception the preceding day. Mrs. George W. Vanderbilt and Mrs. William Gibbs McAdoo presided at the tea table.

Belle was more interested in contributing to the war effort and immediately volunteered for the American Red Cross. The Red Cross proved far too tame for a girl with Belle's energy and enthusiasm, so, typically, she sought something more challenging. She found it in the Women's Radio Corps under the supervision of its director, Edna Owen (Mrs. Herbert Sumner Owen).

Belle studied radio telegraphy, qualifying quickly for her first-grade commercial license. She was appointed junior inspector of radio material for the U.S. Signal Corps and taught Morse code at two aviation camps. (Years later, while Belle was entertaining David Sarnoff, president of the Radio Corporation of America, the two spent the evening tapping out jokes and messages in Morse. Sarnoff, it seemed, had served as a wireless operator early in his career.)

The Women's Radio Corps, along with her work at the American Red Cross, Junior League, and time spent on her mother's favorite charities, satisfied her desire to serve. It was during this period that Belle formed a lifelong interest in rehabilitation of the blind and the lame.

In spite of the war, Anne Baruch considered it her personal duty to see that Belle was properly launched into society. The society pages of the newspapers between 1917 and the early 1920s often had photographs and articles about Miss Belle Baruch, daughter of Mr. and Mrs. Bernard M. Baruch, pictured in uniform while working at the Red Cross Shop at 587 Fifth Avenue or training army aviators. She was frequently photographed at the Islip Polo Club at Bay Shore, Long Island, clad in riding togs atop her mount. Often she was with friends like Sophie Pond or Mary Post, her sister, Renee, or with her famous father. Belle was elated that her father had begun to take pride in his tall, elegantly dressed daughter who shared his love of sports.

Bernard Baruch labored under monumental responsibilities during World War I and its aftermath. He had little time for a debutante daughter, but he tried to fit a few affairs into his schedule and see that she was introduced into the proper social and political circles. Belle's growing reputation as a sailor and equestrian met with his approval, something Belle craved all her life.

It was an exciting time to be young and innocent and just out of the classroom. True, there was a war on, but it added its own sense of excitement and urgency. The young people played as hard as they worked for the war effort, joining the young men who adopted the old adage "Eat, drink, and be merry, for tomorrow we may die."

Ragtime was popular, and for all her height, Belle sparkled on the dance floor, her long legs flashing with energy and grace. She was the first to joke about her height and put her partners at ease. Belle's wit and vivacity attracted many a young man whose pride might otherwise have inhibited him from inviting her to dance.

Belle loved New York, the theater, opera, ballet, and silent films. She was the proud owner of one of the very first Victrolas produced by RCA Victor, and her friends crowded into the Baruch parlor to play the latest hits.

Women's suffrage was on the move, and Belle eagerly joined the fray. Her family was dismayed, particularly her Baruch grandparents, who were singularly intolerant of the new feminism. The grandmother for whom she was named headed the antisuffrage committee of the City Federation, and Belle rolled her expressive brown eyes when she read the *New York Times* article quoting her grandmother's comments that "men have always guided and protected us" and went on to decry, in her words, "the unholy alliance of suffrage, feminism, and socialism."[1]

In January 1919 President Woodrow Wilson appointed Bernard Baruch to serve as economic adviser to the Paris Peace Conference. Baruch asked his wife, Anne, and Belle to join him in France. It was Belle's first trip abroad, her first sight of France. In spite of how shattered and scarred the country was by war, Belle responded to that special ambience of Paris. Perhaps it was due to the training and stories of her French governess, but Belle felt an immediate rapport with the country and its people. She sensed, although she could not articulate it at the time, that this would become her second home.

It was in France that Belle's political awareness began to develop. One could not be caught up in such an important event in world history and remain aloof. As she drove through the bombed-out villages of the French countryside en route to the U.S. Marine cemetery at Belleau Woods, she witnessed firsthand the devastating aftermath of war.

After months of negotiations, the Versailles Treaty was signed in June 1919, and the long, futile quest for ratification by the U.S. Congress began. The United States, led by Senator Henry Cabot Lodge, was in an isolationist mood, beginning to withdraw into itself. President Woodrow Wilson had a dream—a world united in peace, maintained by a common governing body, the League of Nations. President Wilson had begun to fight for that dream even before the end of World War I, selling the concept to the Allies at the Paris conference. Now he had to sell it to the United States Congress.

Wilson's dream fired Belle's imagination. She was not immune to her father's influence and shared his passion for the country's entry into the league. It was a combination, perhaps, of youthful idealism, the desire to please her idolized parent and the influence of Evangeline Brewster Johnson, Belle's closest friend and constant companion. Evangeline, of the Johnson and Johnson pharmaceutical family, came from one of America's most prominent and wealthiest families. She and Belle were introduced into society the same year and became close friends.

The two young women were kindred souls and a physically striking pair. Evangeline was six feet tall, blonde, and given to melodrama. Belle was even taller, somewhat reserved, her brunette coloring the perfect foil for the fair Evangeline. The term *women's libbers* had not yet been coined, but had it existed, it would have been readily applied to Evangeline and Belle. Evangeline was more of an activist than Belle, outgoing where Belle could sometimes be shy. "She was probably good for Belle," Renee Samstag (Belle's younger sister) observed. Belle had never been one for intellectual pursuits, but under Evangeline's influence she began to read more widely.

Belle was the better organized of the two, giving order and direction to Evangeline's sometimes flighty notions. Avant-garde, witty, intellectual, and idealistic, Evangeline dashed dramatically through life taking up one cause after another. She piloted her own plane as early as 1919, a pastime Belle would take up later in life. Evangeline scandalized the Philadelphia Main Line ladies with her antics and reveled in making dramatic gestures.

Evangeline and Belle hated having to follow society's dictates about wearing long stockings with their bathing suits. The mischievous Evangeline suggested a protest. She flew her plane low over the coastline of the vacation spot of the rich and famous on Palm Beach, dropping leaflets on the sunbathers below. She later told a biographer: "It made me so mad to have to wear stockings with my bathing costume. So, I wrote out some articles and flew in my plane, dropping the handbills on the beach, arguing against stockings."[2]

Evangeline aided and abetted Belle in the militant fight for women's rights. To her family's dismay, Belle became even more active in the suffragette movement. She and Evangeline marched, passed out literature, and defended the women's movement at every opportunity. The two young suffragettes celebrated wildly when women finally won the right to vote in 1920.

When not distracted by family social obligations or pursuing separate interests, the two girls were inseparable. Evangeline did not share Belle's passion for riding and happily engaged in other pursuits while Belle was off foxhunting or show jumping. She was a frequent guest at Hobcaw, writing in the guest book on April 30, 1921, "Hobcaw, the very altar of friendship."[3]

Belle and Evangeline shared an apartment at 515 Park Avenue for several years beginning in late 1921. The two young women put their considerable financial resources and personal efforts into the League of Nations Non-Partisan

Association, traveling from New York to Washington and to Geneva, where world headquarters for the league had been established. They were passionate in their desire to do whatever they could to prevent another war. Belle chaired the Information Distributing Bureau of the association and the Woman's Pro-League Council while Evangeline chaired the Speaker's Bureau.

The Bernard M. Baruch papers at Princeton University include an undated letter to Baruch from Edith Bolling Wilson in which she refers to a paper written by Belle: "As you see I am returning this wonderful interpretation of the 'League of Nations' which I think one of the cleverest and most lucid things I have seen on the subject—and which makes me wish your small daughter was a United States Senatoress. The Dr. [Admiral Cary Grayson] and I read it to the President and he was delighted with it but says please ask her where she learned that it was Jefferson's idea—that interests him tremendously and he wants to read what she had studied."

The greatest coup Belle and Evangeline engineered was an unprecedented major radio address by former president Woodrow Wilson on the eve of the fifth anniversary of the Armistice. In 1923 radio was still in its infancy. Not until the presidency of Franklin Delano Roosevelt would political leaders realize its effectiveness as a vehicle for mass communication. It was Belle who saw its potential, and Evangeline listened enthusiastically. They hoped that an address by Wilson might jolt the country out of its isolationist apathy and into the League of Nations.

The two young women wrote asking for an appointment with President Wilson to discuss their plan. Wilson was in failing health and discouraged by the failure of his dream to see the United States assume its role as a leader of world peace via the league. The world had honored Woodrow Wilson with the 1919 Nobel Peace Prize, but, to his unremitting sorrow, he was never able to convince his own Congress to ratify the treaty.

He granted the initial interview because of his affection and respect for Belle's father, but both he and Mrs. Wilson were quickly swept along by Belle's and Evangeline's infectious enthusiasm. The Wilsons invited them to join them for dinner and the theater, promising to allot time in which to discuss their idea. Writing in *My Memoir* years later, Edith Bolling Wilson recounted her first meeting with Belle and Evangeline: "I shall always recall them as they looked that night. They are both over six feet tall, and were dressed in stunning velvet evening gowns of the latest Parisian stamp. Long earrings matched the costumes. In all they were two as stunning-looking creatures as I ever saw."[4] Neither Belle nor Mrs. Wilson realized that this encounter was the beginning of a lifelong friendship.

Wilson found himself incapable of resisting the enthusiasm and charm of Belle and Evangeline. Reluctantly, for he distrusted the newfangled radio, he agreed to speak. Preparation of the address taxed his waning strength to such an extent that Mrs. Wilson was tempted to cancel, but her husband refused. He labored many days over the ten-minute address, and on the night of November 10, 1923, in a faltering voice that gained gradually in strength, he addressed the largest radio audience to date in the nation's history, nearly three million people.

Recalling the day when, five years earlier, the guns of World War I had grown silent, he said: "Memories of that happy time are forever marred and embittered for us by the shameful fact that when the victory was won . . . we withdrew into a sullen and selfish isolation which is manifestly ignoble because manifestly dishonorable."[5]

The next day, as the nation celebrated Armistice Day, an estimated twenty thousand citizens poured into S Street in Washington, D.C., to gather in front of the Wilson residence. Belle and Evangeline had given the ailing Wilson a final opportunity to plead for his beloved league. Belle could not have anticipated the spontaneous outpouring of love and support offered by the American people to their former president, but was humbly grateful to have had a hand in honoring Woodrow Wilson. Edith Wilson never forgot.

Three months later, in February 1924, Woodrow Wilson died, and Belle and Evangeline joined a nation in mourning. Wilson's death only renewed their determination to fight on for the league. Just prior to his death, Woodrow Wilson had written to Mrs. William Gorham Rice:

> I am deeply interested in what Mr. Rice has told me of your plan for a bureau at Geneva which is to be at the service of Americans who wish to see and understand the workings of the League, and it has occurred to me that there are two young ladies in New York who might be of great service to you. . . . They have been working most diligently and intelligently for some time past to make correct information about the League easily accessible to all who desired it, and answers ready to all objections to the League which will silence if not satisfy every honest critic.[6]

Mrs. Rice responded to Wilson that not only had Belle and Evangeline agreed to take charge of such a bureau for a fortnight, they had also promised to finance the venture for that period. Mrs. Rice also expressed confidence that she could persuade them to oversee the running of the bureau for the six weeks it was scheduled to be open.

In September 1924 Belle wrote to her father from Geneva, Switzerland, world headquarters for the League of Nations:

> What there is to learn in this world! Several of us have been giving joint luncheons for Senators, Congressmen and just plain American citizens. . . .
>
> We were fortunate enough to be at the opening of the assembly this morning, being pushed up in the press gallery. . . . There are 350 would-be British spectators and 250 Americans, not to mention tons of others and the ticket fight is better than the Democratic convention. . . .
>
> I have kept my ears open and if I ever remember one quarter of what I have heard that will be a lot.[7]

It was heady and thrilling to be part of a cause in which she so passionately believed. And, for the first time in many years, Belle enjoyed the attention and approval of her famous father, who was too often engrossed in problems of war and the peace conference to draw close to his daughter.

6

Henry Ford and Anti-Semitism

T he United States in the 1920s was introspective, isolationist, and seeking to assign blame for its own entry into World War I as well as for the conduct of the war itself. As chairman of the powerful War Industries Board and, unquestionably, the most renowned Jew in the country, Bernard Baruch found himself the target of speculation and a primary victim of Henry Ford's vicious anti-Semitic attacks.

Henry Ford Sr., the great industrialist who first developed the assembly line, personified the American dream and was a folk hero to the common man. Often called "the man who put a continent on wheels," he was mentioned often as a viable candidate for the presidency. Unfortunately for the nation's Jews, Ford was a vocal and bitter anti-Semite.

Historians and sociologists speculate as to the root of his virulent anti-Semitism and exactly what inspired him to launch his infamous Paper Pogrom. In May 1920 Ford, who owned his own newspaper, the *Dearborn Independent*, wrote a series of anti-Semitic articles blaming Jews for all the world's problems, including—but not limited to—war, strikes, and conspiracies against the United States and, indeed, the world.

According to Ford, Jews were orchestrating an international conspiracy to control the world. As Margaret Coit noted, Ford considered Jews to be "responsible for liquor, short skirts, white slavery and the failing banks in the farm areas. Jews, Ford claimed, controlled the movie industry, sugar, cotton, the packing and shoe industries, grain, jewelry, loan companies and the theaters."[1] Bernard Baruch, Ford railed, was the "Jew of super-power" and the "proconsul of Judah in America." He implied that Baruch had profited from his position as head of the War Industries Board in World War I.

Rebuttals to Ford's prejudice were many. In his book *Henry Ford, "Ignorant Idealist,"* David E. Nye wrote: "It is clear that Ford entertained a conspiracy theory of history." Author William C. Richards said that through the written word, Ford did to Jews "what Nazi Germany was to do a decade later."[2]

In December 1920 Ford accused Baruch, along with the Lewisohns, Guggenheims, and "many a lesser son of Judah" of controlling the copper market on both sides of the Atlantic. He claimed that the Jews, with their Gentile fronts, had sold sixteen-cent copper for twenty-seven cents and made enormous profits on the surplus after the armistice. He specifically cited Bernard Baruch as an "instrumentality in the effort of Judah to control the United States and the world." In all, Ford sponsored 191 such articles, which he later had bound into a book.

It was the vilest anti-Semitic attack the Baruch family had experienced. Baruch had a tough hide and supreme confidence in his own judgment and integrity, but to Anne Baruch it was devastating. Because of their father's wealth and power, the Baruch children seldom encountered such overt anti-Semitism. After reading the charges, Baruch left his office and gathered his family about him. Anne and Renee were in tears, but Belle and Junior were furious and protective of their father. "It's a damned scurrilous lie and Ford knows it!" Baruch told his family. "Just stay calm and it will all blow over. No comments to the press, no talking about it to your friends."

Baruch's younger daughter, Renee, said that is was a dark period in the life of the family. "And," she added dryly, "don't forget Father Coughlin." (Father Charles Coughlin, a Roman Catholic priest who had a popular radio program, launched a bitter anti-Semitic attack just over a decade later when Bernard Baruch was counseling war preparedness. "Jewish War Monger" was one of the kinder epithets he cast against Baruch when Baruch attempted to warn the United States that World War II was imminent and the country must prepare itself. The rabid anti-Semite accused Baruch of being part of an international Jewish conspiracy and claimed that Jewish money financed the Russian Revolution of 1917. He insisted that Baruch was one of the key leaders of the alleged conspiracy.)

Baruch briefly considered suing Ford, but the only public comment he ever made was in response to clamoring newspaper reporters asking about Ford's charges: "Now, boys," he said, "you wouldn't expect me to deny them would you?" With that he laughed and went on his way. The national press did not pursue the issue, but it was a traumatic period for the Baruchs and the barbs of anti-Semitism cut deeply. No Baruch ever drove a Ford, nor did Baruch allow his employees to drive a Ford on Baruch property.

Ironically Baruch was often criticized by the Jews for not being Jewish enough. It was well known that his wife and daughters were Episcopalians, and Baruch attended synagogue only on High Holy Days.

It hurt Belle to see her adored father attacked and to endure the rebuffs and insults she and her brother and sister encountered in response to Ford's attacks. Nor was Belle of a particularly forgiving nature. Nearly thirty years later she argued angrily against her father's decision to give the commencement address at New York's prestigious Chapin School, her mother's alma mater, which had refused admission to Belle and Renee because their father was a Jew.

Belle was young and resilient, however, and recovered her poise much more quickly than did Anne and Renee. She was approaching her twenty-first birthday and was caught up in the excitement of her own life. On that propitious occasion, Bernard Baruch gave his daughter one million dollars, a sum he was to give to each of his children when they reached their majority. Baruch, as he would for all of Belle's life, continued to manage her investment portfolio, but the money was Belle's, to do with as she wished. He hinted that she might want to further her education, but Belle had other plans. The purchasing power of one million dollars in 1920 would be equivalent to more than ten million dollars today. To Belle, the money represented two things—independence and horses.

7

Resolution and Independence

Belle came of age in the Roaring Twenties, the Jazz Age. She was young, rich, and adventurous. The post–World War I era in America was one of turbulent and often painful social and economic change. The war had exposed millions of rural Americans to urban lifestyles and shifting mores. Suddenly, half the population was living in the cities. The age of the automobile had arrived, and Belle witnessed the last of the horse-drawn trolleys in New York.

It was also the age of prohibition, Al Capone, and bloody gangster wars. Hemlines were rising and one-piece bathing suits, once banned from New York beaches, were the vogue. Belle enjoyed her furs and couturier clothes. Patou of Paris was her favorite designer, and Belle visited his salon at least once each year. Shaking his head over her thin body, he lined her skirts with layers of petticoats to fill out her tall, slender form. She loved hats and was rarely seen without one.

Belle was a frequent visitor to the Great White Way, where Katherine Cornell and the Barrymores dominated the stage. The great stars of silent films glittered over America, and Belle rarely missed a new film starring such favorites as Rudolph Valentino, Clara Bow, Charlie Chaplin, Douglas Fairbanks, and Mary Pickford. She had a passion for westerns as well. After all, they starred great horses as well as actors. She loved George M. Cohan, and her eyes would fill with tears at the sound of such patriotic songs as "Over There" and "Grand Old Flag."

There were beaux, of course—dashing young pilots she met while teaching Morse code, European royalty whose interests were equally divided between the tall, elegant young woman with the piercing brown eyes and the Baruch fortune. And there were the sons of other rich, acceptable American families. Few could hold a candle to her beloved, charming father. None touched her heart or kindled her emotions, and, in her secret heart, Belle began to wonder if any man ever would.

Belle visited her share of speakeasies and outshone most of her friends on the dance floor with spirited renditions of the Charleston, Black Bottom, and other popular dances. She loved jazz and frequented Harlem's Cotton Club and other clubs where she could listen to Louis Armstrong and Jelly Roll Morton. She loved the big bands of Duke Ellington and Cab Calloway, but she always preferred small, private parties to large-scale social events. It was easier for Belle to be among trusted friends than among strangers who might seek her out because of her father's wealth and political influence.

She once left a party given by her friend ZaSu Pitts, the film star and comedienne, because of a persistent guest who plied her with questions about her father. Even with her closest friends, Belle did not discuss her father nor the famous guests who visited Hobcaw House and Bellefield.

The Baruch offspring received frequent warnings about unscrupulous people who might attempt to use them for their money or possible influence with their famous father. A close family friend remarked that, perhaps without intending to do so, Bernard Baruch managed to convince his children that they had little personal value outside of being his children. "It's a terrible thing," she observed, "to make a child think she has no personal worth as a human being."

Baruch had enormous influence, especially during the latter years of World War I. It was not unusual for Belle to receive requests from friends, or even casual acquaintances, to use her influence with her father to gain a certain military posting, a draft deferment, a political favor, an introduction, or even a tip on the stock market. The Baruch children knew well that such requests would receive short shrift from their father. For Belle, part of the attraction of France was that, outside diplomatic circles, Bernard Baruch was not a household name.

Belle traveled extensively throughout the United States and Europe and confounded her parents when she moved into the apartment with Evangeline Johnson in New York and also established a pied-à-terre in Paris. Even in the flapper era, it was unheard of for a young single woman to leave the family home for her own residence. The conservative Baruchs were appalled, but even Bernard could not influence his determined daughter to remain under the family's protection. Belle's sister, Renee, younger by six years, marveled at her sister's daring. "She always had such courage . . . not just the physical courage to ride the way she did, but the courage to live as she wanted to."

In a typical gesture of independence, Belle elected to legally change her name from Isabel, which she disliked, to Belle. After all, she reasoned, she had been called Belle most of her life; why not make it legal? Reluctantly, her father cooperated, writing a letter to attest that Belle Wilcox Baruch was one and the same as Isabel Wilcox Baruch.

Belle further horrified her straitlaced parents by adopting the bobbed hair and flamboyant dress of the flapper era, drinking bathtub gin and smoking in public! The high-spirited Roaring Twenties were ideally suited to Belle's restless quest for excitement and independence. As she noted in the Hobcaw guest book: "I'm a little Hobcaw flower; growing wilder by the hour; nobody can cultivate me, Gee! I'm wild!"[1] The Baruchs were secretly relieved when Belle began to spend most of each year in France, out of the public eye in New York and Washington.

In the early 1920s Belle made her first visit to the hunt country of Pau in the French Pyrenees. The capital of the region of Bern and a center of the French aristocracy, Pau was a charming and cosmopolitan city. Belle loved the rolling green countryside with its mild winters and the breathtaking view of the snowy peaks of the high Pyrenees.

The British discovered Pau when Wellington and his troops stopped there on the way home from Spain. By 1860 Pau housed the largest British colony outside the empire, nearly one-third the population claiming British citizenship. The British established shops and held endless teas, foxhunts, cricket matches, and balls. It was also the site of the first eighteen-hole golf course on the European continent, but Belle had little patience for hitting a small white ball across the rolling hills.

Expatriate Americans discovered Pau after World War I, and, once again, Pau resumed its position as a haven for the international foxhunting set. For years Belle leased what she referred to as her "little French farmhouse" during the horse show and hunt seasons. Villa Poeyminau was a charming three-story brick house set in the midst of a small gated estate with stables for the horses.

At the end of each season Belle returned home to America, first visiting New York and, as soon as possible, moving to Hobcaw Barony. She would arrive at Hobcaw for the annual Christmas gathering of the family and stay for a stint of hunting, fishing, riding, and relaxation. Hobcaw, she said, renewed her spirit. Then it was back to New York to continue her work on the Nonpartisan Committee for the league and other business obligations.

Belle went often to Hobcaw in the spring as well, particularly in March and April when South Carolina flora are at their loveliest. Evangeline Johnson and other friends, such as Mary and Langdon Post, shared the pleasures of Hobcaw.

Belle never knew whom she would find at Hobcaw. Barbara Hutton's yacht might be anchored in Winyah Bay; statesmen or foreign diplomats might be in residence. Joseph Pulitzer, Josephus Daniels, Generals George C. Marshall and Omar Bradley, Senators Robert A. Taft and Harry F. Byrd, James Byrnes, Herbert Bayard Swope, and Clare and Henry Luce were frequent visitors. Winston Churchill, a lifelong friend of Belle's father, visited often over the years, both in New York and at Hobcaw Barony.

Baruch had a special fondness for writers and reporters. Jack London hunted at Hobcaw, and Edna Ferber, Hedda Hopper, and Westbrook Pegler also were among the guests. The prince of Monaco, grandfather of Prince Rainier, was another visitor, although he "hunted" rare birds and butterflies. Statesmen and politicians, luminaries of the stage and screen, the famous and the infamous vied for invitations to Hobcaw Barony. Bernard Baruch was a gregarious man, and rarely were there fewer than fifteen or twenty guests at the evening meal.

8

Lois Massey

The one special person who shared Belle's dreams and vision of Hobcaw Barony was Lois Massey, who served as social secretary to the Baruchs at Hobcaw and later to Belle at Bellefield. Lois loved Hobcaw almost as much as Belle and was often her companion when Belle visited Hobcaw.

Lois's uncle was Captain Jim Powell, and her first memory of Hobcaw was at the age of five: "I remember riding on a horse named 'Big Jim' with my uncle over the woody roads and across the rice field banks where hundreds of Negroes were working in the fields. . . . The rice mill was on a canal where flats, or lighters, loaded with rice were to be towed to town. The sound of music filled the air as their [the workers'] favorite songs were sung in unison as they worked."[1]

In 1922, when Lois was still in her teens, Baruch hired her father as a master mechanic, and the family moved to a house provided for them on Hobcaw Barony. The Baruchs liked the cheerful young girl who was so willing to do anything asked of her. Baruch hired her as his social secretary at Hobcaw, and later she worked for Belle in the same capacity.

Both Jim Powell and the Baruchs decided that Lois had to learn to ride and shoot. "I got so I could stay on the horse pretty good after a fashion." Shooting did not go as well. "Really, I couldn't hit the side of a barn," Lois admitted, "and Uncle Jim would get disgusted with me."

Belle decided to take Lois in hand and improve her marksmanship. After careful instruction, Belle took Lois duck hunting one morning, and to Belle's delight, Lois brought down four ducks with a single shot. "Dead-eye Dick," Belle crowed. "I didn't hear but one shot!"

"It never happened again," Lois admitted ruefully. "But I kept trying."

Belle teased Lois unmercifully about her adventure with the snake in the chicken coop. Near the Massey house was a chicken coop large enough to accommodate about one hundred chickens. Every morning Lois would gather eggs to be delivered to the big house. One morning Lois reached into a nest and found herself clutching something very cold. Startled, she snatched back her hand and saw a huge chicken snake that had happily devoured all the eggs in the nest, then curled up to nap and digest its meal.

"I rushed to the house," Lois said, "picked up a pistol, came back and 'bang!' into the nest." Everyone came rushing out, but to Lois's chagrin, when the smoke cleared the snake was still sleeping peacefully.

Even Bernard Baruch took a hand in training Lois to shoot and took her on her first deer hunt. When a beautiful buck came into view, Baruch gave her first shot. "I froze," Lois recalled.

"Lois, shoot!" Baruch shouted.

Woefully Lois shook her head. "No can do!" she croaked.

Belle loved to tell about the time Lois discovered a "dead" opossum by the side of the road. She was on her way to Hobcaw House, and, rather than let the creature lay there and rot, Lois picked it up, heaved it atop the luggage rack of the car, and continued down the rutted, bumpy road.

As she drove through the gates at Hobcaw House, people gathered about the car, pointing and laughing. Puzzled, Lois climbed out of the car only to see a terrified opossum, its tiny paws clinging with all their might to the rungs of the luggage rack. "It must have had a wild ride!" Belle teased.

"The best times," Lois Massey reminisced, "were when the whole family was there. Belle would take a notion to go foxhuntin' by moonlight. The stable hands would saddle the horses and have them waitin,' and then the colored men, with the hounds, would leave early to scent a fox, and when they finally got him in fast pursuit, their voices in rhythm would sing a song which could be heard for miles. We'd be sitting down to dinner and if, in the middle of the meal the men ran in to say they'd found a fox, why, Belle and whoever else was going would jump up from the table, say 'excuse me,' leap on their horses and take off after that fox. She was a foxhunter from her heart, I'm tellin' you!"

Foxhunting at night on Hobcaw Barony was not for the fainthearted. Even full moonlight had difficulty penetrating the dense woods to illuminate the sandy, rutted roads as the horses raced pell-mell after a fox. There were deep ditches marking the boundaries of the various rice plantations, and often the chase took them beyond the acres of Hobcaw to neighboring properties. Belle reveled in the thundering pursuit, giving full rein to her wildest nature.

There were more organized foxhunts during the day as well. Massey recalled: "We fox chased over every acre of ground from Hobcaw to Waverly Mills. In those days the colored men would leave around three or four o'clock in the morning with the horses and hounds if we were going to DeBordieu Beach, Waverly Mills, or Arcadia Plantation to hunt. We would ride up in buckboards and arrive at daylight when the chase would begin.

"After hours of hunting, we would stop for breakfast. At DeBordieu, Mrs. Emerson from Arcadia brought breakfast to the beach house. At Waverly, Phil Lachicotte would treat us to mint julep made from good ole stump hole corn. Then eat!

"Ralph Nesbit of Caledonia [Plantation] served us breakfast in a huge dining room, at a long table accommodating about twenty, set with china and silver goblets. An old colored butler would carry in a silver platter bearing a huge egg omelet that had been cooked over an open fire in their fireplace."

Christmas at Hobcaw House was a special time for everyone on the plantation. There would be a huge Christmas tree and a bag containing fruit, nuts, and candy for each man, woman, and child. "Candy came in fifty-pound tubs," said Lois Massey, "nuts by the fifty-pound bag, and oranges and apples by the boxloads. We shopped for weeks before the holidays and had bagging sessions each night after dinner.

"There were presents for each person on the plantation—shirt, pants, and tie for the men and boys; dresses, sweaters, and other clothing for the women and girls. . . . The parties were gay, fun, and very simple but gracious in every way. Black and white had fun."

Lois worked closely with the blacks of the plantation and was loved by them for her unfailing good cheer and concern for their welfare. She loved to tell how the servants rescued her family when their summer place at Clambank was destroyed in a sudden, violent storm.

"The bridges were washed out and the water was coming through the house in waves," she related. "The chickens were sitting on the top rung in the hen house, cars were full of water, the boats at the dock sunk. The marsh between Clambank and the woodland looked like a huge lake with waves. There was nothing to do but wait and pray."

After the tides and wind subsided, Lois, her mother, and her uncle Jim Powell looked longingly across the marsh toward home. Suddenly, at the edge of the woods, they saw the people of Friendfield Village coming to their rescue. Black people in the village had waded through three miles of water infested with poisonous snakes, alligators, and dangerous debris, the men dragging and carrying rowboats.

"The men rowed across to pick us up," Lois said. "When we got home to the mainland house, whose pantry had been emptied and taken to the summer house, the women brought rice, canned food, fried chicken, and coffee. I'm not ashamed to say we all cried."

When black people needed or wanted something special, they always asked Lois to intercede with either Powell or the Baruchs. "Laura Jenkins [mother of the preacher Moses Jenkins]," Lois recalled, "was the oldest woman on the plantation. She lived in a one-room cottage with a fireplace that covered one whole side of the room. There was a small iron pot hanging inside and a comfortable rocker nearby where Laura would sit and smoke her pipe. I stopped one day to check on her, and she told me she wanted Mrs. Massey (my mother), to make her a shroud. She wanted to look at it and be sure it was exactly what she wanted."

Lois consulted with Mrs. Baruch about the unusual request. Anne stated emphatically that Laura should have her wish and that she herself would purchase the material. "Mom made the shroud," Lois said, "a gown-type, trimmed with lace and ribbons with a cap to match. Laura was very happy."

As Lois matured, she grew closer to the Baruch family. "Mr. Baruch," she said, "was tall, handsome . . . had a deep searching look in his eyes. If he looked at you over those glasses, you better be perfectly sure you were telling the truth. Tomorrow he might ask you the same question again and could repeat your earlier reply word for word.

"Mrs. Baruch was tall, stately, soft-spoken, sincere . . . a perfectionist. She was generous, more so than most folks knew. She always told me she was for the underdog.

"Mister Junior was an excellent shot. He loved bird shooting and clay-pigeon shooting, boats, and horseback riding.

"Miss Renee was quiet, reserved, intellectual. She was a good pianist, a bookworm, and loved tennis. She had a nice sense of humor, a wonderful person! She enjoyed nice, quiet horseback rides through the woods.

"Miss Belle had a wonderful smile, an enormous sense of humor. She had an unending love for horses, dogs, fox chasing, and the outdoors. Just a great person! Loved peas, corn-on-the-cob, asparagus, oatmeal, custard, and picnics on the beach."

9

Travels with Edith
Bolling Wilson

I n the spring of 1925 Edith Bolling Wilson planned her first European trip since the death of her husband in February 1924. Belle, along with Lucy Moeling, was to be her traveling companion. They sailed for Europe on the *Majestic* on May 17. Mrs. Wilson sought rest, anonymity, and complete freedom from formal receptions, press interviews, and the like. Belle, her sister Renee, and Evangeline Johnson, who joined them in Europe for part of the trip, were to protect Mrs. Wilson from the press and any unwanted publicity.

There had always been close ties between the Wilsons and the elder Baruchs. Not only had Bernard Baruch been head of the War Industries Board, he had also worked tirelessly for President Wilson both during and after his presidency.

When Woodrow Wilson left the White House, he moved to a lovely house on S Street in Washington. Baruch and other Wilson supporters arranged the mortgage. Baruch even bought the adjoining lot, leaving it in its natural, wooded state to protect the privacy and quiet of the Wilson household. He had been one of the few people admitted to the house on S Street during the former president's final illness, and he served as a pallbearer at Wilson's funeral.

Baruch's loyalty and devotion to Mrs. Wilson continued after her husband's death. He, Cleveland Dodge, Vance McCormick, Jesse Jones, and others created a trust fund to provide for Mrs. Wilson's expenses during the first year of her widowhood while Mr. Wilson's estate was being probated and her financial affairs arranged.

Fortunately, Edith Wilson was reasonably wealthy and could live comfortably by most, if not by Baruch, standards. The Baruch family showered her with little "extras": flowers and candy, vacation trips, a silver-fox stole for Christmas. According to Belle's secretary, Belle saw that Mrs. Wilson had a new car when needed. The devotion of the Baruchs to Edith Wilson was expressed in a lifetime of caring.

Edith Wilson was astute enough to rely on the counsel of Baruch and other advisers. She particularly turned to Bernard Baruch concerning memorials to her husband, the archiving of his personal papers, and, later, her own autobiography. She often referred to him as her publicity adviser. Entrusting Mrs. Wilson to the care of his daughters on this first trip abroad following her husband's death was just one more gesture of concern and affection. Belle would become much more than simply the daughter of an old friend.

Arriving in France, they left the ship to drive through Normandy to Paris where Belle, who spoke French, German, and a smattering of other languages, proved to be a knowledgeable and vivacious guide. She was full of energy, life, and fun—just what Mrs. Wilson, who was still mourning her husband, needed.

Edith Wilson knew Europe well, but traveling with Belle was a new adventure. Her fresh, youthful perspective made everything more exciting. Belle planned interesting side trips and was full of ideas for picnics, quiet luncheons, and intimate dinner parties where Mrs. Wilson could rest and bask in the warmth of caring, loving companions.

Belle lived most of the year in France and knew of the latest plays, ballet, and opera events and frequented the salons of the finest couturiers. Mrs. Wilson had always favored Worth, but she enjoyed visiting the other salons of Paris with Belle and Evangeline. Naturally, Belle insisted that Patou be included in their shopping expeditions.

Belle was at home on the Left Bank and in the expatriate community, introducing Mrs. Wilson to delightful and interesting people she would never have met in her official capacities. Belle's youth and gaiety made Edith Wilson feel young again and able to forget her recent months of mourning. An unbreakable bond formed between the two women.

Belle's respect and admiration for Mrs. Wilson, coupled with the age difference of more than twenty years, prevented Belle from ever calling Mrs. Wilson "Edith" or "Miss Ede" as intimate family and friends addressed her. She always called her "Ma'am" (later shortened to "Mam"), much to Mrs. Wilson's amusement. As their friendship grew, it soon became a joke between them. "Mam" evolved into Belle's pet name for Edith Wilson, and so she addressed her as such in letters and conversations and Edith Wilson signed her letters to Belle by the same appellation.

Belle had a talent for being there when she was needed and for gracefully extending whatever privacy she felt Mrs. Wilson required in order to enjoy the many friends who called. Never intrusive, Belle cheerfully went about her own affairs when Mrs. Wilson wanted to visit someone's home for a few days or go to lunch or dinner with old acquaintances.

They traveled to Venice in July, then, in August, Belle took the group to Scotland to Fettersee, the ten-thousand-acre estate in County Kincardine that Bernard Baruch rented for the grouse season. Belle would usually join her father there, or sometimes in Czechoslovakia, for a few days of shooting each year.

Shooting with Baruch was an experience in luxury. As Kitty Carlisle Hart described her visit to Baruch's hunting lodge: "Everything was done by Fortnum and Mason, down to the chewing gum (!) on the night table; and we were piped into dinner with bagpipes every night."[1]

While shooting on the moors, Baruch served his guests with elaborate lunches, complete with linen, silver, and wine in silver coolers, served on huge trestle tables. But even Baruch's millions could not spare his guests from the specters that visited Fettersee. The Scottish castle was reputed to be haunted, and nothing would ever convince Edith Wilson that it was not. She often regaled friends with tales of the dreadful apparitions she witnessed while a guest there.

One of her biographers, Alden Hatch, wrote, "It [the castle] reminded her of the peculiar construction of the Bolling house in Virginia, because each room had a separate staircase. The first night, she carried a candle up the winding vaulted stairway to her room and nervously closed the heavy wooden door, which had no lock. Then the haunts began. Such moans and groans and rattles sounded through the door that Edith with the strength of terror pushed a big armoire against the door. To this day no one can convince her that the castle was not full of ghosts."[2]

Leaving Scotland and its ghosts behind, the party traveled to Geneva, where Mrs. Wilson made her only public appearance of the journey at the League of Nations. In late October they set sail for New York, joined at that time by Anne Baruch. Mr. Baruch met them at the dock, and Mrs. Wilson visited with the Baruch family in New York before returning to Washington.

Later that year, a seemingly natural and joyous occasion would alter profoundly Belle's self-perception. It would bring her face to face with her most intimate and heretofore hidden sexuality.

10

❧

An Awakening

In late 1925 Evangeline Brewster Johnson fell in love with the brilliant conductor Leopold Stokowski. Nothing would do for Evangeline but for Belle to share her ecstasy and participate in the plans for the wedding. She chortled as she told Belle about her staid family's reaction to her fiancé. When she announced her plans, her brother demanded to know just who Stokowski was. When Evangeline replied that he was a conductor, her brother said loftily: "In this family, one doesn't marry conductors."

"Darling," she told him, "not a streetcar conductor!"[1]

Belle joined in the laughter, but a cold dread was building within her as she struggled to share Evangeline's happiness. She tried to articulate her feelings but did not fully understand them herself.

In a letter written January 6, 1926, to Edith Wilson, Evangeline expressed her dismay over Belle's unhappiness: "Belle I hope and pray will become reconciled to the idea, though in what possible way she is 'losing me' is impossible for me to understand. But I want to have her happy too for her love and devotionate [*sic*] friendship are among the most precious things in my life."[2]

Reluctantly, Belle joined in the preparations and was among the select guests when Evangeline married the man she described as "a child, a man, and a genius all at once."[3] Mourning Evangeline's marriage, Belle came to the painful realization of why no man had ever lingered in her heart. Her feelings for Evangeline far exceeded those of friendship. With agonizing insight, Belle recognized that she loved Evangeline and would prefer the affection and intimacy of other women to that of men.

In the 1920s America was a homophobic society. The very subject of homosexuality was taboo. One did not dare mention the terms *lesbian* or *homosexual* in polite company. Such individuals were ostracized, called perverts, and thought to be mentally ill. She had no one to whom she could turn. Whatever trauma or pain such revelations caused Belle remain forever private. Baruchs did not discuss such personal feelings, particularly those of such an intimate nature.

As always when she was troubled, Belle went to Hobcaw Barony, seeking peace and understanding. She had a tough, practical streak, was a realist and totally honest, but her sense of isolation was almost overwhelming. In time she came to terms with her self-discovery and accepted this aspect of her nature. Although twice she came close to marriage, her enduring relationships were extended liaisons with other women.

While many homosexuals seek comfort in the society of those who share their sexual orientation, Belle's strength of character was such that in her younger years, she did not allow herself to become isolated from so-called normal society. Homosexuality for her, she decided, was normal, but she refused to define herself by her lesbianism. It was part of who she was, but not *all* of who she was. Her friendships were many and varied. Such was the force of her personality that those who knew of her lesbianism accepted it or simply denied it in order to enjoy the companionship of such a remarkable woman.

Belle's wealth and riding prowess, coupled with her generosity and charm, ensured her acceptance in European society, which was more tolerant of alternative sexual lifestyles. Already an intensely private person, Belle's lesbianism only increased the cool hauteur with which she faced the world. She had the wealth and social position to live her life as she wished as well as the courage to do so.

As for the Baruch family, no one knows, or will reveal, at what point they became aware of Belle's sexual orientation. Indications are that it was sometime in the 1930s before Belle became quite open about her lesbian liaisons. Not that there were public displays of affection; Belle's innate sense of privacy and propriety would never have permitted such behavior.

The family created a conspiracy of silence, shrouding Belle's lesbianism with denial. It was ignored, unmentioned. Her companions were treated as friends or houseguests or simply ignored. Bernard Baruch's nurse/companion of twenty years, Elizabeth Navarro, stated that not once in the two decades they were together did he refer to his daughter's homosexuality. "He knew that I knew. . . . I'd have to be nutty not to know."

Only her brother, Junior, reacted with open disgust and revulsion. He once confided to Elizabeth Navarro that he discovered his sister's lesbianism in the most shocking manner. Arriving in New York with his British bride, Winifred Beatrice Mann, he happily planned a surprise visit to his sister's New York apartment. Laughing and happy, he entered her apartment unannounced, only to discover her in a passionate embrace with her lesbian partner. Disgusted and humiliated in front of his bride, he stormed from Belle's apartment and rushed to confront his mother, insisting that she speak to Belle, that she demand that Belle cease her perverted lifestyle.

"But you know, mother," he said bitterly, "she just went about with her head in the sand."

Junior refused to visit his sister again except on rare family get-togethers. He would visit his father at Hobcaw House, his Kaminski cousins and William Kennedy in Georgetown, but he would not go near his sister's home at Bellefield.

11

La Belle Équitation

In the spring of 1926 Belle went to France, where she plunged into a whirl of social engagements. She sighed with pleasure at the beauty of Paris, the Paris immortalized by Hemingway and Fitzgerald, where the wide avenue of the Champs-Élysées bloomed with chestnut blossoms and brilliant flowers instead of the tourist kiosks of today. It was not in Belle, however, to join the "lost generation." Too many things were happening in the world, and she wanted to be a part of them.

Edith Wilson returned to Europe that summer, and Belle eagerly sent her advance copies of all the latest theatrical and musical events. She welcomed Mrs. Wilson and her brother, Wilmer Bolling, and their small party headed once more to the haunted castle in Scotland for the hunting excursion.

Leaving Scotland, they drove to Eastern Europe, destined for Prague, Czechoslovakia, where they were to be the guests of President Jan Masaryk. Then it was on to Geneva once again for a session at the League of Nations. Mrs. Wilson left for the United States, and Belle journeyed to Pau.

Belle was restless. The world was changing so quickly! Marvelous electronic and aeronautic advances were being made. There had already been radiotelephone communication between New York and London, and the first airmail service had been established between New York and Boston.

The months flowed into 1927, and Belle was in France when Charles Lindbergh flew his *Spirit of St. Louis* solo from New York to Paris. It was an exciting time, and Americans basked in the reflected glory of "Lucky Lindy," who was the toast of Paris. Babe Ruth set a new home-run record, and the amazing Holland Tunnel opened connecting New York and New Jersey. Belle wanted new challenges to add to her own accomplishments.

While hunting at Pau, Belle met Paul Larregain, a brilliant rider and teacher. Larregain was highly respected as a horseman, breeder, and trainer and was among those who organized and established the standards for international equestrian competition. Belle was a frequent visitor at Larregain's stables.

Sir Alfred Munnings, one of the great equestrian artists of the world and president of the British Royal Academy from 1944 to 1949, wrote of Larregain:

> A fine horseman and an expert in what is known as Haute École, was a man called Larrigain [sic]. He had been an instructor at Samur [the French National Riding Academy]. His stables and enormous riding school—a converted aeroplane hangar—stood in the valley near the Garbe river. Here I used to watch French attendants with their short-handled whips, lashes many yards long, standing at attention whilst two horses, being schooled for international high jumping came on to the wide, sanded floor. These horses were without saddle or bridle. Perfectly free, wearing thick cotton bandages and knee-caps to prevent damage from the iron jumping-bars, they would, at the movement of a long lash, turn at the far end. Then, one following the other at a canter, measuring their stride, they jumped over the unbendable iron bars, more often than not without a fault.
>
> Continuing their beautiful free action around the big arena, on the far side they met with and jumped a similar obstacle. These bars would then be raised an inch—two inches—three—until the jump was somewhere near seven feet. The horses, knowing such bars did not easily give, seldom hit them. It was a thrilling sight for one trying to understand the miraculous live mechanism of the horse.[1]

Larregain had watched Belle ride among the foxhunting set at Pau. "La Belle," as he saw her, was fearless in headlong pursuit of the fox, firm in the saddle, her long legs guiding her mount. She did not shy from the most dangerous course, taking each jump with exhilarating, almost intoxicating joy. Strong and powerful, the Junoesque American was in total control of her mount and, more importantly, of herself. What elegance and style! Belle looked magnificent in riding kit, the high polished boots, hand-sewn and fitted by Maxwell of London, her hunt jackets perfectly tailored. Her imported English saddle was purchased at M. J. Monheimer in New York. In top hat, she appeared even taller and leaner, an elegant silhouette.

"Belle should always be seen on horseback," gushed a friend. "She looks so magnificent!"

"That would be a bit awkward," Belle observed.

The more Larregain saw of Belle Baruch, the more he liked her. He was aware of the quiet, anonymous philanthropy of the young American who gave generously to local orphanages and hospitals, particularly those involved in physical rehabilitation. More than one poor patient found his medical bills paid by a mysterious benefactor. A condition of Belle's gifts was that the donor remain anonymous.

Larregain suggested to Belle that while foxhunting was great sport, she should consider competing, particularly in high jump. Privately, he did wonder if the rich young American would have the discipline and determination to excel at the dangerous, demanding, and male-dominated sport of international show jumping.

Belle considered Larregain's suggestion. She had done a lot of show jumping as a girl and young woman, but the average American courses just after World War I had a meager variety of obstacles, possibly six or eight jumps. The courses were fairly straightforward as well, lacking the complexity and challenge of their European counterparts, which usually featured from fifteen to twenty difficult and dangerous obstacles.

Some American riders sneered at what they called European "trick jumping." However, the highly respected American equestrienne Katharine Dunlap challenged that attitude in an article published in *Horse and Horseman* magazine:

> Just what is really meant by that expression—what really *is* "trick jumping"?
>
> If it means that a horse and his rider have the skill and training necessary to negotiate a series of difficult obstacles arranged in such fashion that the horse must be constantly in hand, and that his rider must be capable of keeping him there, and of giving him the right lead and balance to make his performance the best possible, then, perhaps, the "trick" is a good one, being simply what is otherwise known as good horsemanship! . . .
>
> The high degree of proficiency demanded in order to make a fair showing in the larger European shows presupposes a long, arduous schooling. But horsemen as well as horses are developed in the process. The "trick" seems to consist of setting a high standard in the courses and of working hard and patiently to attain it. In that case it might almost be a trick worth our while to turn.[2]

Belle was twenty-eight years old and had been riding most of her life. She knew she was good, a "natural." The challenge, the opportunity to ride against the best in the world was irresistible.

Together, the Frenchman and the American girl began to train. Belle was as tireless as Larregain was demanding, driving herself and her mounts, striving for the perfect jump, the perfect course. Recovering quickly from inevitable falls, she remounted without coddling or encouragement. She had a rare patience with her horses, strong but loving and sensitive hands on the reins.

She also began to expand her stable with Larregain as her mentor. Perhaps the greatest expression of confidence the Frenchman gave to Belle was arranging for her to buy the prized Anglo-Arabian, Souriant III.

Souriant means "smiling," and Belle was grinning from ear to ear when she first mounted the magnificent chestnut. She had many fine horses through the years, including Hunter, Yankee Doodle, Interdite, Paleface, and Dame—all champions—but Souriant, whom Belle called Toto, was her favorite and by 1931 the envy of all Europe.

By 1928 Larregain decided Belle was ready to launch her amateur riding career. But it was not going to be simple. Riders in the international shows were required to have a license from their respective national riding federations. In vain, Belle pleaded with the United States embassy in France to issue her a license. Officials at the embassy were adamant in their refusals. Only the United States Cavalry teams represented the country in international competition, she was told. Granted, a few individuals competed in an unofficial capacity, but certainly not women.

Belle in a temper was intimidating. She would draw herself up to her full six-foot-plus height and glare down her impressive nose at her offender, dark eyes flashing, a raptor ready to strike. But neither her unbendable will nor her imposing demeanor could win this particular battle. The embassy staff might quail before her fury, but they steadfastly refused to issue a license.

Belle's frustration was enormous. To come this far and be denied the right to compete was unthinkable! Typically she refused to accept defeat. Through the intercession of Larregain and other supporters, she obtained a French gentleman rider's license. In spite of her profound annoyance with the embassy, Belle always rode under the U.S. flag.

In the international competitions, a rider's national flag was always flown over the jury box as the rider entered the ring. Also flown was the national flag of the rider who was leading the competition at that time. Thanks to Belle, the U.S. flag was flying regularly in the international arenas of Europe. Her first year as an amateur rider was exceptional. She quickly earned the respect of the international equestrian community, placing in half the shows she entered and taking six first-place wins.

Belle once wrote to Edith Wilson: "When I enter the ring the Stars and Stripes go up, which makes it really very impressive."[3] The strains of the national anthem would bring tears to her eyes. It galled her, however, to see the

U.S. ambassador or his representatives smiling and nodding, sharing the lime-light when "our wonderful Miss Baruch" triumphed in the international shows. Belle drew deeply on her rigid social training to maintain a semblance of civility toward the very men who tried to stop her from competing.

It was always Belle's dream to represent her country in the Olympics, but it was not until 1949 that the United States Equestrian Team was formed, one year after the army dissolved the cavalry. Even though women were members of the USET, it would be 1956 before women could compete in Olympic equestrian events. Kathy Kusner, in 1964, would have the honor of being the first equestrienne to bring an Olympic medal home to the United States.

At the end of the show-jumping season, Belle cabled Edith Wilson to join her in Europe for a few weeks' vacation. Headquartered at the Ritz, the women shopped, dined, patronized the theaters and concert halls, and traveled. Flushed with success, fulfilled and happy, Belle came home to Hobcaw Barony in December for the family's annual Christmas gathering.

Belle noted that the country's economy matched her optimistic, ebullient mood with a fast-rising bull market. Her father, however, did not share the nation's euphoria. He grumbled about the plight of the farmer and the de-pressed market for farm produce as well as for farm-related industries and ser-vices. For years Baruch had labored in vain to bring a share of the industrial boom to the farmers. He did not trust an economy in which one-fourth of the nation's population was in dire economic straits.

Belle's father growled that the stock market was artificially high. Plain com-mon sense, he insisted, dictated that prices could not continue to rise indefi-nitely. Belle and the family listened and smiled, unconcerned, content to leave such matters in Bernard's capable hands. But not even the wily "Wolf of Wall Street" foresaw the economic chaos awaiting the world in the coming year.

12

Success and Romance at Home and Abroad

The year 1929 began like any other year for Belle. She celebrated the New Year at Hobcaw with her family, then headed north to New York to see a few plays and look after her business affairs before setting sail for Europe.

Unaware of the crisis looming in America, Belle reached France in the spring for the start of the riding season. She entered fewer shows that year, riding mostly in Paris and Pau with only one trip each to Fontainebleau, Vichy, and Biarritz. She acquitted herself well, finishing in the top three in half her meets. Miss Baruch, it was noted in the European newspapers, was frequently the only American and the only woman competing.

While foxhunting at Pau, Belle met Barbara Donohoe, the daughter of a prominent family from Menlo Park near San Francisco. Barbara was tall, elegant, every inch a lady. Barbara and Belle liked each other on sight, each recognizing in the other a kindred spirit and shared interests. Both were independent and adventuresome, eager to meet life head-on, relishing all of life's pleasures. It was Belle who persuaded Barbara to join the horse-show circuit, offering to board Barbara's beloved Malicorn with her own mounts since Barbara had no stable in France. The two women traveled through Europe together, foxhunting, competing in horse shows, and hitting the high spots. Once again, Belle had a close friend with whom to share her life. Barbara was her first great love.

The secret to their enduring friendship, Barbara once observed, was that "I was myself and she was herself and we wouldn't dream of trying to influence one another. I shouldn't like it and I know she wouldn't."

When not at home with her family or visiting friends, Barbara was a frequent visitor at Hobcaw Barony and traveled extensively with Belle. They were devoted to each other, and Belle grew restive when Barbara was not at her side.

Through the summer of 1929 Belle rode and hunted, and toured in Italy, France, and England. Her father's misgivings over the state of the market had long since slipped from her mind. But fortunately for Belle and the rest of the Baruch family fortunes, Bernard Baruch had been keenly attentive.

Baruch was increasingly restless and intuitively mistrustful of the aggressive bull market. As early as late 1928, he began to sell out of the market. "Repeatedly," he wrote, "in my market operations I have sold stock while it still was rising—and that has been one reason why I have held on to my fortune. Many a time I might have made a good deal more by holding a stock, but then I would also have been caught in the fall when the price of the stock collapsed."[1]

As he stated more succinctly to Helen Lawrenson, writer and former managing editor of *Vanity Fair* (and with whom Baruch had an extended affair): "I have a talent for making money, the way Fritz Kreisler has a talent for playing the violin and Jesse Owens has a talent for running. I buy when stocks go down, I sell when they go up. When prices go up, production increases, consumption decreases, and prices then fall. When prices go down it's vice versa. I got rich, Madame Fathead [Baruch's pet name for Lawrenson], by remembering those words."[2]

By the time "Black Tuesday" struck in September 1929, Baruch had divested himself of nearly all his holdings. It was not that he foresaw the coming of the Great Depression, rather that his common sense and intuition warned him that there had to be a limit to soaring prices. On the night of the crash, Baruch hosted a dinner for his friend, Winston Churchill. Financiers, bankers, and political friends gathered at Baruch's Fifth Avenue residence to honor his British guest. One man stood to toast Churchill and address the group as "friends and former millionaires."[3] For Baruch the millions were still secure. He had come out of the crash with nearly all his wealth and that of his children intact.

Belle hurried home from Europe to find devastation throughout the financial world. The country was sliding rapidly into the abyss of a depression that was to last more than a decade. Thanks to her father's sagacity, however, Belle's carefree life changed very little. Banks failed, millions were unemployed, soup kitchens and bread lines struggled valiantly to feed the hungry, but the house of Baruch stood solidly on the foundations of Bernard Baruch's financial acumen.

In December 1929 the Baruchs gathered at Hobcaw for their annual Christmas festivities. Old friends, Dick Lydon (New York State Supreme Court justice Richard T. Lydon), and Senator Key Pittman of Nevada were among the guests.

Early one evening, fire broke out in the house. Seeing the flames, William Kennedy and his family hurried to help. As the flames roared into the night sky, everyone on the plantation rushed to the scene. "It was the biggest fire I had ever seen," recalled Minnie Kennedy. Men rushed into the house carrying out furniture and whatever belongings they could grab. But the fire roared madly through the wood-frame house before an effective fight to save the "Old Relick" could even be organized.

Lois Massey had been sent by Mrs. Baruch to carry a message to the neighboring plantation of Arcadia. She had delivered her note to Dr. Isaac Emerson and was headed back to Hobcaw when she saw flames lighting the sky. By the time she reached Friendfield House it had burned to the ground.

"Everyone was kind of in shock," she recalled, "but, thank God, nobody was hurt." Strange things had been removed from the house—Mrs. Baruch had rescued a huge bouquet of flowers, someone else had dragged out a mattress, and Junior had rescued his Victrola. Someone strolled over to see what record had been playing, and everyone laughed somewhat hysterically when they saw the title: "I Don't Want to Set the World on Fire, I Just Want to Start a Flame in Your Heart."

One other essential item was rescued from the fire—a barrel of corn liquor. As Bernard Baruch later described it: "We were standing on the front lawn, watching the flames, when suddenly Senator Pittman exclaimed: 'My gosh, Bernie! You've got a barrel of good corn licker in the basement which will go up like a bomb when the fire hits it.' Whether it was the threat of an explosion or the prospective loss of good liquor that worried Key, I don't know, but he and Dick Lydon tied wet handkerchiefs over their faces, dashed into the basement, and came out rolling the barrel before them."[4]

It was a sad family group that straggled back to New York. An era had ended at Hobcaw, and though Bernard Baruch built the magnificent new Hobcaw House—made as fireproof as possible—the Baruchs felt that something irretrievable had been lost.

By 1930 there was a worldwide depression. Millions were unemployed and banks were closing across the nation as Americans lost their life's savings. In ironic contrast to the poverty and chaos in the land, construction of the beautiful Chrysler Building and the magnificent Empire State Building, then the world's tallest skyscraper, was completed in New York.

Belle went back to France only to find that Europe was suffering too. England estimated two and a half million unemployed; Germany, five million. In the midst of the strife, Adolph Hitler's Nazi Party won a majority in the Reichstag, and an insidious malaise began to drift across Europe.

Still, life for Belle remained largely unchanged. Those of her friends who had not lost everything in the depression still followed the show circuit. There were the hunt balls and shooting and riding to hounds and new triumphs for Belle in riding competitions. Then the unexpected happened: she fell in love—with a man.

Dashing, handsome Charles A. "Chita" Davila, nephew of composer Franz Liszt, was the Rumanian minister in Washington, D.C. Belle met Chita through her friend Ella Mano, then married to General Demistroski, a close friend and confidant of King Carol II of Rumania. "There was so much laughter when the three of them got together," Ella Severin recalled. "They had such humor among them."

Belle and Chita's romance covered two continents with meetings in Bucharest, Paris, Washington, and New York. On one occasion, when she toured Rumania with Edith Wilson, Davila was there, serenading them each night with a different Gypsy orchestra. The two lovers shared many interests—a love of horses and shooting, dancing and music, a sophisticated view of the world. Belle was incredibly happy. She had thought this type of love would never come to her. Reports of marriage between the handsome couple were rumored throughout Washington. In a letter dated February 9, 1931, Edith Wilson wrote to Bernard Baruch:

My dear Baron:

. . . What is this that I have just heard over the telephone from Daisy Harriman concerning Belle and the Roumanian Minister? She tells me that the whole of Washington is stirred up over a report that he and Belle are engaged, and that when he gave a dinner on Saturday night it was rumored to be the occasion of an announcement; but as the dinner proceeded, and no announcement came, he was asked the direct question, and his reply was that if such an honour came to him it would certainly not be his place to make the announcement—and that he was at a loss to know where such a thing could have got started. Mrs. Harriman asked me if I had heard it, and I told her I was such a cave-dweller that I never got gossip; and her reply was, "Well then I know it is not true, for you would know it."[5]

The New York newspapers of February 26, 1931, headlined the story:

DENIAL FAILS TO DOWN STORY OF BARUCH-DAVILA TROTH
Despite denials the rumor persists, not only in this city but also in Washington, that Miss Belle Baruch and Mr. Charles A. Davila, the Rumanian Minister to the United States, are about to announce their engagement. The

parties to the betrothal, I hear, have declared the story to be without foundation, but in both social and diplomatic circles, and especially in the latter, the tale is not unbelieved. . . .

Miss Baruch, who is a member of the Junior League, and a familiar figure in society, is known for her interest in matters other than those which are purely fashionable. She has long been an ardent advocate of greater participation of women in civic and national affairs and has for some time been a student of international politics.[6]

Just what reply Bernard Baruch made to Mrs. Wilson's letter is not known, and the Baruchs declined to discuss the relationship between Belle and Chita Davila. Renee Samstag said vaguely that it was, after all, over fifty years ago, but as she recalls, the family did not sanction the marriage. "He was a foreigner, you know, and they let her know in many little ways that they did not approve."

There was no such subtlety in Bernard Baruch's cruel words to his older daughter. "Davila is nothing but a fortune hunter," he thundered, "all he wants is your money. He doesn't care about you!" Belle shared the Baruch iron will and determination and, as much as she loved her father, she was determined to marry Davila. "He can't give you any more than I can," her father protested, and offered her two million dollars if she would go back to France and forget the Rumanian diplomat.

Belle refused, but in the end civil war and political expediency ended the relationship. Rumania, like all the Balkan countries, was fraught with intrigue and turmoil during the pre–World War II era. King Carol II of Rumania struggled constantly to maintain his throne against political enemies like the notorious Iron Guard, known for its rabid anti-Semitism and passionate nationalism. The Iron Guard had claimed responsibility for numerous political assassinations and had wiped out entire villages of Jewish people. For Chita Davila to marry the daughter of one of the most prominent Jews in America, and quite possibly the world, would hardly have been conducive to a long, healthy life in his native country. One might dally with a wealthy Jewess; one did not marry her and live to enjoy the liaison. It did not matter that Belle was Episcopalian. In the eyes of the fanatics, one drop of Jewish blood was a contaminant. King Carol strongly protested the liaison to Davila.

It was a tumultuous, dangerous period of Rumanian history, and Davila's energies were focused on the survival of his nation and his person. Reluctantly, they ended their passionate relationship. Proud and bitter, Belle advised her father of their estrangement and, in typical, pragmatic Baruch style, collected her consolation prize of two million dollars, which she used to build one of the finest stables in Europe.

Nearly a decade later, Edith Wilson sent Belle newspaper clippings concerning Davila's political activities and return to the United States. One concerned then-exiled King Carol's wish to enter the United States from Mexico and establish a free-Rumania movement within the United States.

> Charles Davila violently opposes Carol's plan to head a free Rumanian movement in the United States. Davila was deprived of his Rumanian citizenship in 1938 after he had criticized Carol as a dictator; the citizenship later was restored by Premier Antonescu whom Davila assailed only a few weeks ago for helping Hitler. A year ago Davila organized the American Rumanian Alliance for Democracy.
>
> Declaring that he spoke in the name of Rumanian democrats, he said the Rumanian people are overwhelmingly on the Allied side.
>
> "There will not be any kind of Rumanian organization; headed by Carol Hohenzollern either on American or Canadian soil or anywhere else," he added.[7]

The other column, by *Washington Post* writer Elizabeth Henney, was in a somewhat lighter vein:

FORMER MINISTER OF RUMANIA BACK IN CAPITAL
SETTING FEMININE HEARTS AFLUTTER

> Don't look so startled. That isn't a ghost with the group in the corner by the punch bowl. That's Charles A. Davila, in the flesh. Yes, I know, I heard he was dead too. I also heard earlier rumors that he'd been married, and that after his tour as Minister of Rumania, he had become persona non grata with his own government. Well, his presence in town would seem to indicate the first rumor was highly exaggerated; he says he isn't married; and anyone knows he couldn't get an answer on the third question from a diplomat. . . .
>
> And so again, debutantes will be sighing over, and setting their caps for, the gentleman who reigned so long in Capital Society as Washington's most eligible and most uncatchable bachelor.[8]

Perhaps for Belle, her liaison with Davila was merely an experiment in heterosexual love. Once again, the Baruch cloak of intense personal privacy shrouds the affair.

Many years later Nolan "Red" Taylor, Belle's superintendent at Hobcaw Barony, asked about a photograph of a handsome, dark man in splendid military uniform who bore a startling resemblance to the young Bernard Baruch.

Belle identified him as Chita Davila and said, "I never stopped loving him." Taylor said he particularly remembered the incident because it was so unusual for Miss Belle to make such a personal comment. Ella Severin said that Davila visited Bellefield at least twice in the 1950s. He was still single and, to her knowledge, never married.

After the breakup with Davila, Belle retreated to Hobcaw to the new Georgian manor house her father had built in 1930 to replace the "Old Relick." The gracious brick and concrete building, with six two-story white columns supporting a wide balcony, was decorated by Mrs. Raoul Fleishman, then a noted interior decorator in New York, later part owner of the *New Yorker* magazine.

In lowcountry tradition, Hobcaw House faces the waters of Winyah Bay. There are nine bedrooms in Hobcaw House, each with its own bathroom and fireplace. The large living room stretches across half the front of the house and is divided from the library and downstairs bedrooms by a spacious entrance hall. Off the living room is a baronial dining room that could comfortably accommodate twenty-five to thirty people. Near the back entrance was a large combination gun and mud room where hunting parties would shed their muddy boots and heavy outdoor clothing and rack their guns.

In spite of its grandeur, to Baruch, Hobcaw House was still just a hunting lodge. It was a splendid and beautiful home offering every convenience, but the Baruch children nostalgically preferred the Victorian "Old Relick."

By March, Belle was back in France, foxhunting at Pau. The French countryside was dear and familiar, and if Belle was pining after a lost love, it was not readily apparent to her hunting companions. Belle was in her element, relishing the ritual of the hunt, the bay of eager hounds, the sight and sound of riders reining in their restlessly prancing mounts, awaiting the signal of the hunting horn. Barbara Donohoe was at her side.

The elegant, charming F. H. Prince was master of the hunt at Pau and welcomed Belle as one of the most splendid horsewomen of her day. Hunts were held three times weekly over one of the most demanding terrains in Europe. Riders gathered promptly at 11:45 A.M., and the first horn sounded at noon precisely.

The Paris edition of the *New York Herald*, which often wrote about the hunt activities at Pau, listed Belle's companions: Master F. H. Prince, Mrs. Prince, Miss Hutton, the Marquis and Marquise de Guadalmina, Comte and Comtesse H. de Bearn, Mr. and Mrs. Kingsland, Baronne Glutz, Colonel and Mrs. Heathcote, Comte and Comtesse de Toulouse-Lautrec, M. and Mme Merillon, the Vicomte and Mlle de Vaufreland, the Baron and Mlle de Palaminy, Miss Donohoe, Comte de Baillet-Latour, and a dozen others.[9]

Though Belle did not ride often in the show-jump circuit that year, she finished in the top four 63 percent of the time. She made the decision, however, that she would enter the Paris Horse Show at the Grand Palais on April 11, 1931. The Paris Horse Show was the crème de la crème of show jumping, the one every competitor dreamed of winning.

Belle arrived at the Grand Palais around noon. Since no one was about, she walked the course, studying the twists and turns and challenging jumps of one of the most difficult and demanding courses in the horse-show world. Belle's starting position was 108, so she returned to her hotel to rest, not returning until late afternoon, after nearly half of the 119 entries had performed. She noted that no one had yet attained a perfect score.

She sat in the grandstands for a while, then wandered back to where Souriant was stabled to discuss strategy with Larregain. Finally she mounted Souriant, taking him to the exercise paddock. Other discouraged riders returned, complaining about the dreadful course and the terrible demands it made on their horses, some calling it a horse killer. Finally, her number was called. Souriant and Belle entered the ring. Bowing to the jury, suddenly they were off, completing the course in record time with no errors—the only perfect ride of the day.

Belle and her supporters waited anxiously, watching the rest of the competition. She admitted to her parents in a letter that she and her friends were "in a most un-Christian frame of mind and beamed approval if the others unfortunately sent flying a bar or splashed merrily in the water."[10] Finally, the last horse made the circuit, and Belle's number 108 stood alone at the top of the list—the only perfect ride.

The Paris edition of the *New York Herald* reported:

Riding against 118 horsemen, among them the outstanding gentlemen riders of France, Miss Belle Baruch, daughter of Bernard Baruch, of New York, took her great chestnut, Souriant III over a severe course yesterday to win the Prix de la Coupe and the trophy offered by Gaston Doumergue, President of the French Republic, and the enthusiastic applause of the spectators at the Concours Hippique.

The American girl's brilliant ride was greeted by the most spontaneous outburst of this year's show and as the award was being made the crowd swarmed into the ring to form a great circle about the winner, who sat top-hatted and smiling on her handsome mount.[11]

There were joyous celebrations afterward, for the Paris Horse Show was as much a society as a sporting event. Belle wired triumphantly to her parents: "One hundred nineteen entries Coup de Paris Trophy given by President of Republic. Stop. Souriant and I won being only perfect performance. Stop. Very happy. Love."[12]

A German-language overview of show-jump history, *Geschichte des Pferde-Sports,* by Max E. Ammann, referred to 1931 as the "year of the amazons . . . 1931 was the first great amazon siege against the mighty conquering males. . . . In Paris, Belle Baruch, trained in Pau by Larregain, won the Coupe Civile with Souriant III. The Coupe de Vichy went to Baroness Louise Hasselbalch, then living in Switzerland, riding Baladine. Stella Pierce, riding Girlie, won the Daily Mail Cup, repeating the win in 1932."[13]

After her Paris triumph, Belle was approached by the German cavalry team with an offer to buy Souriant as a gift for Adolph Hitler. She flatly refused, not even bothering to hide her contempt. Belle despised Hitler and, in later years, refused to ride in the international horse show at Aachen, Germany. German wines were not served at a Baruch table. Belle had a very strong Jewish side in spite of her Episcopalian upbringing. Her friend Varvara Hasselbalch Heyd recalls that Belle frequently poked fun at her own hooked nose and referred to other Jews in her fluent German as *krummnasen* (hook nose) or *unsere Leute* (our folks).

In June 1931 Edith Wilson and her niece Lucy Moeling arrived in France aboard the *Leviathan* for a trip that included a visit to Poland to witness the unveiling in Poznañ of a statue of Woodrow Wilson by Gutzon Borglum. The event was in conjunction with Poland's commemoration of the U.S. Independence Day on July 4, and Mrs. Wilson was to be the guest of honor. The Poles had never forgotten Woodrow Wilson's staunch support of Polish autonomy following World War I. Ignacy Paderewski, whose amazing life included a brilliant career as a concert pianist and the premiership of Poland, had arranged the unveiling.

Bernard Baruch's limousine was waiting for Mrs. Wilson and Miss Moeling, and they were driven to Paris. The Baruch family joined them for parts of their eastern European tour. Baruch ancestors had come from Poznañ, once part of East Prussia and now part of Poland.

The Wilson party, traveling by train, was met at the Polish border by a delegation from President Ignacy Móscicki and escorted to Warsaw. After much celebration, they boarded the train once again for Poznañ. Quoting from a letter from Lucy Moeling to her husband, Edith Wilson's biographer, Isabel Ross, describes the event:

"Our arrival at Poznan was the most dramatic thing I have ever been privileged to see," Lucy wrote to her husband. A mounted escort with pennants flying escorted them to Wilson Park. Edith sat on a raised dais with the President, two ambassadors and the Minister of Foreign Affairs. The sun blazed down on them as the President unveiled the statue. Even with many eyes focused on her Edith could not conceal her dismay, and Lucy wrote to her husband, "I almost shrieked when I saw it—it's so terrible aside from not having the slightest resemblance . . . the statue is unbalanced. The queerest impression."[14]

Although appalled by the statue, Edith Wilson was touched by the outpouring of sincere affection from the Polish people and their genuine regard for the memory of her beloved Woodrow. From Poland, the party traveled through Germany and on to Switzerland. Bernard and Anne Baruch left the group to return to Paris. Belle stayed on with Lucy and Mrs. Wilson in Geneva.

Paderewski, who had arranged the events in Poland, had been unable to attend, remaining in Switzerland to comfort his wife, who was gravely ill. Edith Wilson wanted to drive from Geneva to visit her old friend at his country home, so Belle arranged for a car. Because of Mrs. Paderewski's illness, it was not a joyous occasion, but the old friends reminisced, and the memory of one amusing incident would evoke laughter from Belle and Edith for years to come.

Belle had taken Mrs. Wilson and Paderewski for a long, pleasant drive through the Swiss countryside. As they climbed the hill leading back to Paderewski's house, the car stalled. Pragmatic as always, Belle assessed the situation and advised Paderewski that if he'd give them a good push, she could restart the engine. The world-renowned pianist gasped in dismay and reluctantly but firmly informed Belle that there was no way he could push the car and risk injury to his "precious fingers."

The two women exchanged glances, and Edith, every bit as practical as Belle, climbed out of the car and, as the famous concert pianist watched from the roadside, began to push! Belle and Edith managed to contain their giggles until they were in private, but the incident became a favorite "remember when . . ." story. Belle saw Lucy and Mrs. Wilson off on their return trip to the United States and rejoined the horse-show circuit.

13

Triumphs with
Souriant and
Rumors of War

I n 1932 Belle hired a Frenchman, Jean Darthez, as her head groom and
trainer, beginning a relationship that would span three decades. The
doughty Frenchman maintained what he considered to be the neatest, cleanest
stables in all of France. Belle was an exacting employer, especially where her
horses were concerned, and in Darthez she found someone who met her expectations. The primary responsibility for the care and training of her stables was
henceforth in the capable hands of Darthez.

It was sometimes hard to say who loved her horses more, Belle or Darthez.
Both were especially devoted to Souriant (or Toto, as they called him). In
fact, sometimes Jean's devotion to the handsome chestnut exceeded even Belle's
expectations. Planning to compete in Italy, Belle instructed Jean to make
arrangements to ship Souriant to Florence. To her dismay, the Frenchman reserved an entire car on the Rome Express for the champion jumper. When Belle
objected to such extravagance, Darthez insisted: "Miss Baruch, your horse must
have the very best!"

Toto must have enjoyed the ride, because he and Belle scored another great
triumph, winning the Premio Primavera Florentine, setting a woman's amateur
high-jump record of 2.10 meters. At the ball following the show, Belle was again
asked to sell Souriant, this time to the Italian team who wished to present the
Anglo-Arab to "Il Duce" (Mussolini).

Belle laughed and said, "Tell me, how many lira are there in the bank of
Italy?"

"Why, millions, signorina," she was told.

"Well," said Belle, her brown eyes sparkling, "it's not enough. There isn't enough lira in all of Italy to buy Souriant."[1]

In August of that year, Belle commissioned Sir Alfred Munnings to paint her astride Souriant. She arranged to meet Sir Alfred at Biarritz and drive him to the Hôtel de France at Pau.

In a letter dated Monday, August 29, 1932, Sir Alfred wrote to his wife, Violet:

> Here I am for a few days. Miss Baruch is here. Has been waiting for me. Hot —but not that heat of Spain. The Pyrenees—faint—a long way away, and the town very nice. . . . I'm ready to do Belle's wonderful horse. Soon I go down to the stables to see the horses and the young ones in the school [Larregain's school] where Miss Baruch is going to jump. . . .
>
> Miss Baruch just loves it all, and rides with her friend. She has eight horses and a mare and foal, and gets on anything in her skirt and silk stockings and high-heeled shoes, and goes round those horse show jumps—I never saw anything like it, and her toe never moves in the iron,—it's beyond me.[2]

Belle was the ideal hostess for Sir Alfred. He delighted in her luxurious, specially designed Chrysler, only twenty-five models of which were made each year. Sir Alfred would start painting early in the morning while it was cool. Belle would bring gourmet lunches to share at noon, always including his favorite juicy melons and, of course, a treat for Souriant. In the evenings they dined with Belle's friends in tiny local restaurants where the food was plain but delicious.

Sir Alfred fell in love with Souriant and inscribed on his early studies for the painting: "The most charming horse I ever painted. He stood alone like this whilst the groom kept away the flies." In later years, when he published his autobiography, Sir Alfred wanted to include Souriant's portrait as one of the illustrations. Prompted by her passion for privacy, Belle refused permission but later regretted that she had not allowed her beloved Toto's painting to be included.

Sir Alfred noted in a later letter that when he and Belle went to Biarritz where Belle was to ride in the show, she had to withdraw because of illness. A series of minor illnesses plagued Belle throughout 1932.

As was her custom, Belle visited Geneva while the League of Nations was in session. She had been delighted the previous year when American Jane Addams was awarded the Nobel Peace Prize. Miss Addams, who led the Women's League for Peace and Freedom, had been nominated several times by both her own organization and the League of Nations.

In the fall of 1932 the League Assembly devoted most of its sessions to the Japanese incursions into Manchuria. The debates extended into the early winter months of 1933, but in the end, the league failed in its first test of the collective security system, unable to muster the will and votes to do more than verbally chastise Japan. Japan simply announced its decision to withdraw from the League of Nations, effective in two years' time. The scene was set for the expansion of Japanese aggression in the Far East.

In Germany, Hitler watched closely, encouraged by the league's lack of resolution. He was well aware that the cohesiveness of the European nations was diminished by severe economic straits and that each country scrambled to protect its own interests.

Franklin Delano Roosevelt was elected to his first presidential term in 1932, and his primary concern was rebuilding the U.S. economy. He protested the Japanese action but had little influence with the European nations. After all, the United States was not even a member of the league. Belle no longer took an active role in the League of Nations, but she retained an active interest in and concern for the league's role in world peace. She was not encouraged by what she heard in Geneva.

Belle sailed for home in December, staying for only a few months. She was determined to have a better riding season in 1933 and left for Europe on the *Ile de France* in March. She wrote Lois Massey to say that she was trying to force herself to get up early enough in the morning to take part in the shooting matches aboard ship: "Bertha [her gun] is under my bunk. Shall have to shine her up for the occasion. From the top deck clay birds are thrown out over the sea. If they get caught in a cross air current, heaven help me." To her delight, Belle won the ship's clay pigeon championship.

Illness continued to plague her throughout 1933. She placed only four times but was honored by the Republic of France with the La Croix de Chevalier du Mérite Agricole for her contributions to equestrian sport.

Ella Severin recalls that in December 1933 she was in Paris with Belle and Barbara Donohoe. Ella and Barbara saw Belle, who was feeling ill, off by ship to America, and they traveled up the continent by train, Barbara to Finland and Ella to Sweden. "Belle told me later," Ella said, "that she was so ill by the time she reached New York that she had to be helped from the ship."

Her repeated bouts with tonsillitis resulted in a tonsillectomy, but infection had already spread throughout her system, triggering an acute arthritic reaction that placed Belle in a wheelchair for some weeks. Belle was determined to recover and walk again. She spent considerable time at Hobcaw recuperating.

Belle listened attentively as her father groused about the country's decision to desert the gold standard. He was opposed to many of the new administration's financial policies, and relations were not as cordial as he would have liked. President Roosevelt did not listen to the distinguished adviser as attentively as had his predecessors.

Baruch and Belle also discussed Hitler's announcement that Germany would rearm itself, an act contrary to the Versailles Treaty. In May 1933 Hitler had asked the league for permission to rebuild Germany's armaments industry. France withheld its approval, and in October Hitler simply announced that Germany would rearm anyway. Like the Japanese before him, Hitler said that Germany would withdraw from the League of Nations within two years. Hitler managed to calm France's fear with the offer of a bilateral pact limiting the size of its military. France refused the pact but was somewhat mollified. Once again, the league was unable to stem the rise of militarism in the world's more aggressive nations.

Belle may have felt twinges of concern over the future of Europe, but she was not by nature contemplative. She was a doer, a pragmatist. She did not dwell on "what-if's" nor govern her life by fear of the future. As long as it was practical to do so, she would continue to live in Europe most of each year. Ignoring the pain and discomfort of her arthritis, she sailed for France in the early spring of 1934 to join her friends and beloved horses.

14

⚜

European Friends
and a Fleeting
Betrothal

Belle had developed an international coterie of close friends, some Europeans and other Americans who, like Belle, lived in Europe several months of the year. Nearly all shared her passion for riding.

There was petite, blonde Eleanor McCarthy, born of American parents, reared in France. Eleanor and her family lived at the Ritz where Belle frequently stayed. Eleanor rode like a small whirlwind, whether in pursuit of a fox or over the high jumps. She was an excellent pilot, high-spirited, and great fun. She had a passion for American Indian jewelry and had a magnificent collection in both turquoise and coral. She married a Frenchman whom she later divorced, then married Geoffrey Cuthbertson, brother of Belle's good friend Munro. When war threatened, Eleanor went home to New Orleans and was a frequent guest at Hobcaw Barony.

Danish-born Louise Hasselbalch and her daughter, Varvara, were very close to Belle. Born Baroness de Plessen, Louise was the granddaughter of Baron Otto de Plessen, minister of Denmark to the court of St. Petersburg from 1850 to 1876. He married Princess Varvara Gagarine, who was closely related to the court of Czar Alexander II. Through the Gagarines, the family traced its origins to Rurik, the founder of Russia. Friends speculated that it was her Russian blood that caused Louise's wild mood swings from deliriously happy to tragically depressed. Louise surrendered her title to marry Erik Hasselbalch, a wealthy textile manufacturer with factories in Denmark, Sweden, and Norway.

Hasselbalch died in 1925 leaving his thirty-three-year-old widow with a five-year-old daughter.

Louise assuaged her grief and loneliness with a fanatical interest in horses. She lived mostly abroad, participating in international show jumping. Vivacious and popular, she was one of Belle's most successful, and friendliest, competitors.

Guy Arnoux was another of Belle's favorites. A superb rider, he rode mostly in the Camargue in the South of France but lived in Paris. He was a member of France's Deuxième Bureau (similar to the FBI in the United States), had a devilish wit, loved practical jokes, and was excellent company. Arnoux tickled Belle's sense of fun and was a frequent visitor in her home. Arnoux was also a painter whose murals decorated many restaurants, including La Belle Aurore, where Belle gave many dinner parties.

He once teased young Varvara Hasselbalch by asking, "Why don't you go to bed with me?" Shocked, Varvara managed to mumble an embarrassed refusal. Arnoux laughed and said: "You are silly because then you could brag about having been in bed with the whole French army because I have been in the marines, the cavalry, the infantry, and the Goumiers [North African regiment]."

Hunting at Pau, Belle met Eugène Blocaille, a French gentleman of no particular occupation. Blocaille was well-to-do, though certainly his income did not approach that of Belle. He developed a passionate admiration for Belle and was determined to shepherd her about, whether she liked it or not!

He was a rather quiet, shy man, very nearsighted with thick-lensed glasses. His hobby was painting on china, and Belle displayed many examples of his excellent work at Bellefield. Blocaille created a complete set of china with hunting motifs as a tribute to Belle. Varvara Hasselbalch Heyd said of Blocaille: "I never understood why he should always be around, but his admiration for Belle was beyond limits! I gather he didn't have much money. Maybe it was just another of Belle's gracious gestures."

Belle's affection for Blocaille was genuine. Belle was generous and open-handed with her friends, always the first to pick up a restaurant or bar check, even paying travel expenses for many of them. But she could not abide anyone who attempted to take advantage of her. She might succumb once, but never twice. Blocaille would never have been a "hanger-on" if Belle had not wanted him there.

Belle was fond of the Meunier chocolate family, of which several members were frequent hunting companions. There were many titled Europeans in her circle, but Belle was never impressed with titles, preferring to judge her companions as individuals. Belle's father had always used a man's behavior while shooting as a yardstick of character. Belle judged a great many people by the way they handled their horses and competition.

One titled friend who was always welcome at Belle's homes in France and America was Count Gabriel de Suares d'Almeyda. An excellent rider, "Coquelicot" or "Coco," as his friends called him, was considered something of a character, "but only in the nicest way," said Barbara Donohoe Jostes. Coco was a gifted mimic with an irreverent sense of humor. Belle liked to visit him and his wife at their castle in France.

Coco was accustomed to servants, rarely having to fend for himself. When he visited Belle in the States, Belle had only a cook at Bellefield, and Coco had a wonderful time not only hunting and riding but also helping with the household chores, a unique experience for him. On one occasion he flew with Belle and Ella Severin on a western trip in Belle's private plane. Upon arrival at one of their stops, he stood watching as Belle and Ella, who is a mere five feet tall, struggled with suitcases. Exasperated, Ella finally snapped, "Don't just stand there, Coco, help with the luggage!" "He was really a good fellow," Ella laughed, "it just never occurred to him to carry his own bags!"

Unlike most of Belle's friends, who were wealthy, Ella Severin was a working girl in the international division of Banker's Trust in Paris. They had met socially, and Belle later discovered that Ella was employed at the bank where she did business. The friendship developed. Ella was a petite, charming young woman whose dark hair was in striking contrast to her fair Nordic skin. Her mother was a famous actress, one of the first Scandinavians to star on the Broadway stage. Busy with her career, she left Ella to be reared by relatives in Sweden.

"In those days," Ella said, "you had to be twenty-one to become emancipated. Until you were twenty-one, you had to do what the family told you to." Ella shocked everyone by saying that she intended to leave and go out on her own. The family laughed at the idea of their "little Ella" trying to be independent.

"How will you live?" they asked. "You don't know how to do anything!"

"Well, maybe you think so," she replied, "but I can speak French, I can speak English, I can speak German, and I can speak Swedish. That's a lot going for me, isn't it?" They were even more amazed when she told them she was going —not to Stockholm as they expected—but to Paris. This was the kind of spunk and spirit that Belle admired, and they became fast friends in the 1930s.

Belle also befriended a young seamstress whom she employed while in France. As happened so often in post–World War I Europe, the woman was stricken with an incurable form of tuberculosis. She was sent to a sanatorium at Berck-Plage near Le Touquet in the north of France. Belle not only visited regularly but also paid all her medical bills.

No one would have known of this generosity had Belle not asked Varvara Hasselbalch, whose mother had a summer home at Le Touquet, to call on the woman whenever Belle was away and unable to visit. Sometimes Belle would take Varvara with her to the hospital. Varvara recalls, "Belle would go down the aisle of the dormitory of some forty sick people, all lying flat on their backs with mirrors above their heads, which they could direct. As Belle came in with presents, there was a loud metallic clicking as all mirrors were turned in her direction. Visitors were rare in those days." Generosity, as Varvara and many other friends attest, was one of Belle's strongest attributes. "Not just writing a check out," Varvara said, "but also going to the trouble of cheering up this person until she died."

Among Belle's dearest companions was Munro Cuthbertson, a young Englishman Belle met while foxhunting. Munro was an officer in the British army, and Belle always called him "Colonel." His less respectful friends nicknamed him "cuff button" because of his button nose. Although an excellent rider, Munro did not compete but was often present at the hunts, house parties, and balls Belle enjoyed so much. He was somewhat reserved and rather nervous, but a very kind young man. They became great friends, and it was to Munro that Belle turned in a rare moment of vulnerability.

Belle confided to Munro that she had become aware recently that her mother had a drinking problem. Anne Baruch was what society then called a "closet toper," and it was becoming more apparent each year. As her husband's fame and reputation grew, Anne's reticence and dislike of his too-public life increased. She was often withdrawn and unwilling to undertake the social obligations his international status demanded. She hated Washington, D.C., and simply did not care to practice her accomplished social skills outside the circle of close family and friends, where she was safe from the insults and slurs of anti-Semitism.

Baruch had encountered prejudice most of his life and had developed the skills and strength to deal with it, as would his children. But sensitive Anne, raised in the protected conservative environment of Anglo-Saxon Protestantism, had been shocked and wounded by the anti-Semitic attacks against her husband and children and unbearably hurt by the snubs from old friends and acquaintances as, one by one, social doors once opened and welcoming were closed because she had married a Jew. Her husband's ascendancy to wealth, power, and international fame did not assuage or heal the wounds she suffered as a young, idealistic bride.

Anne Baruch was astute enough, and sensitive enough, to know that the Baruchs were often tolerated as the "token" Jews in political and social milieus. She never developed Bernard Baruch's tough hide and suave insouciance in the face of prejudice. Anne was an acknowledged leader in her own circle of New York society, and she did not care to move out of that safe inner circle. More and more, Anne remained at home in New York while the glittering, vivacious women of international society willingly attached themselves to the charming, handsome, bon vivant to whom she was married. More and more, she retired quietly to her own suite to find solace in alcohol.

Like any child of an alcoholic, Belle felt enormous sorrow and guilt, believing that her lesbianism contributed to her mother's drinking. In her anxiety, Belle blamed herself, knowing that her mother had such high hopes for her older daughter. Anne expected that Belle would make a brilliant marriage and give her grandchildren to love, children that might help to fill the void left by her often absent and philandering husband.

Munro sympathized with Belle's agony. Himself a homosexual, he was finding it increasingly difficult to conceal the fact from his family, who was pressuring him to marry and produce an heir. Perhaps, he suggested, they could resolve both family problems. There was no woman he liked and admired more than Belle. She was among his dearest friends, and marriages based on solid friendship were often the best unions. Many European marriages were arranged on a far less solid foundation. Together, he reasoned, they could achieve a more "normal" lifestyle, perhaps even children. He eagerly proposed marriage to a surprised Belle.

At first Belle hesitated, but the more she considered the possibility, the more plausible it seemed. After all, she did love Munro in her own way. Her affair with Chita Davila had proved her capable of heterosexual love. Marriage to Munro might solve a lot of problems, perhaps help her mother's alcoholism. Above all, it would present a facade of sexual "normality" that would be acceptable to both families. Munro would also understand that she had certain needs, just as he did. Belle accepted Munro's proposal, assuring Barbara Donohoe that it would not affect their relationship.

Once committed, Belle threw herself eagerly into the preparations. Immediately she wired her mother, telling her the wonderful news and inviting her to come to Europe to chaperone and help plan the wedding. Belle rented an Italian villa at Il Conventino, St. Michele, in Rapallo, and Anne Baruch arrived to chaperone the couple. On August 14 Belle wrote to her father, who was at Vichy for his annual "curative" visit:

Dear Chick [her pet name for him],

Well here we are very comfortably installed. The villa is charming and I think mother is really enjoying the quiet and rest. She will go walking at noon but luckily the sun has not been too hot. I think it amuses her to see how simply we live. Munro is the Italian scholar of the crowd and helps order the meals.

How is your cure getting along? Would you care to come here as a sort of after cure? It would be so nice if you did.[1]

Edith Wilson was informed and cabled to Belle that as soon as the date was set, she would happily come to Europe for the wedding. Belle responded:

Dear Ma'am,

Your sweet cable made me very happy to think that you would come over here for wedding festivities. Father remains abroad such a short time that we have decided not to rush matters as he will probably sail for New York early in September which means we shall have to come to America. The red tape in Europe is dreadful and especially as I insist on keeping my nationality. No definite plans have been made and no announcement will appear in the immediate future. It will probably not take place until the New Year so rest assured, dear Mam, that you will be the first to be posted.

Have rented a charming small villa on the sea for a few weeks where Munro and I are doing our best to see if we can pick a fight with one another under mother's excellent chaperonage. So far we have gotten on quite famously. He is rather exceptional in comparison to the average individual one meets, having many interests besides being extremely cultured and a student of several languages at his finger tips. He came with mother and myself to a reception you had in Paris at the Prince Murat's house during the Peace Conference.

Will let you know the plans as soon as they are made. Am still working on getting a small plot of Hobcaw. I must have a little American soil to cling to.[2]

The marriage never took place. After several blissful weeks in Italy, Munro left Belle to return to England. Several days later Belle was shocked to read in a British tabloid that Munro was embroiled in a public scandal involving the questionable death of a young homosexual male who died in his London apartment. Anne Baruch was appalled, and Belle's father demanded that Belle end the relationship. Belle, who abhorred scandal and publicity, acquiesced, relieved that no public announcement of their engagement had been made.

Although she broke the engagement, Belle always maintained a deep affection for Munro. She never went to Europe without seeing him, and he visited her several times in America. When she died, she bequeathed twenty-five thousand dollars to Munro as a final gesture of affection. When told of Belle's critical illness in April 1964, Munro wrote to her father: "Just a note to say how much my thoughts are with you also in these days of anxiety about Belle. In spite of differences of interests, environment, & circumstances she is one person I always cared for, and we always remained pretty good pals. Still, one hopes against hope."[3]

In spite of, or perhaps because of, her broken engagement, Belle had a good year in international show jumping. She competed only sixteen times but finished in the money in most of her competitions. Still suffering from arthritis pains in her legs, Belle declined her father's invitation to shoot in Czechoslovakia, writing: "Wish I could have had a little shooting too but when I was told it was all walking on rather uneven ground, decided it was best not to try, especially lugging those heavy guns along. The last vestiges of 'twinkles' are in my legs and I feel them more while walking than riding."[4]

Belle sailed for New York that winter, eager to reach America and the comparative warmth of South Carolina, where she could recuperate further from the arthritic pains in her legs and back. Once again, her father spoke of the inevitability of war and urged his oldest child to come home. Living in Europe eight or nine months of the year, Belle was even more aware of such possibilities than her revered parent. She was politically savvy and well informed. She had intimate knowledge of the attempted coup d'état by the Hitler-controlled Nationalist Socialist Party in Austria. But she was reluctant to leave her friends —desert them, as it were—to seek the safety of American shores.

A part of her yearned for a permanent place to call her own, that "American soil to anchor to" as she had written to Edith Wilson. She knew that the uneasy peace that had existed in France after World War I, "the war to end all wars," was tenuous, growing more fragile each day. She was astute enough to know that not only peace was threatened but the very fabric of life. War would not only bring catastrophic physical changes but also destroy the societies of the European nations. And who was to know what would spring up in their place.

From time to time her father, who was in his sixties, spoke of dividing Hobcaw Barony, a notion that was appalling to Belle. A deep, abiding love of the land lay within her, and the thought of losing Hobcaw stirred an instinctual fear, as though the foundations of her life were shifting irrevocably. Over the years, it had become clear that Hobcaw was the anchor she was seeking.

At the family's annual Christmas gathering, Belle wrote in the guest log: "When the bones get too brittle for Pau, I shall abide here *always*." She called her father aside during the holidays and asked him to sell her a part of the barony. He grumbled that he would think about it, secretly pleased that his daughter shared his love of his native South Carolina. Typically, however, he gave no definite answer.

15

Bargaining
for Bellefield

In January 1935 Belle went to New York with thoughts of Hobcaw on her mind. Planning to return to Europe immediately, she took a short lease at a residential hotel, The Surrey, on East Seventy-sixth Street. She had confided to Lois Massey her wish to buy a piece of Hobcaw Barony and had asked her for support and assistance. Lois, dismayed by the possible breakup of the property, promised her help and gathered information and statistics concerning prices, boundaries, and so on.

With typical pragmatism and organization, Belle presented the facts to her father and once again asked to purchase a part of Hobcaw. Her father listened, did not refuse, but again gave no firm answer. Refusing to be discouraged, Belle wired to Lois: "Thanks to your excellent list of figures was able to make most efficient plea for Hobcaw today which made good and hope lasting impression. Had uninteresting trip. Mother about again but weather dreadful. Cheerio."

Later she wrote that she was "being detained in town by the doctors—a good crowd to keep away from." Delayed in New York, Belle made use of the time to see the latest films and plays. She wrote to Lois: "Have seen David Copperfield, Clive of Judea, and Man of Aran—all good pictures but not extraordinary. Mother and I saw Katherine Cornell and Basil Rathbone in Romeo and Juliet on the legitimate stage. What a swell actress she is."

Finally released by the doctors, Belle sailed for France on January 22. She found a delightful little house at 5 Rue Dosne Prolongée in Paris and settled in for the season. But Hobcaw was still very much on her mind. In May she wrote again to Lois:

Renee had already written me a little about Hobcaw and I always get very upset at these regular yearly upheavals. I only wish something would be decided, then we could act. Of course, it is father's to do with as he sees fit and if anything happens to Hobcaw it would really be my last tie in America other than my family. . . .

Miss Donohoe arrived 10 days ago and she is fairly speechless as I have dragged her around to balls, dinners, horse shows in record time.[1]

As though she knew her days of international show jumping were drawing to a close, Belle placed in thirty-three events that season, taking first- or second-place honors eight times and rarely falling below fifth or sixth place in fields of over one hundred riders, most of them the cream of European cavalry.

In June, Lois Massey wrote to Belle, telling her of the rumors that her father was once again talking of dividing the barony, and also that Belle's beloved Uncle Sadie (Jim Powell) was ill. Belle wrote in reply:

I, too, am distressed to hear what you have to say. For the moment I am rather helpless but I am sure everything will come out in the wash. I can't bother father much from so far away but hope to have a long talk with him upon his arrival here—whenever that is—and try to straighten out several matters. I have heard vague ideas about Hobcaw being divided for the last 20 years but I still don't own an inch of property. I could get quite discouraged but I won't allow myself to as it will certainly not prove a thing.

Am perturbed about your news of Uncle Sadie. I am so sorry to hear that his legs are bothering him so much now. I just can't picture Hobcaw without him as he meant half of it to me. I guess I am still living in childish dreams. Perhaps a spill I took smack on my head several weeks ago did not improve matters. I have however, a staunch supporter in Renee.

Hope to do a good season of shows here during the summer and then see what the winter holds in store.[2]

Belle's sister, Renee, does not recall exactly what Belle was referring to in this letter. Lois Massey, who was Baruch's secretary and hostess at Hobcaw at the time, states emphatically that Bernard Baruch had intended to divide Hobcaw Barony among the three children with Hobcaw House and its immediate acreage going to Renee, the tract near the highway that Belle eventually purchased going to her, and the lower end of the property known as Fraser's Point to Junior.

"Renee," Lois said, "wasn't especially fond of living down here. She liked New York and had her life there with Bob [Samstag]. She would come down on Christmas and different holidays and maybe for a couple of weeks during the spring. She really didn't want Hobcaw House. And Junior—well, if he couldn't have it all, he didn't want any of it."

That year, two major occurrences profoundly changed the character of the land on the Waccamaw Neck in Georgetown. In July the Lafayette Bridge opened, the final connecting link for U.S. Highway 17 that followed the eastern coastline from Maine to Florida. One no longer had to travel to Hobcaw from Georgetown by boat. Then in November the final cut was made to open the Inland Waterway between Little River and the Waccamaw River.

These traffic links opened the area to development and tourism. Myrtle Beach, about thirty miles north of Hobcaw Barony, would become one of the most popular tourist areas on the southeastern coast of the United States. The sixty-mile stretch of pristine beaches between Little River and Georgetown would attract thousands of tourists, and development of beaches and wetlands would destroy habitat and drastically impact the flora and fauna of coastal Horry and Georgetown counties. Only those lands donated by Archer M. Huntington to the state, parts of Arcadia, and Hobcaw Barony would form a buffer for the preservation of at least some species. But they were not enough to halt the gradual diminution of wildlife Belle had known and loved from childhood.

Belle sailed for America on the *Aquitania* in November, and on December 9 she wrote to Lois Massey from New York: "The time is drawing near for the Christmas trip to Hobcaw. I am nearly afraid to go as I live terribly on the past and I can't quite picture what to expect this year but I suppose since I am well launched in middle age I can not expect to go on with childhood dreams. How glad I shall be to see you and Uncle Sadie again."[3]

On December 14, obviously upset, Belle wrote again to Lois:

The definite date of departure next week has not been decided upon but it will be Fri., Sat. or Sun. Would you mind inquiring in G'town if I can get any Nouilly Prat [French vermouth] or if not could you order me 6 bottles from Charleston.

I may as well tell you but I only intend being at Hobcaw until the day after Christmas. Times and conditions have changed as you undoubtedly know so don't be surprised if I arrive without a gun or riding breeches—what for after all? Want to see you and have lots to say.[4]

Bernard Baruch was secretly pleased that Hobcaw meant so much to his daughter. More than Renee or Junior, Belle had always shared his love for the vast property. He was also anxious to lure his independent oldest child from Europe. Like any parent, he worried about his daughter's safety, especially with her Jewish heritage.

Hitler had reinstituted compulsory military service in July 1935, once again violating the Versailles Treaty. The European nations scrambled to make individual treaties with Germany, lending tacit consent to his abrogation of the Versailles accords.[5] In the meantime, Benito Mussolini had moved against Emperor Haile Selassie of Ethiopia, hoping to add that country to Italy's African colonies. Ethiopia was a league member and appealed for help. The league voted for trade embargoes against Italy, but they had little effect. Baruch viewed these events as further signs of inevitable war. Certainly he was not as sanguine about Hitler's intentions as his European friends. In October 1935, at the Aberdeen Proving Grounds, where he received the Army Ordnance Association's medal for outstanding service, he said: "Today, twenty-one years after the outburst of the volcano that shook the world, we see humanity in arms and embattled. . . . Hitler and peace! The very terms are antithetical. He is today the greatest menace to world safety."[6]

At the annual Christmas gathering that year, Baruch announced that he would sell a part of Hobcaw to Belle, finally ending her depression and anxiety over the future. Baruch was a wily old gentleman who liked to have his way. He was willing to let her have the property, he said, but he wanted her to think seriously about taking over the management of the entire barony. Thus, he hoped to entice Belle home to America through the challenge of running his vast acreage in the southern lowcountry.

In late December Baruch worked out the tax ramifications and wrote to his secretary, Mary Boyle, in New York:

My present plan is to sell Alderly and Bellefield to Belle at the fair market value which, they say (as per enclosed) is worth $25,000. Then give her ½ the purchase price. This (enclosure) is her check for the property.

I have to give her $12,500—I have already given her $12,500 this year (500 lbs) so that you can give her $7,500 this year and $5,000 next year.[7]

Belle was elated, and the sale was duly noted in a 1936 issue of the *Georgetown Times:* "Bernard M. Baruch, owner of Hobcaw Barony, has sold to his daughter, Miss Belle W. Baruch, Alderly and Bellefield plantations. . . . The two plantations are composed of 4,519 acres and extend from the Waccamaw River to the Atlantic Ocean. . . . Miss Baruch plans immediate construction of a winter lodge."[8]

The news excited the blacks on the plantation as well. Everyone knew of Miss Belle's fascination with Bellefield. She had always hoped to use the foundations and part of the structure of the unfinished plantation house as a basis for her new home once she gained permission from her father. But that past winter a forest fire had destroyed the walls that had stood for over two hundred years. The superstitious among the plantation residents interpreted this to mean that the ghost of the young planter who inhabited the house knew of the impending sale and destroyed the house rather than let anyone occupy it.

According to legend, the young man, who was building the structure as a manor house for his beautiful wife, died before the building was completed. During its construction, it had been his custom to visit the building site each evening after the plantation work was finished to inspect the day's work. The plantation slaves would see his lantern moving from room to room, and floor to floor, as he wandered about checking the finished work, perhaps dreaming of how it would look when his wife and daughter, and the children still to come, would inhabit the handsome building.

When he died from a sudden illness, his wife and child moved away, and no family ever occupied the house. Renegades and cutthroats were said to have used the abandoned house as their headquarters. Runaway slaves were known to have hidden there. One such slave swore he encountered the ghost of his former master, who urged him to return to his current owner and beg forgiveness.[9] Then came the evil spirits, the haunting, and the plat-eyes. Travelers on the Waccamaw River swore they saw mysterious lights in the deserted house.

When Belle bought the property, rumors and murmuring swept through Hobcaw Barony as the superstitious plantation folk insisted that it was the planter's ghost who had smashed his lantern against the dry timbers of the mansion that cold winter night and flames from the house that started the forest fire, not the other way around. The young master, they said, didn't want Miss Belle living in "his" house.[10]

Even today, Bellefield guests tell of mysterious lights and ghostly footsteps. One lady who stayed there many months told Ella Severin that she often saw the soft glow of a moving light and heard someone walking in the corridors. "Belle and I certainly never saw or heard anything," Ella insisted, "but then maybe we don't have ESP or something. . . . Everyone tells me that there is a ghost and every night when I go to bed I wonder if I'm going to see him tonight.

But I don't, at least not so far. . . . The ghost has pity on an old lady because he knows I wouldn't sleep." A young Canadian couple who visited Bellefield in the late 1980s also spoke of strange lights and ghostly meandering.

Belle dismissed the idea of ghosts and evil spirits, plunging immediately into plans for the property that she would call Bellefield after the nineteenth-century plantation that once stood on her land. In the few weeks that Belle spent in New York before returning to France, she hired architects Murgatroyd and Ogden of New York to design her Bellefield home, utilizing some of the old foundations of the burned house. The actual construction contract was awarded to LaFaye and LaFaye of Columbia, South Carolina.

With her customary organization and decisiveness, Belle approved blueprints, issued instructions, and ordered construction to begin. Letters and telegrams flew across the Atlantic from Paris to New York and South Carolina. Belle was never one to dither. She knew and demanded exactly what she wanted, relying heavily upon Lois Massey and Jim Powell to supervise matters at Bellefield and to keep her informed of any problems that might arise.

Nor did Belle neglect her riding while she supervised the building of Bellefield from across the Atlantic. She placed in over twenty shows that year, finishing among the top three in half of the events. She also kept a close eye on Germany and Italy.

16

⤡

Lois Massey and Prewar Europe

I n May 1936 the Italian army took control of Addis Ababa, the capitol of Ethiopia, making it a part of Italian East Africa. To Belle's disgust, the League of Nations decided to accept Italian rule for Ethiopia. Noting the dithering by the league, Hitler repudiated the articles of the Versailles Treaty that declared the Rhineland to be a demilitarized zone. There were talks and protests but no decisive action by the league. To calm the fears of neighboring European countries, Hitler offered nonagression pacts.

In July the Spanish civil war began, again without interference from the League of Nations, which considered the matter to be an internal affair. Italy and Germany aided Generalíssimo Francisco Franco while Russia and France helped the Republicans.

By August 1936 Japan had issued its new national policy, stating that it was "Japan's destiny to be the dominating force in all of eastern Asia."[1] By the end of the year Japan and Germany signed an Anti-Comintern Pact, agreeing to share information and collaborate in suppressing communism. Again, the League of Nations was powerless. By the time Belle came to Hobcaw for the family's Christmas gathering, the two aggressor nations had formed their unholy alliance.

Bernard Baruch was relieved that his eldest child had begun construction on her new home in the South Carolina lowcountry, but he pressed for an immediate, permanent return to the United States. Belle was not ready, however, to leave France for good. While at Hobcaw, she visited the construction site of Bellefield daily, making minor changes in the layout and discussing landscaping ideas with Barbara Donohoe, who was to help design the grounds and gardens.

These were halcyon days for Belle. Her life was filled with challenge and pleasure—riding, Bellefield, and Barbara Donohoe. Her relationship with Barbara was one of the happiest of her life, and the two women were devoted to each other. When Belle was involved in riding or other business that did not interest Barbara, it was not uncommon for Barbara to come alone to Bellefield to work on the gardens. She and Lois Massey traveled all over the Carolinas, Georgia, and Alabama seeking out choice plants and trees for the grounds of Bellefield. Barbara would make full use of the indigenous flowering plants of the South, planting huge banks of azaleas, rhododendrons, and camellias and interspersing the magnificent live oaks on Bellefield's lawns with flowering dogwoods.

Barbara loved Bellefield. "I had a favorite walk," she said, "along a path to a log across the creek, ending near a holly tree. One day I stepped upon the log and encountered a huge snake coiled on a branch of the holly tree. It was like an Audubon painting; the scene is forever imprinted on my mind."

For her home, Belle chose a comfortable, rambling, white frame country house with brick trim, reflecting the lifestyle she enjoyed most. Belle eschewed ostentation, preferring simple comforts. Visitors often commented on the peace and serenity of Bellefield and that it was very much Belle Baruch's home, her interests and personality evident throughout.

Marie Glinn of Chez Vous of New York designed the interior, using Belle's favorite hunter green throughout the main living and dining areas and in Belle's bedroom and study. Sir Alfred Munning's portrait of Belle astride Souriant hung above the living-room fireplace, just as it was displayed for years at her home in France. A grand piano, covered with photographs of family and famous guests, dominated the spacious room with its casual, comfortable chairs and couches arranged in conversational groupings. Belle's love of hunting and nature was abundantly portrayed in the Audubon nature studies and English hunting prints adorning the walls of the spacious rooms.

The heart of the house was the sunroom, with its massive fireplace, ballast brick floors, and vaulted ceiling with hand-hewn wooden beams. An imported zinc bar from France stood in one corner, and mounted hunting and riding trophies and sports memorabilia adorned the walls. At the end of the bar was a ten-cent slot machine, a gift from Edith Wilson. It was here that Belle liked to relax and entertain, sharing cocktails, laughter, and conversation, playing bridge and canasta.

The outside door of the sunroom opens onto the spreading back lawn of Bellefield, overlooking a small pond that Belle ordered to be enlarged. On the stoop was a handmade doormat of inverted bottle caps, their corrugated edging designed to discourage the ubiquitous snakes from sunning themselves at the entrance to Belle's favorite room. One also kept a sharp eye out for the alligators that wandered overland from the barony's creeks and marshes to establish residency in the new lake. Belle put up fences to keep out the wild hogs, but the deer simply bounded over the top to drink at the lake and nibble at the shrubs. Fortunately, Ella Severin once observed, they are not fond of camellias.

In March 1937, after numerous secret conferences with her parents and Barbara Donohoe, Belle announced a surprise trip to Europe for Lois Massey, who had served the Baruchs at Hobcaw House for fifteen years and now was Belle's strong right arm in the construction of Bellefield. Lois, Belle told her, was to put everything on hold and join her and Barbara in France in late April.

After rushing to get a passport and visa, Lois left for New York by train on April 21. Belle had reserved a room at the St. Moritz Hotel on Central Park South, and Marie Glinn took Lois on a shopping spree for coat, dress, and hat. On her first night in New York, Miss Glinn also hosted a cocktail party for Lois at the St. Moritz, inviting many of the people who had enjoyed Lois's hospitality and care at Hobcaw House over the years.

The next day she made a whirlwind tour through Radio City Music Hall and the old Trinity Church, stopping for lunch with Anne Baruch, who presented her with a beautiful black handbag. That evening it was dinner with Belle's Swedish friend Olga de Stroumillo, who taught at the Julliard School of Music, then off to the theater to see *The Masques of Kings* with Pauline Frederick and Dudley Digges. Lois was especially thrilled to find she was seated directly in front of Edward G. Robinson, who was in New York for the opening of his latest film.

The Baruchs and their friends kept Lois too busy to feel homesick and arranged for her to travel to France with Miss Glinn. Lois wrote in her diary on April 24: "People thick as ants in a molasses pot down bidding folks goodbye. What a mess. Miss S [Stroumillo] brings me a corsage of gardenias. A cable from Miss Belle and Miss Donohoe arrived and letters and cards from folks at home. Left at eleven o'clock and it is a beautiful sight watching the huge buildings of New York disappear from sight and such a lonesome feeling when all land disappears."[2]

Lois was not sad for long, throwing herself into all the shipboard activities. Rudy Vallee was on board and agreed to sing one evening. Marie Glinn was a delightful and knowledgeable companion, the food was excellent, and gregarious Lois found delightful companionship among her fellow passengers. Lois's unsophisticated, innocent delight in the ocean voyage charmed the more jaded travelers.

Belle and Barbara met Lois and Marie at the train station in Paris, welcoming them with a champagne supper. Lois wrote to her family:

> Well, here I am in gay Paree. I have to pinch myself to be sure it's me.
> . . . Can you imagine having two maids unpack *my* bags. Hot dog, what
> a shock for them! . . .
>
> I really feel like Alice in Wonderland. . . . Am going to send you a pic-
> ture of myself in my new Paris dress. It is a dream, black crepe and a real
> Patou model. The girls [Belle and Barbara] guessed at my measures and
> had it made for me.[3]

From then on it was a dizzy whirl of touring and partying, interspersed with trips to the Grand Palais for the Paris Horse Show in which Belle was competing. She scored a disappointing sixth place that year, but Lois was thrilled just to witness the costumes and pageantry of one of the most important social and sporting events in Europe.

When Belle was not riding, she took Lois to Notre Dame, the Louvre, and up to Montmarte at night to the Sacre Cœur. She sent her off with Barbara to Rose Valois, Belle's favorite hatmaker, for a new chapeau. They dined on frog legs and watched Josephine Baker's new show. There were trips to Chartres, Versailles, and Fontainebleau and visits to the great châteaus in France's Loire Valley.

Lois met the delightful Louise Hasselbalch and her daughter, Varvara. As she described it to her sister Dot:

> We didn't get to bed until four this morning. We went to the horse show yes-
> terday afternoon . . . didn't get in until almost one and had just started a raid
> on the ice box for some food and a bottle of beer when the doorbell rang and
> in walked Mlle. Hasselback [*sic*] and her daughter and most of the Austrian
> army. The boys who rode yesterday . . .
>
> Oh boy, speaking of raids this house looks like Sherman had been through
> it. . . . Being Austrian they all spoke German and could they dance, espe-
> cially waltz! I haven't quite gained my equilibrium yet.[4]

The evening spent dancing, singing, and laughing at Belle's Paris house was among the last carefree moments for her Austrian friends. Later that year Hitler began to talk privately of *Anschluss,* political unity between Germany and Austria. He forced the appointment of Nazi sympathizers to key Austrian government posts. In March 1938 German troops marched into Austria, and the *Anschluss* became a reality.

But in Paris in the spring of 1937, there were parties and balls, picnics and luncheons at elegant French restaurants, sumptuous teas and visits to the couturier showings of Patou and Jonelle. The cocktail hour was often spent at Belle's favorite, Grillar Bar. Lois and her hostesses saw all the latest films: *Moonlight Sonata*, Fred Astaire and Ginger Rogers in *Shall We Dance*, Sylvia Sidney and Henry Fonda in *We Live But Once*, and Pearl Buck's *The Good Earth*.

On May 12 they listened to the coronation ceremony of King George VI on the radio. A few days later Barbara Donohoe and Glinn whisked Lois off to England, where they were still celebrating the coronation. Belle stayed in France to spend time at Maisons Lafitte, where she stabled her horses that year.

Another whirlwind tour of the famous sites of London followed, interspersed with visits to the finest gardens in England. Because Miss Donohoe was a member of the International Garden Club, they had access to many private gardens, which were not usually open to the public. They were guests at a garden party at the home of the archbishop of Canterbury, where Lois was thrilled to catch a glimpse of Queen Mary.

Then it was back to France for a few final days of exhausting activities before Lois boarded the *Ile de France* at Le Havre for her return to the United States. It was the trip of a lifetime for Lois Massey, one the Baruchs enjoyed as much as she. The Baruchs, particularly Bernard Baruch, were known for their generosity to longtime employees. As Kitty Carlisle Hart commented, Bernard Baruch's private secretary had "an ermine coat and a diamond necklace, and his valet died leaving a million dollars."[5]

Belle sensed that 1937 might well be her last year of major competition and rode superbly, winning thirty-four trophies, finishing among the top four in over half the events.

In August, Belle was asked by General John J. "Black Jack" Pershing to attend the dedication of the war monument at Montfaucon, France, honoring the more than 122,000 Americans who died on French soil during World War I. Designed by John Russell Pope, the towering granite column, topped with a symbolic figure holding olive branches in his hand, was outlined against a brilliant blue sky in the Lorraine Valley. As Belle stood at the top of the broad stairway ascending to the monument, she wondered privately how long it would be before more American blood would be spilled on French soil.

She glanced at the assemblage of dignitaries, which included French president Albert Lebrun; General Pershing, leader of the U.S. expeditionary forces in World War I; Marshal Philippe Pétain, one of France's great wartime commanders; William C. Bullitt, U.S. ambassador to France; and the Baruchs' good friend Josephus Daniels, U.S. ambassador to Mexico.

President Franklin D. Roosevelt gave an unprecedented transatlantic speech, broadcast over the speakers at Montfaucon from his yacht anchored in the Potomac. As General Pershing dedicated the war monument to the "American and French soldiers who died here and to the ties of friendship which exist between France and America," he paused to pay signal honor to Bernard M. Baruch, whose inspiring accomplishments as head of the War Industries Board mobilized the country for war and insured victory for the Allies. He then introduced Belle, who touched the electric switch that raised the immense United States flag up the face of the column, where it snapped and fluttered in the cool breeze. It was a bittersweet moment, for everyone feared that the "war to end all wars," fought nearly twenty years ago, was about to be repeated.

17

Varvara Hasselbalch's American Sojourn

During that final summer of competition in 1937, Belle noted with concern the growing disharmony between her friend Louise Hasselbalch and her teenaged daughter, Varvara. Varvara was increasingly rebellious against Louise's almost tyrannical insistence that Varvara pursue a professional riding career.

It seemed to Belle that Louise, widowed at an early age, often seemed puzzled as to just what she should do with the child. For the first few years after her husband's death, Louise had left Varvara alone with a nanny and her grandmother in the ninety-room Palais Plessen built by Varvara's grandfather, while Louise lived abroad and rode in the international horse shows. When Varvara reached age nine, Louise settled briefly in Switzerland and placed her daughter in boarding school there. Later Louise moved to Fontainebleau, France, and Varvara was transferred to a nearby school. Louise also kept a pied-à-terre in Paris and a summer residence in Le Touquet in northern France overlooking the English Channel.

Louise decided to train the child for a riding career and unceremoniously yanked her out of school whenever she wanted the child to compete in various riding competitions. It was an unsettling experience for Varvara who, like any child, wanted to please her mother but resented always being behind at school. She never knew when her mother would descend and pull her from what should have been the reassuring routine that all children crave.

Belle saw herself in the young teenager who would one day be called "the richest girl in Denmark, the most beautiful girl in Denmark, and the most fun girl in Denmark!" But in the summer of 1937 Varvara was an unhappy teenager, taller than her contemporaries (over six feet), confused and hurt by those who pursued her for her wealth, and often thrust into situations she was too young to cope with. Louise was known for her numerous affairs and kept a log in which she rated the sexual prowess of her lovers.

"Belle," Varvara recalls, "became my savior and refuge."

> Her home at 5 Rue Dosne Prolongée was always open to me and the telephone number Passy 30-32 still sticks to my memory!
>
> No. 5 was a lovely, spacious house with a tiny green garden in front where one could sit outside. The house was at the end of a dead-end street. As you came into a big hall, you were faced by that lovely painting of Belle on Souriant III by Munnings. . . . There was a piano on which there were, apart from family portraits, photographs of Mr. [Woodrow] Wilson, and Pade-rewski.
>
> We used to gather in the smaller drawing room facing the garden. Charles, the chauffeur, would drive the green Chrysler (with white rings painted around the tyres supreme luxury in those days!). There was Albert, the man-servant, a cook, all in style. . . . Belle . . . was a very good and gener-ous hostess.
>
> There was a dog called "Pou," a bastard breed, a terrier, a real French "concierge" dog. Belle loved him, but it was mostly Barbara who had to air him.[1]

Varvara came often to Belle's home that summer to escape what she viewed as her mother's constant criticism. Belle sympathized with Varvara and shared her pain and embarrassment when, at one of the hunt balls, someone tapped Varvara's shoulder and asked for a dance. Turning, she looked up into the eyes of a handsome Italian, delighted to find someone taller than she. Delight turned to humiliation when she suddenly realized that her cavalier was actually sitting on the shoulders of a fellow countryman in order to achieve the height of the young Dane. Belle certainly knew the awkwardness and pain of towering above most eligible males.

Varvara possessed the beauty of a young Ingrid Bergman but, like many teens, thought of herself as awkward and unattractive. Belle enjoyed Varvara's visits and took her to the theater and films. "Her favorite play at the time," Var-vara said, "was *The Three Waltzes* with Pierre Fresnay and Yvonne Printemps."

She just adored Yvonne Printemps' singing, Je t'aime, quand-même, and would play the record over and over again on her enormous gramophone, as big as an icebox, which would automatically change records . . . a wonder of a mechanism unknown in Europe in 1937!

She loved to take us all to the fashionable nightclub, "Le Bœuf sur le toit," where Fats Waller and many famous pianists would play. . . . Mother knew Paris probably better than Belle and once they both, accompanied by Guy Arnoux and someone else as chaperone, went to the famous brothel, "Le Spfinx." . . . They only sat at the bar and observed. Belle was always very prudish.

She [Belle] wasn't exactly what you call a beauty, though she nicknamed herself "Beauty." When you think of how handsome her parents were, something must have gone wrong! . . . Her masculine way of dressing didn't make her more attractive, the only feminine touch were her hats. She would go to the best haute couture fashion houses, and would sometimes take me to see the collections. But her style, was her style. . . .

Her sense of humor was contagious and catching. She would make fun of herself, hence all the nicknames, Beauty, or Bellie-dear, which she signed on her scarce notes or letters to me. . . . She was also very gadget-minded.

Belle liked to command and expected her orders to be executed immediately. No nonsense. Her imposing stature and character—that's when the eyes would flash lightning—insured that everybody respected her.[2]

Belle knew Louise loved her daughter but simply did not know how to express it. She felt they could use a respite from each other and persuaded Louise to allow Varvara to come to the United States for a visit. "When mother and Belle agreed on letting me go to Bellefield," Varvara recalled, "our groom gave mother hell for putting her daughter into the hands of a lesbian. Mother laughed it off. I didn't worry. I hardly knew what it meant."[3]

On October 9, 1937, Louise accompanied her daughter, Belle, and Barbara Donohoe to Gare St. Lazare to see her daughter onto the train for Le Havre, where she would board the S.S. *Normandie* to sail for America. Varvara remembers that all Belle's servants were there to see them off. Belle's good friend Munro Cuthbertson, bearing two bottles of excellent champagne, traveled on the train with them to the docks of Le Havre. Varvara recalls, "The 'au-revoirs' and the 'bon voyages' were humming in my ears. . . . I sniffled something to my mother through my carnations (a gift from Belle) and was answered by another queer sniffle which sounded like . . . 'don't drink too many cocktails . . . be sure and behave . . . don't put beans up your nose or your feet on the table.'"

Munro broke open the champagne, and it was a gay trip to Le Havre. At the docks, Barbara Donohoe spotted a last bit of green grass for Pou and rushed the dog to relieve himself. Unable to secure a porter, they struggled with the luggage, including Varvara's numerous bags.

Varvara was awed by the luxurious liner and dragged Munro, who had helped them locate their cabins, through two of the saloons and as many other ornate rooms as they could manage before the loudspeaker signalled for visitors to leave. Barbara, Belle, and Varvara hung out the windows on the promenade for a last glimpse of France and Munro Cuthbertson. Unable to locate Munro on the crowded dock, Belle resorted to the shrill, piercing whistle she had learned from Jim Powell at Hobcaw and spotted the Colonel waving in response from the roof of the docks.

Belle quickly learned what traveling with a teenager could be like. Recalling a storm at sea, Varvara related: "Everybody was seasick, except us, so we had all the available caviar and champagne for ourselves. Elevators got stuck, people broke bones (the corridors were too large!) and I found out that the swimming pool was fun!"

With the fearlessness and carelessness of youth, Varvara discovered that the violent yaw of the ship stabilized her body in the center of the pool no matter how she might try to reach the sides. A thoroughly frightened steward rescued her and restored her to Belle who, Varvara said, "gave me hell, quite rightly too!"

Belle, Varvara recalled, "could be temperamental, but always fair. She would be strict with me. . . . I'm sure I needed that, but how she could put up with me for nine months at Bellefield is still a riddle to me! If she had been too harsh, she was never too proud to ask forgiveness."[4]

Varvara was welcomed warmly by the elder Baruchs at their Fifth Avenue home. Mrs. Baruch organized a full program for the coming days, including a Fritz Kreisler concert, the rodeo at Madison Square Garden, an appearance by Helen Keller (whom Belle knew and admired), and tours to the Empire State Building, Radio City Music Hall, and other New York landmarks. Then it was off by train to Hobcaw Barony.

"Life at Bellefield was just heaven for me!" recalled Varvara. Belle had an employee, Bill Kramer, teach the girl to shoot, first on empty Coca-Cola bottles tossed into the air. Varvara took great pride in producing two ducks she had shot only to have Belle express her horror when she learned that they had been shot *"on the water,* not flying, a sportsman's disgrace!"

Under Kramer's and Belle's tutelage, Varvara became an expert shot, shooting alligator, deer, fox, and rattlesnakes. She was not allowed, however, to shoot the wild turkeys, which were becoming scarce and which Belle particularly loved. She would sit for hours waiting for them to come gobbling to their feeding place.

Belle taught Varvara to drive, and everyone laughed and teased her when she showed off her new South Carolina driver's license with her named spelled Hasselbelch instead of Hasselbalch. Thereafter, Varvara proudly fetched the mail and groceries at Georgetown, went for oysters at Clambank, and, like any teenager with a new driver's license, happily ran any errand requiring the use of an automobile.

Varvara had brought her camera and was already showing the sense of composition and light that would earn her an international reputation as a photographer. It was during her stay at Bellefield that Varvara took the correspondence course in photography that would launch her career.

Belle indulged her hobby although she hated to have her picture taken. Lois Massey laughingly recalled: "That child always had a camera in her hands, always taking pictures. I told her if she didn't stop taking pictures of me while I was asleep, I was going to wrap that camera around her neck."

At that time, blacks still lived in all three of the old slave villages on Hobcaw Barony. "There was order on the Plantation," Varvara remembers. "The Baruchs were very punctual people . . . very organized. The villages, the school, everything Mr. Baruch had done for the resident Negroes, was a very modern concept—seemed like a happy kibbutz."

Varvara, of course, lived at Bellefield with Belle. The Baruchs were in residence at Hobcaw throughout the fall and early winter. Belle was having the small lake at the back of the house dug and was building stables designed by John D. W. Churchill of Park Avenue in New York. The stables would guard the entrance to Bellefield Plantation, and visitors would enter through the wide double doors of the stables, across the brick courtyard to the crescent-shaped road approaching the house.

Varvara blossomed under the eyes of the Baruchs. Always self-conscious about her height, she felt at home among the Baruchs, some of them much taller than she. "Mr. B," she said, "would give me a friendly pat on the back and say, 'stand up, you are amongst grownups!' I was never to forget it, it helped me, for the rest of my life I was to stand straight."

At first shy with the legendary Bernard Baruch, Varvara soon became close friends with him and all the family. She marveled at his restless, searching mind.

"How many inhabitants in Denmark?" he would ask. "Around four million," I guessed.

"How many refrigerators per capita?" I certainly couldn't answer! "A shame. You could have come in on the ground floor of Birds Eye frozen peas and be an agent in Denmark," he said. "There's a great future in that."

Frozen peas? I had never heard such a wild idea and thought Americans were mad! Little did I know with my 17 years that it was to become a universal success.[5]

With the good life at Bellefield and its wonderful food, including lots of cornbread with butter that Varvara found irresistible, the teenager began to put on weight. The Baruchs teased her, at first calling her "Butterball" but later changing it to "Feather," a loving nickname they called her all their lives. Bernard Baruch once told her that she would always be able to reach him, wherever he was, if she would just give the code word "Feather." Neither was to know that Feather would reach out to the Baruchs from German-occupied France.

Varvara was impressed with the orderliness with which Belle ran her household. Annie Griffen Baruch had trained her daughters in the art of housewifery. Anne knew to the last fork and sheet the style and number of silver and linens at her homes in New York and Hobcaw House. She maintained written inventories of crystal, china, vases, silver, linen, paintings, furniture, and so forth. She knew exactly what foods, wines, liquors, and condiments were in the pantries of each household. Belle, too, was an inveterate list maker and even maintained an inventory of her personal library.

Lois Massey was always at Bellefield, and the teenager was particularly impressed with the large checkbook for household expenses that Lois would present for Belle's signature. Belle personally reviewed the bills from the local merchants, checking both the math and content of each invoice. "The American way of life was so new to me," Varvara said.

Varvara was curious to see Belle's interaction with the black residents of Hobcaw Barony. She was well aware that, in general, Belle had little tolerance for blacks. One of the few quarrels Louise Hasselbalch and Belle had was over Varvara's wish to dance with Bambi Santerre, a young black man, at a horseshow gala at Le Touquet in France. Belle had forbidden her to dance with Bambi. Varvara appealed to Louise, who had a heated argument with Belle before allowing Varvara to dance with the young man who was the same age as Varvara.

Belle's attitudes were ambivalent and sometimes contradictory. She unquestionably loved some members of the household staff, especially those whom she had known since early childhood. She nevertheless expected excellence in their work, although she could be indulgent and kind. Belle did not consider any black her equal and, with the exception of William Kennedy, never elevated a black to a supervisory position at Bellefield. Varvara sometimes wondered if Belle herself understood her own feelings.

Belle had a turbulent relationship with her head housekeeper, Daisy Kennedy. Belle, with her penchant for perfection, could be brusque and domineering, often careless of her tone or manner, and occasionally unreasonable. Daisy Kennedy knew her own self-worth and refused to be treated with disrespect. She was well able to hold her own when she knew she was in the right. On one occasion when she and Belle had argued violently over some trivial matter which neither could remember a few days later, Daisy whirled around, lifted the back of her skirt to Belle, and said, "Kiss my butt!"

If there was one thing Belle admired, it was spunk, and that is undoubtedly why Daisy was not fired on the spot. Belle also knew when she was in the wrong. She often would not concede the point to the individual with whom she was arguing; rather, she would simply drop the issue, stomp off, and allow her opponent to do as he or she pleased. Daisy worked for Belle a number of years. Theirs was not a comfortable, happy relationship, but it was one of grudging, mutual respect.

Once during Varvara's stay, cigarette cartons were disappearing rapidly from the household cache. Belle was not one to tolerate petty thievery. She questioned everyone. Finally, one of the young black employees admitted the theft, saying, "Sorry, Miss Belle, but I didn't really steal them, they just stuck to my fingers!" Belle had difficulty in controlling her laughter and let him off with a reprimand that time. When he was caught again a few weeks later, he was fired immediately.

Francena McCants, housekeeper at Hobcaw and at Bellefield for over thirty years, said of Belle:

> I'll tell you what about Miss Belle. . . . If something wasn't right, she'd sit down and explain it to you. She liked things done her way. And if you made a mistake, she'd take you aside and tell you private-like, never embarrass you in front of folks . . . and never talk behind your back like some do. You didn't ever have to worry 'bout where you stood with Miss Belle . . . you knew. . . .
>
> She always took care of you. If you was sick, she'd see that you got to the doctor, do everything she could for you. You always knew that no matter what, Miss Belle was gonna take care of things.[6]

Prince Jenkins, born and raised at Hobcaw and an employee of the Baruchs for most of his life, commented: "Some folks thought Miss Belle was hard to get along with, but I never had no troubles . . . as long as you did things her way." He laughed and added: "Miss Belle . . . she am what she am and she did what she do. I sure do miss her."

No doubt the Reverend Moses Jenkins contributed to Belle's stern reputation. Varvara was amused to hear the preacher tell his congregation at Friendfield church that they must never steal because "Miss Belle will get after you with her shotgun!"

Belle was the self-appointed, unofficial truant officer of Hobcaw Barony. The Baruchs valued education, and Bernard Baruch provided the schoolhouse and teacher. Belle, when in residence, made sure the students attended class. She once discovered that two boys were absent and set off in search of the truants. Spotting them on one of the dusty trails of Hobcaw, she urged her horse to a canter. Seeing Belle bearing down on them, the boys ran into a nearby swamp, knowing Belle would never risk her horse in the dangerous waters.

Undaunted, Belle reined in her horse, dismounted, and waded into the knee-deep murky waters to find the two miscreants hiding behind a cypress tree. Taking each by an ear, she hauled them out of the swamp to the road, mounted her horse, and herded them back to school. The plantation youngsters always spread the word when Miss Belle was at Hobcaw. They knew they didn't dare skip school.

The days were peaceful and happy at Hobcaw Barony. With Bernard Baruch in residence, numerous visitors stopped by, including the film star Walter Huston who thrilled Varvara with an autographed photo.

Jim Powell taught Varvara to chew tobacco. Much to her amusement, the lanky Carolinian chewed a brand called Old Denmark. "I could never spit as far as he," Varvara said, "and gave it up very soon." Belle laughed, remembering how she and Junior learned to spit and chew when they were youngsters tagging after Powell. Powell liked Varvara, seeing in her the young Belle who had tagged after him all those years ago. He would sit for hours with Varvara on a log at Clambank, spinning yarns of the Carolina lowcountry.

Christmas of 1937 was Belle's first holiday in her new home, and the Baruch family gathered for a celebration. Lois Massey, Belle, and Barbara Donohoe planned an elaborate meal, and Lois kept the menu: creamed oysters, roast turkey with chestnut dressing, sweets in orange shells, cranberry sauce, peas, persimmon and avocado salad, and mince pie with ice cream.

There were small green trees on the sparkling white tablecloth, small green and white candles glittered at each place setting, and white bells were filled with green and white mints. It was a festive, memorable occasion, the first official party at Bellefield Plantation.

A few days later, the elder Baruchs hosted what was to be Anne Baruch's final New Year's celebration at Hobcaw House. Invitations to the annual party were highly coveted, and among the more than 150 guests were Mr. and Mrs. Archer M. Huntington, Mr. and Mrs. George Vanderbilt, Mr. and Mrs. Thomas Yawkey, Mr. and Mrs. Henry Luce, Mr. and Mrs. Solomon Guggenheim, and Miss Varvara Hasselbalch, who was awed by the splendid occasion and august assemblage.

Later that month, Belle was given the final deed to Bellefield.

Shortly after the beginning of the year, Bernard and Anne Baruch prepared to leave Hobcaw. Varvara insisted on assembling the family and guests who were there for a group photo on the steps of Hobcaw House. Handkerchief in hand, Annie Griffen Baruch is waving good-bye. It was the last photograph of her; she died on January 18, 1938.

Belle had already been summoned to New York when her mother failed to recover from a heavy cold that developed into pneumonia. She called Lois Massey and Varvara and asked them to come to New York for the funeral.

Lois Massey was glad for the company of the younger woman so that she could share her memories of Mrs. Baruch. Anne Baruch had not been a dedicated sportswoman and had not shared her husband's passion for Hobcaw, but she loved having family and friends gather there for the holidays. The activities she enjoyed most were long walks along the manicured paths of the grounds at Hobcaw House or drives by carriage along the winding roads of the barony. It was Lois who usually accompanied her and who earned the nickname Swivel Eye, because it was Lois who first spied a bright-plumaged bird, deer, or squirrel.

The funeral service was private, held in the family home on Fifth Avenue. "I'll always remember," said Lois Massey, "she had the most beautiful blanket of flowers on her casket that I've ever seen . . . huge, multicolored pansies. . . . She would have liked that."

Belle, Varvara recalled, was grief-stricken for many weeks. Belle's lesbianism had placed insurmountable barriers between mother and daughter. Given Annie Griffen Baruch's Victorian-style upbringing, her daughter's homosexuality was a grievous burden, evoking guilt, betrayal, and carefully suppressed disappointment and anger. No matter how they might love each other, Belle's sexuality precluded a warm and loving intimacy between mother and daughter. Belle, after all, had rejected the feminine standards that bounded Annie Griffen Baruch's life, choosing instead to pattern herself after her father.

As noted earlier, denial was the Baruch method of dealing with Belle's lesbianism. After the initial shock and despair, the subject simply was not mentioned between mother and daughter. Certainly it was never discussed with outsiders. Belle's sorrow was exacerbated by the knowledge that she had failed to fulfill her mother's dreams and hopes for her oldest child. She mourned the proud, sometimes lonely woman, knowing that she would be forever denied the total loving acceptance that every child craves from its mother. Christiane Darthez recalls: "She [Belle] always kept a red rose in front of her mother's photograph."

Varvara, Lois, and Barbara Donohoe did their best to cheer her. Friends and family gathered in mutual support. Bob and Renee Samstag visited in February, and Bernard Baruch returned to Hobcaw House. Belle hunted and fished, went foxhunting at night, filling the hours with activity. Marie Glinn joined the group and renewed Belle's interest in completing the decoration of Bellefield House.

Belle had been training her horse, Keepsake, also called Kiki, to harness, and she found great solace in working with the docile animal. She proudly took Lois on Kiki's first ride with the buggy.

Word came on February 15 that her good friend Admiral Cary Grayson had died, and Belle mourned the man who had been personal physician to President Woodrow Wilson. She knew the pain his death would bring to Edith Wilson and her father.

Barbara and Varvara did their best to divert Belle's thoughts, planning picnics in the woods where they dug violets and jasmine to be transplanted at Bellefield. Knowing how she loved westerns, they coaxed her into Georgetown to see the movie *Wells Fargo*.

Belle took an interest in the building of the stables and was eager to see them completed. She planned to move her horses from France and wanted everything ready. She knew that time was running out for Europe.

Belle did not return to France in early spring as was her custom. She preferred to remain at Bellefield and to spend time in New York with her father, who was mourning the death of his wife. Bernard Baruch was known as a philanderer who had numerous affairs both before and after the death of his beloved Anne, but he had an old-fashioned, chauvinistic attitude about his affairs. He considered them of little consequence, and certainly they had no bearing on his respect and regard for his lawful wife. He genuinely mourned her loss and the absence of the stable, comfortable home she had provided. Years later, Baruch confided to a woman reporter:

"I have been studying women for almost eighty years, and I still don't know anything about them. My wife was the most wonderful woman in the world. . . . She never criticized me, not one word in all the years we were married. And whenever any question arose, she always left things to me. She always said: 'You know best.' . . . When you've lived with one woman forty years, and she's borne your children and shared your griefs—well, there's nothing left for any other woman either here," touching his heart, "or in here," touching his head.[7]

Years later, just after Belle died, Bernard Baruch asked Anne Johnston, who had been a private-duty nurse for both him and Belle, to accompany him to the family cemetery. On the way, he stopped at a florist shop and asked the chauffeur to buy two dozen yellow gladioli. When they arrived at the cemetery, the then ninety-three-year-old Baruch asked Johnston to lay two gladioli at the foot of each marker in the family plot.

With tears in his eyes he wandered amid the family graves. "This is my wife I loved all my life," he said to Anne. "This is Renee's 'Fraulein' [Renee Baruch's governess], a big part of our lives . . . a wonderful woman."

"It was very sad, very moving," Johnston recalled.

Baruch's will instructed that his remains be cremated and placed in an urn at the foot of his wife's grave.

The woods and streams of Hobcaw Barony and the development of Bellefield were a solace to Belle, and gradually her spirits rose. She planned a party for Varvara's eighteenth birthday on April 16. The teenager planned a surprise of her own.

Varvara went shopping in Georgetown and discovered a rare delicacy on the shelf at Ford's Grocery. She paid five dollars a can for the unusual meat, a great deal of money in 1938. As Varvara opened the cans to prepare her "surprise," Rose the cook kept muttering "Jesus!" in horrified tones.

Varvara carried the dish into the dining room and announced that she had received a birthday present from Denmark, a delicacy called *sild* ("herring" in Danish). Everyone ate a sample and agreed it was delicious. Varvara could no longer contain her giggles and announced that the "delicacy" was actually rattlesnake. "Dead silence," Varvara recalled, "until one of the guests left the table to throw up. Belle was furious!"

Eventually Belle saw the humor in the situation but insisted that Varvara apologize. Things settled down to normal once again, and the women of Belle-field enjoyed the long, beautiful spring of the Carolinas, fishing, crabbing, boating, and gardening. Belle had a great fondness for asparagus and grew it and many other fresh vegetables on the plantation.

Barbara Donohoe had invited Varvara to travel cross-country with her to California, and Varvara was eager to make the journey. She was dying to see more of the United States than New York and South Carolina. She had written to her mother for permission and received a letter from Louise announcing dramatically that she was "dying of hunger, having to sell my horses and rent the house out." Varvara, she claimed, was using all her money, and she wanted to kill herself. Varvara canceled her plans and rushed back to Europe, only to be greeted with the words: "What are you doing here? I wasn't expecting you!"

"It appeared," said Varvara, "that it was not her money I was spending but my own! And she had no intention of killing herself. It was all nonsense." It was also typically Louise. Her capriciousness often made Varvara feel more the mother than the daughter.

The months at Bellefield had given Varvara perspective and crystallized her determination to pursue a career in photography. Belle's genuine affection and concern, and her rock-solid strength and dependability, gave the young Dane the confidence to follow her own dreams rather than live out those of her mother. Belle, she knew, would be there if she needed her. "I realized much later in life," Varvara said, "that Belle might have had certain hopes where I was concerned, but she never made any indecent advances to me. I dearly loved and respected her."[8]

18

✂

*Life Stateside
and War Abroad*

After seeing Varvara off to Europe on the *Queen Mary,* Belle, Lois Massey, and Barbara Donohoe stayed in New York for a month. Belle wanted to buy a small apartment in New York since, in the future, she would be living primarily in the United States. In the meantime, she leased a house in Bedford, New York, just outside the city, and brought two of her favorite horses from Hobcaw.

Her sister, Renee Samstag, had a house at Pound Ridge, and the two sisters saw a great deal of each other that summer, drawing closer after the death of their mother. "We always regretted that we weren't closer," Renee commented, "especially as we grew older. But there was such a difference in age. Six years is a lot when you're ten and sixteen, or sixteen and twenty-two. We just didn't have the same interests. Later, of course, it [age] didn't matter so much."

Renee apparently accepted her sister's lesbianism, and they saw a great deal of each other once Belle settled at Bellefield. She always maintained the Baruch conspiracy of silence, declaring such matters "personal, and no one's business."

Belle savored life and was never one to sit quietly. She kept her group on the run with cocktail parties, trips to Bear Mountain, Woodstock, and West Point, and dinners at a favorite restaurant, Boots 'n' Spurs. On June 22 they celebrated Bob and Renee Samstag's third wedding anniversary by attending the Max Schmeling–Joe Louis fight. In just two minutes and four seconds, the "Brown Bomber" defeated the German, who had handed him the only defeat of his career when Schmeling knocked Louis out in the twelfth round of a fifteen-round match the previous year. The fact that Schmeling was a German, honored earlier by Adolph Hitler as representative of the superiority of the Aryan race, made Louis's victory all the sweeter.

They decided to stay in the city for a few days to shop at Macy's, consult with Marie Glinn on plans for Bellefield, lunch at Schraft's, see the film *Mayerling*, and take in some Broadway shows. Two of Belle's favorites, Alfred Lunt and Lynn Fontanne, were starring in Chekhov's play *The Sea Gull*.

Bernard Baruch sailed for Europe on a fact-finding tour for President Roosevelt, and his daughters and his secretary, Mary Boyle, saw him aboard ship. Belle then returned to South Carolina to prepare for her last trip to Europe until after World War II, a catastrophic event that would change forever the boundaries and societies of that great continent.

Arriving in France in August, Belle wasted no time organizing the transfer of her horses, including Barbara Donohoe's Malicorn, to the United States. She had persuaded Jean Darthez to move his family from France and had built a white frame house for them near the Bellefield stables. Jean needed little persuasion. The specter of war drew ever closer, and he wanted to protect his family. Also, the thought of parting forever with his beloved Toto was unthinkable. His wife and children did not share his enthusiasm.

In the early fall of 1938, just as the Sudetenland succumbed to Nazi intimidation, the Darthez family arrived at Hobcaw Barony. Robert, who was twelve, recalls: "It was raining the day we arrived and I remember thinking, *What a dark and dismal place.*"

The Darthez children were greatly intimidated by Belle. Christiane, the youngest, recalled the first time she met Belle. "I was five or six years old at the time. We were living in Maisons Lafitte near Paris, having moved there from Pau. . . . Standing beside my father, I was completely awed when I looked up at, what seemed to me at the time, the tallest person I had ever seen!"

The children were constantly warned by their parents that they were not to disturb Miss Belle in any way, and such reminders only increased their awe and fear of Belle, who could intimidate most adults, let alone small children. "I had the distinct impression," Robert said, "that she did not like children."

Belle liked children but was not comfortable with them, seldom having occasion to interact with them. Neither her brother nor her sister had children, so there were no nieces or nephews. She could be aloof and haughty and, when uncomfortable, doubly so. Belle's uncertainty as to how to deal with children, coupled with Jean's old-world attitude about relationships between employer and employee, exacerbated the children's fears. Yvette, the oldest of the three, recalls: "When we were children, we were made to feel by our parents that she was someone to fear, but as we grew older this was not so! She was actually a very nice person."

Between Belle and the new arrivals, however, it was a standoff, with the children avoiding Belle whenever possible. They had great difficulty adjusting to their new home, and it was a lost and lonely time. Christiane said, "It was, at first, a very traumatic experience for me. My little friends had been left behind in France; here I was in this isolated place where I saw no other children until I was placed in a school where no one spoke my language and all made fun of me! . . . Loneliness was a real problem for me on the plantation."

"Because we lived so close to the 'big house,'" said Robert, "we could not play as kids normally do. I was not allowed to have friends come home from school to play." This was undoubtedly Jean's restriction rather than Belle's, since other families living on the plantation frequently invited friends and family to call. No one, however, was allowed to shoot on Bellefield or Hobcaw property without the knowledge and consent of either Belle or Bernard Baruch.

The children adjusted, however, becoming caught up in life on the plantation, awed by the abundant wildlife. Robert recalls: "I had secret places where I would go to observe the deer and wild boars. I loved to stalk the animals and see how close I could get to them."

Christiane's favorite place was the stable loft, where she would go to dream and play and peep fearfully down at Belle as she visited her beloved horses. Belle came often to the stables, her pockets bulging with lumps of sugar for Toto, Lionclau, Nonesuch, Hydravion, Malicorn, and Keepsake.

"To me," Christiane said, "her most likeable trait was her love for her horses and dogs and, indeed, her love of nature. This was the strongest bond between her and my father. His whole life was centered around 'his' precious horses, especially Toto." Jean made the easiest transition because he was with his beloved horses and, with Belle's encouragement, had a huge garden that he and his family tended, helped occasionally by Belle when the mood struck. She particularly liked to hitch up the mule and plow or cultivate the fields.

Jean and Belle had a somewhat volatile relationship, part employer-employee, part friendship. Darthez was by no means a "yes" man, nor would Belle have respected or employed him if he were. They often disagreed angrily and loudly, in voluble French, usually over some minor point on the care of the horses.

"Both of them," Christiane said, "were extremely stubborn, each would 'stick to his guns' until there was an impasse. She [Belle] would then storm away and would avoid him for days at a time! . . . Sometimes she could be quite sulky and leave for New York without telling him, then some days later he would receive a short, curt letter with instructions where to forward her mail. That was her way of giving in to his idea. . . . Upon her return all would be forgotten."

Darthez and Belle also shared laughter and good memories. They would reminisce about their riding careers, old friends, the particular qualities of certain horses, and the state of international show jumping. Both loved a good story, and Belle would seek out Jean at the stables to regale him with the latest jokes and ribald tales she had heard from visitors or on trips to New York. "She had a habit," Christiane recalled, "of ruffling her hair until it was quite disheveled, usually while chuckling over something she would hear or read that she found amusing."

Hobcaw was especially lonely for Lucie Darthez, Jean's wife. Locked in the loneliness of near silence because of impaired hearing, it was impossible for Lucie to learn English. Separated from family and friends, she had only the comfort of her husband and children, each of whom soon found outlets for their homesickness. For Lucie there were none, but she endured, never complaining, taking what happiness she could from her family.

Belle was very fond of Mrs. Darthez, but the two women had little in common. Lucie, a superb needlewoman, liked to stay busy and undertook the mending of the most delicate laces and linens at Bellefield. She was also an excellent cook, and while she did not work as such at Bellefield, Belle always insisted that she trusted no one but Madame Darthez to clean and prepare shellfish, especially shrimp, for the guests of Bellefield.

Both Yvette and Christiane happily recall the picnics that Belle would organize at Clambank. "Miss Belle," Yvette said, "would have the cook prepare a picnic and we would all go to Clambank for the day . . . those were fun times."

"It was lovely," Christiane said, "to sit on the dock with a crab line dangling in the water, smelling the salt air and the marsh. At low tide, there were millions of fiddler crabs 'playing their violins.' It was so peaceful."

It was isolated and often lonely, but gradually the Darthez family became an integral part of Hobcaw Barony. "Only after leaving Bellefield," Christiane said, "did I realize what a unique and interesting youth I had had!"

In the meantime, Belle's father had returned from Europe, disheartened and discouraged by the Munich Pact and the obvious military weakness of both France and England. He knew it was inevitable that the United States would be pulled into the war and immediately urged war preparedness.

According to several biographers, Roosevelt apparently agreed but knew that, politically, the country was not in a mood to accept the truth. Without official sanction and being careful to state that the views he expressed were his own, Bernard Baruch waged war on the country's apathy and isolationism. Margaret Coit wrote: "Baruch's task was to focus public opinion. The President outlined his instructions: 'You put a burr under their tail, Bernie, and if I hear 'em holler, I'll know you're doing all right.'"[1]

So Bernard Baruch took the heat, announcing often and persistently that the United States must arm for war. Father Coughlin, joined by the Reverend Gerald L. K. Smith, began his attacks on the "dirty Jew war monger." Even Adolph Hitler vilified Bernard Baruch. As Jordan A. Schwarz commented in his Baruch biography, *The Speculator:* "It was a mixed blessing to be the most famous Jew in America. He was both a convenient symbol for American Jews' successes and a target for hatred of them. He was everybody's favorite Jew when a token representation was required to demonstrate America's opportunities. At the same time, bigots, ranging from ordinary cranks to the extraordinary Henry Ford, heaped abuse upon him as a representative of the oldest continuing international conspiracy."[2]

Bernard Baruch bore their insults with stoicism and dignity, secure in his conviction that his duty was to alert Americans. Belle alternately raged and wept over the injustice to her beloved father, less able than he to calmly accept the vilification. Better than most, Belle knew he was right in his evaluations.

Bernard Baruch calmed his daughter and told her to concentrate on Bellefield and enjoy the coming holidays. Old friends came to Belle's new home for Thanksgiving. Evangeline had divorced Leopold Stokowski and brought her new Russian husband, Prince Alexy Zalstem-Zalessky. Caroline K. Post and Hugh Johnson also celebrated the holiday with them.

Shortly after their departure, Belle began preparations for Christmas, wanting to make it a memorable occasion. She especially wanted to start new traditions for Bellefield. The Christmas celebrations at Hobcaw Barony are among the happiest memories of the Darthez family. "The Christmas trees for the 'big house' [Bellefield] and for the stables were selected and cut by my father," Christiane recalled.

> The tree for the stables would be set in the middle of the stable yard and strung with colored lights. Each horse had a stocking beside his box, filled with carrots and lumps of sugar. . . .
>
> About a week before Christmas, my father would take my brother and me to find and cut our own tree. This was one of my favorite rituals! Another was the burning of the Yule log. He always kept a very large special oak log that would burn slowly throughout the night and most of Christmas morning. We would sit around the fire roasting chestnuts in the embers.

Belle would usually have guests at Bellefield for Christmas Eve. Her sister, Renee, and her husband, who always stayed at Hobcaw for the holidays, were usually there. Belle always asked my father to bring his family to the "big house" after dinner where the guests were gathered in the living room. Everyone would be dancing and singing, Renee Samstag seated at the piano. . . .

Later everyone would go to Friendfield [one of the black villages on Hobcaw] for the annual Christmas prayer meeting. Although my family would later go to Midnight Mass at St. Mary's Catholic Church in Georgetown, I always enjoyed this service on the plantation more. . . .

There were welcoming speeches for all the visitors from the preacher. Each person's name would be mentioned beginning with Miss Belle, or on the occasions when Mr. Baruch was there, he was honored first.[3]

After the first Christmas at Bellefield, the Darthez children were a little more resigned to their new home. They still dreamed of France, but South Carolina had its own fascination.

In the early spring, Eugène Blocaille arrived from France for a visit, as did Edith Wilson. Mrs. Wilson had published her memoirs with the help and guidance of Bernard Baruch, and she came to Bellefield to rest after the initial flurry of promoting the new book. Belle was happy to have two of her dearest friends to share her dream house. Only the tragedies of Europe marred their happiness.

By March 15, 1939, Hitler had occupied Czechoslovakia, and in April, Mussolini invaded Albania. With each advance of the German army, Belle recognized yet another change in the rhythm of her life, the surrender of old dreams not yet replaced with the new. She kept busy in a conscious effort to fill the vacuum, concentrating on Bellefield, consulting daily with the housekeeper and her secretary, Lois Massey. She visited the horses daily, talking with Darthez, setting up a training routine for the jumpers. She no longer had to pack the joys of Hobcaw into a few weeks each spring and fall but found endless pleasure throughout the seasons of South Carolina. She went fox and boar hunting at night, gigged for flounder by lantern light, and began to adapt to life in the United States.

Belle rode in very few horse shows in America. The painful arthritis in her knee and back hampered her performance, and being a perfectionist, Belle had no interest in mediocrity. Developing Bellefield was a challenge but did not fully occupy her active mind or satisfy her driving energy. She missed France and her many companions, the rigors of training, the physical and mental demands of international competition. It was hard to let go, to surrender the

thrill of soaring effortlessly over jumps at heights few riders—male or female—
had yet to achieve. Belle, who thrived on challenge, sought new goals and found
them in flying.

Belle's close friends Evangeline Johnson and Eleanor McCarthy were among
the first women pilots in America. It was a pastime Belle had always thought
to take up "one of these days." The time had come, she decided, and with typical efficiency and concentration, Belle began to study for her pilot's license at
a field just outside Newark, New Jersey.

In the meantime, Easter arrived. Hobcaw House was opened and aired for
the season. Bernard Baruch, guests, and family arrived at the barony, some to
stay at Hobcaw House, others at Bellefield. The Darthez children were delighted to participate in the annual Easter egg hunt for the children of the plantation. Belle moved the site to Bellefield from Hobcaw House that first spring.
Christiane recalled: "Easter eggs were hidden among the grass and trees.
. . . The children were given baskets to fill. It was amusing to see a very tall Belle
taking the hand of a tiny tot to go in search of the Easter Bunny's cache."

Belle and Lois Massey would insure that every child received candy. Belle
would then convert the garage to a theater, inviting all the children, their parents, and, of course, Bernard Baruch and any guests visiting at Hobcaw House,
to participate. "First of all," Christiane said, "the children would perform for
the guests. Prompted by their teacher, each child gave his recitation or song,
from the smallest first-grader to the oldest teenager. . . . Belle would then
become the entertainer, operating the movie projector. There would be squeals
of delight as the children watched the antics of Mickey Mouse and Donald
Duck on the garage wall."

There were visitors and parties, hunting and fishing. Belle had found her
"American soil to anchor to." She went to Virginia, leasing a house in Middle-
burg for the foxhunting season. When she felt the need for bright lights and
theater, she traveled to her New York apartment on Seventy-fifth Avenue.

The first summer at Bellefield, Belle moved the Darthez family and the
horses to Bedford Falls, New York, for the summer to escape the heat and mosquitoes. For the next three summers, the entourage moved to Monkton, Mary-
land, where Belle leased a small farm. She was seldom there herself, but the
Darthez family enjoyed the change from the summer heat and mosquitoes at
Hobcaw. Robert was allowed to ride Bellefield horses in the local shows, as were
the daughters of the Bosley family, who owned the farm next to Belle's leased
property. Jean, Christiane recalled, enjoyed teaching the finer points of show
jumping to the two young ladies. Belle would occasionally join in the instructions, and while the Bosley girls admired her riding prowess, it is doubtful they

realized their mentor was considered by Europeans to be one of the great equestrians of the world.

Belle continued her flying lessons, qualifying as pilot in a single-engine plane and copilot for two-engine planes. Never one to do things by halves, Belle bought two aircraft—one single-engine and one two-engine craft. She parked her planes in a hangar at the Georgetown Airport. After World War II she built a landing field and moved her planes, hangar, and equipment to Bellefield Plantation. She had found a new passion and would become a familiar sight to Georgetown County residents, flying her single-engine Stinson every afternoon that weather permitted.

Delighted with her new interest, Belle sat down with Barbara Donohoe, and the two women planned a trip in Belle's two-engine Beechcraft, flying from New York to the West Coast. With her customary efficiency, Belle carefully planned the routes, and the following schedule was found among her papers:

WESTERN FLIGHT
AUGUST 11 TO SEPTEMBER 2, 1939

AUG. 11	NEW YORK TO CHEYENNE
AUG. 12	CHEYENNE TO SAN FRANCISCO
AUG. 13	SAN FRANCISCO TO SANTA BARBARA
AUG. 21	SANTA BARBARA TO LOS ANGELES
AUG. 24	LOS ANGELES TO SAN DIEGO
AUG. 25	SAN DIEGO TO ENSENADA
AUG. 28	ENSENADA TO LOS ANGELES
AUG. 30	LOS ANGELES TO DALLAS, VIA BOULDER DAM AND GRAND CANYON
AUG. 31	DALLAS TO GEORGETOWN [4]

It was an exciting journey and helped lift Belle's deep depression after her mother's death. Flying would become the great joy of her later years. She flew her own plane until a few weeks prior to her death.

Another joy of Belle's new life was her increasing closeness to her father. They had many common interests, and at sixty-nine, Bernard Baruch was still vigorous, sharing her love of hunting and fishing. Gradually, however, Bernard Baruch spent less time at Hobcaw and more and more time in Washington, agitating for mobilization and price-stabilization plans for what he saw as inevitable war. His acquaintance with U.S. Army chief of staff George C. Marshall ripened into friendship, as the two men joined efforts to strengthen the nation's defenses. At Marshall's request, Baruch was instrumental in influencing congress to allot four million dollars for an air base at Anchorage, Alaska. Marshall considered Baruch to be "a pipeline to the centers of influence."[5]

Throughout Bernard Baruch's life, Marshall was a frequent visitor to Hobcaw, Bellefield, and Little Hobcaw at Kingstree, South Carolina. He often celebrated his New Year's Day birthday at either Hobcaw House or Bellefield.

In September 1939 Hitler invaded Poland. Stalin, who had signed a secret protocol with Hitler, invaded Poland on a second front. Belle wept when she read the reports of the gallant Polish cavalry charging on horseback the German panzers. Many of the courageous officers had competed with Belle in the international horse shows, and she lost many friends in the battle. In a matter of days, the two conquerors partitioned Poland between them.

Russian might forced Estonia, Latvia, and Lithuania to sign treaties allowing Russian military bases on their soil. They tried to force Finland as well, but the brave Finns fought the Russian army through the fall and early winter until, overwhelmed by sheer numbers, they were forced to the treaty table after four months of battle.

On April 9, 1940, the Germans invaded Norway and Denmark. Belle's one consolation was that Feather (Varvara Hasselbalch) was in France. The Bellefield contingent had all sent birthday cards to Varvara early in the month. To Belle's relief, a letter from Varvara arrived dated April 13:

Darling Beauty,

Your letter was more than welcomed the other day, it cheered me up, I can't tell you how much. It arrived just a few days after the German invasion of Denmark. And we all expected that day to come, but why so soon? . . . For the first time in my life I am looking for a job.

Varvara went on to explain that she had found work as an ambulance driver with Ann Morgan at the Comité Américain de Sécours Civil at Bellac.

We live in an old "chateau" with mice and drafts, no running water and just a little wood stove to heat this enormous room I share with another girl.

How I love thinking back on the sweet memories of Bellefield. You don't know how many friends have disappeared in the Finnish war. And we haven't seen the end of this war yet. . . .

You wouldn't believe it, but I met one of your great admirers the other day, the old deaf Comte de Cordon. He lives in a chateau a few miles from here. I bumped into him on one of our tours . . . had tea with him and the whole family. . . . He had to bring out . . . with a lot of pride . . . a photograph of you and all of us at the Vichy horse show.

You knew that Castries [Count Christian de Castries attained the rank of brigadier general and was one of the heroes of France] got the Croix de

Guerre and a couple of other decorations. He has been on the front the whole
time. LePan was killed. The rest of the horseshow gang is still going strong,
I think.

Thanks so much, all of you, for your amusing Birthday cards. I had completely forgotten about it . . . fancy 20 years old. Sounds very old. It is as if
I were to begin a new century.[6]

Belle's relief was short lived. On May 10 the Germans invaded the Nether-
lands, Belgium, and Luxembourg. By early June the Germans had driven the
Anglo-French forces onto the beaches at Dunkerque. They entered Paris on
June 14, taking control within days. The German-French armistice was signed
on the 22nd of that month.

Varvara had been driving an ambulance for the French Red Cross and, with
her unit, had fled to Pau in the free zone only minutes ahead of the invading
German army. The situation was desperate, and somehow, through contacts at
various embassies, Varvara got a message to Belle.

Belle flew into action, asking her father for a rare favor in her attempt to get
Varvara out of France. Bernard Baruch readily agreed to use his influence to
rescue the Danish girl. The United States still was not at war with Germany
and maintained an embassy in Paris. The Baruchs arranged for money and a
coveted ticket on a plane to New York to be sent via diplomatic pouch to
Homer Butler, a U.S. diplomat and friend of Belle. Now Varvara had to find a
way into the occupied zone!

"To get a place on a plane when millions of people were trying to flee to the
U.S. was more than reaching for the moon," Varvara recalled. With false identity papers, she entered the occupied zone and contacted Homer Butler. Everything was in order. Belle had not failed her.

Despite Butler's urging that she not leave the relative safety of Paris, Varvara
managed to reach Le Touquet and found her mother in dire circumstances.
It was impossible to get funds from German-occupied Denmark, and Louise
Hasselbalch had no money for food or fuel. She wept when she saw her daughter, begging her not to leave her alone in Europe. Freedom was so close, but
there was only one coveted seat on the plane. Varvara knew she could not desert
her mother. With her small salary from the French Red Cross and the money
Belle had sent, Varvara knew she could keep them alive for several months.
Praying that Belle would understand, Varvara wired Belle, through Homer
Butler, that she was staying in France and would repay the money when the
war ended.

Belle was heartbroken and afraid for both Varvara and Louise. She later
learned that Varvara continued to drive an ambulance, then later eight-ton

trucks loaded with supplies for the prisoner-of-war camps the Germans had established for French and other European prisoners on French soil. Through Butler, Varvara got involved in rescuing escaped British prisoners and, on one occasion, joined a friend in smuggling a man out of one of the POW camps.

In late 1942 the Germans decreed that no foreigner or Jew was to work for the French Red Cross and must leave France. Varvara and Louise traveled to occupied Denmark, where the courageous young Dane acted as a courier for the resistance, smuggling microfilm secreted in a hollow key into Sweden. While maintaining the facade of a frivolous, wealthy socialite, Varvara worked with the resistance and, almost single-handedly, managed the escape of an Italian diplomat, his pregnant wife, and child from Denmark to neutral Sweden. Throughout the long war, Varvara thwarted the Nazis whenever possible. It would be 1946 before Belle and Feather reunited in London.

Infant Belle with her mother,
Annie Griffen Baruch, 1899.
Courtesy of the Belle W.
Baruch Foundation

Belle at Long Branch, N.J.,
ca. 1901. Courtesy of the
Belle W. Baruch Foundation

Belle in the pony cart, ca. 1905. Courtesy of the Belle W. Baruch Foundation

Junior, Renee, and Belle dressed in Scottish kilts, ca. 1908. Courtesy of the Belle W. Baruch Foundation

The Baruch cousins with their grandfather Simon Baruch (seated) and grandmother Isabelle Wolfe Baruch (standing in the back at right). Also standing are Belle, Renee, a cousin, and Junior, ca. 1910. Courtesy of the Belle W. Baruch Foundation

Belle and Renee play with a rocking horse near the "Doll House," Hobcaw Barony, ca. 1910. Courtesy of the Belle W. Baruch Foundation

Belle with a bird dog, ca. 1910. Courtesy of the Belle W. Baruch Foundation

Renee Baruch and Belle, ca. 1915. Courtesy of the Belle W. Baruch Foundation

Belle winning the "Queen of the Bay" sailing cup, Great South Bay, Long Island, 1916. Courtesy of the Belle W. Baruch Foundation

Belle's graduating class from the Rayson School, 1917. Belle is standing at the back, far right. Courtesy of the Belle W. Baruch Foundation

Captain Ed Chamberlin, Mrs. Coster, and Belle at the American Cemetery, Belleau Woods, France, 1919. Courtesy of the Belle W. Baruch Foundation

Portrait of Belle by the photographer Guith, N.Y., ca. 1920. Courtesy of the Belle W. Baruch Foundation

Munro Cuthbertson on the dock at Hobcaw Barony, ca. 1923. Courtesy of the Belle W. Baruch Foundation

Belle with plantation children at Hobcaw Barony, ca. 1925. Courtesy of the Belle W. Baruch Foundation

Belle and Edith Wilson at Hobcaw Barony, ca. 1925. Courtesy of the Belle W. Baruch Foundation

Edith Wilson and Evangeline Johnson on tour with Belle, Paris, ca. 1925. Courtesy of the Belle W. Baruch Foundation

*Portrait of Belle, ca. 1925.
Courtesy of the Belle W. Baruch
Foundation*

*Jim Powell and Belle in the
yard of Old Relick, ca. 1928.
Courtesy of the Belle W. Baruch
Foundation*

Bathing beauties: Eleanor McCarthy, Bernard Baruch, and Belle in Italy, ca. 1929. Courtesy of the Belle W. Baruch Foundation

Edith Wilson crabbing at North Inlet, ca. 1930. Courtesy of the Belle W. Baruch Foundation

19

Personal and National Turmoil in 1941

Belle and Barbara Donohoe worked tirelessly to complete the grounds at Bellefield Plantation. Landscape architects Umberto Innocenti and Richard E. Webel of Long Island's Studio Roblyn designed the entrances to the stables, the house, the forecourt, gates, and terraces of Bellefield. All bricks in the courtyards and exterior walls were ballast bricks from the old Charleston Conservatory of Music. The gates were cypress with handwrought iron fixtures and working parts made of bronze. Barbara planted Lady Banksia yellow climbing roses that still bloom today against the mellow brick walls of the Bellefield courtyard. "They are like sunshine when they bloom," said Ella Severin.

In late 1940 Barbara Donohoe's father fell ill, and she was called home to California, never to return. Leaving her horse, Malicorn, her saddle, boots, and belongings behind, Barbara rushed to her father's side. A few months later Barbara married Fred Jostes and never saw Belle again. Asked about it many years later, Barbara said quietly, "That part of my life was over. . . . One couldn't go on riding in horse shows forever."

Barbara was Roman Catholic, devoted to her family. There is no question but that reminders of familial and religious duty and other pressures were exerted to keep Barbara in California. Belle was heartbroken and devastated when she learned of Barbara's unexpected marriage. She could not believe that Barbara would leave her for a man, ignoring the two times that she had betrayed Barbara's love through her alliances with Chita Davila and Munro Cuthbertson.

Malicorn remained at the Bellefield stables, pampered and cared for until his death from old age. Barbara's sidesaddle remained in Bellefield's tack room, regularly oiled and polished, until it was donated to the Davis Institute in 1988, long after Belle's death. Photographs of Barbara abound at Bellefield, but Barbara admitted that she had not a single photo of her days in Europe and America with Belle. Clearly, she had decided to end their long relationship and did not look back.

Putting aside her grief for Barbara, Belle joined her sister, Renee, in plans for a memorial to their mother and in January 1941 attended the formal dedication of the new x-ray department at Knickerbocker Hospital in New York, given by Belle and Renee in honor of Annie Griffen Baruch. Belle stayed in New York for a time, seeing old friends, attending the theater, and visiting her father and Edith Wilson in Washington, D.C.

Bernard Baruch was deeply involved in his efforts to influence Franklin Delano Roosevelt to institute price controls and prepare to defend the country. Baruch and the president had a somewhat tenuous relationship. Both were men of enormous ego, each wanting to be the focal point of any gathering. Their relationship was exacerbated by the jealousy of the White House inner circle, who declined to share power or prestige with an outsider. As Jim Bishop noted in *FDR's Last Year:* "A few in the Roosevelt circle tried to drive a wedge between the men. The male gossips wove their webs of innuendo, but Roosevelt made a point of defending 'Barney' while, as counterpoint, he kept Baruch from becoming too close a friend."[1]

Roosevelt knew well that he could not afford to offend a man of Baruch's power and prestige and, further, a man who donated enormous sums of money to the Democratic cause. Few Wall Street millionaires were numbered among the Democrats. There were times in the Wilsonian era when it was Baruch's money that kept the Democratic party afloat. As Jordan Schwarz noted: "He [Baruch] had an understanding with Roosevelt, even if they did not always see eye to eye. Roosevelt knew his value, both in public relations and in political contributions. . . . They needed each other, they used each other, they were comfortable with each other."[2]

Baruch, in the meantime, had developed his own conduit to the White House: a strong friendship with Eleanor Roosevelt. Oddly enough, the supposedly liberal Eleanor originally harbored prejudices against Jews and blacks. She had been furious when pushed to attend a party that was given in honor of Bernard Baruch. Baruch, however, charmed her with his courtly, attentive manner and his willingness to dispense both valued advice and dollars in support of her many causes. "From what we heard at the White House," Lillian

Rogers Parks wrote, "Eleanor had been bigoted at first but had grown to admire both Jews and blacks and became good friends with them after she became acquainted with people such as Bernard Baruch and Mary McLeod Bethune. As a matter of fact, we heard that Eleanor overcame her prejudices first and had to gently lead FDR into open-mindedness."[3]

In March 1941 Bernard asked Belle to travel back to Hobcaw Barony with him and help prepare for a visit from Eleanor Roosevelt. Eleanor had visited Hobcaw before and knew the Baruch family well. Belle and her father met her in Charleston, a little over sixty miles from Hobcaw, and drove her to the property. She was so thrilled with the delights of the barony that she wrote about it twice in her syndicated column, "My Day," enthusing about the peace, beauty, and harmony to be found there. She shared with readers her pleasure in the simple joys of crabbing under the tutelage of a young black man and feeding peanuts to the squirrels. Mrs. Roosevelt also was impressed by Belle's prowess with her horses:

> We also spent a little time watching Miss Belle Baruch show her beautiful horses. She has schooled them herself and trained them so they obey her voice and are perfectly familiar with what she wishes them to do. One young one was full of pep and cavorted around, putting his head down and kicking up his heels in pure joy of living.
>
> However, when she started him, riderless, on the real business of going over the jumps, he obeyed orders without question. At the end of his performance, he trotted up at the word of command to receive his lump of sugar.[4]

Belle liked Eleanor Roosevelt and enjoyed her visit. Her father, she knew, was delighted. His vanity and need to be liked and admired were viewed sometimes with exasperation but more often with amused resignation. Belle and Renee had long accepted that they existed on the periphery of his life, that he loved them in his abstract way and certainly wanted to influence their lives, particularly as they might reflect on him. It was important to him that he maintain the appearance of a devoted family man, and, indeed, in his mind, he was. Either Belle or Renee acted as his hostess in New York and Washington, while Belle usually did the honors at Hobcaw Barony. Both did escort duty when he requested their presence at occasional public functions.

The sisters were vastly amused at their father's new title of "Park Bench Statesman" when a "passing photographer" snapped a picture of Bernard Baruch holding court on a park bench in Lafayette Square across from the White House in September 1941. Sharing the bench were Leon Henderson, director of the

Office of Price Administration, and OPA counsel David Ginsburg, while Henderson's assistant John E. Hamm and John Maurice Clark, a professor of economics at Columbia University, were seated on the ground at the great financial guru's feet. Jordan Schwarz called it "a masterpiece of public relations that brought him power without accountability."[5] President Roosevelt was disgruntled by what he considered grandstanding and groused, "There's Bernie on the bench, the star on the stage."[6]

With her father occupied in Washington, Belle assumed more responsibility for the oversight of the entire barony. There were managers, of course, but Bernard Baruch was anxious for his daughter to become involved, and Belle was challenged and fascinated with the intricacies of managing the huge property. Hobcaw Barony was larger than many small townships and sufficient unto itself. Belle became familiar with the maintenance of the various water systems and power and refrigeration plants, laundry, ninety miles of roads, four bridges, three black villages, the church, two schools, the dispensary, docks and water towers, boat landings, and several houses for various white employees on the property.

There were motor launches and boats to be maintained and repaired, gasoline storage tanks and pumps at Hobcaw House, Bellefield, and the airstrip. Hobcaw Barony housed vehicles and farm equipment, a road grader, Belle's two airplanes, and other sophisticated machinery, all of which had to be serviced regularly.

There were the formal gardens of Hobcaw House and Bellefield to be tended as well as vegetable gardens, chickens, milk cows, domestic hogs, mules, and, of course, the stables of both Bellefield and Hobcaw House. Hobcaw Barony raised its own corn, hay, and other feed crops for the horses and cattle.

Belle gained a working knowledge of forestry, although little tree cutting was done on Hobcaw Barony until the government asked for timber for the war effort. Still, the forest had to be inspected for disease, and an effort made to balance the deer herds and curb the feral hog population.

From time to time, alligators roamed too close to the living areas and had to be destroyed. Bobcats and other predators would raid the chickens or destroy domestic animals, and Belle would join the hunt. Oyster beds were seeded and maintained and creek beds and streams checked periodically to make sure that beaver dams did not interrupt critical water flow or flood precious timberlands.

Belle reveled in the challenge, and her passion for the land of Hobcaw grew until all else was subordinate to it. Someday she wanted it all—every tree, bush, bird, animal, drop of water, and grain of sand. She wanted to nourish and protect it, to walk the land, cherishing every acre. She often felt that, like Adam in the book of Genesis, God had given her dominion over her own Eden, Hobcaw Barony.

The Baruchs employed well over one hundred people: cooks and domestics, farmers, mechanics, drivers, hunting guides, gardeners, and general laborers. Most lived on the property. In true baronial style, the Baruchs were responsible for the welfare of the people on the vast estate. Elderly and sickly individuals were given make-work so they could draw a small wage. Some old retainers were given charge accounts at Ford's store in Georgetown so they could buy the small necessities not provided by plantation life. The expectations of the barony's blacks were best summed up in an incident that touched Belle's heart and lingered in her mind.

Bernard Baruch's superintendent had come to him saying that he wanted to move a black man off the property because he was lazy. Baruch summoned the old man and asked what he had to say for himself. With simple dignity, the man, named Morris, said: "Mist' Bernie, I was born on dis place and I ain't agoin' off." Pacing up and down, the gray-haired man continued:

Mist' Bernie, I was born on dis place before Freedom. My mammy and daddy worked de rice fields. Dey's buried here. De fust ting I remember are dose rice banks. I growed up in dem from dat high. . . .

De strength of dese arms and dese legs and of dis old back, Mist' Bernie, is in your rice banks. It won't be long before de good Lord take de rest of pore ole Morris away too. An' de rest of dis body want to be with de strength of de arms and de legs and de back dat is already buried in your rice banks. No, Mist' Bernie, you ain't agoin' to run ole Morris off dis place.

He went on to tell Baruch of the problems he had raising his daughter and grandchild all alone, saying "De Missis [Mrs. Baruch] will understand me."[7] Morris stayed at Hobcaw Barony and is buried there near his family. Memories of her father's compassionate handling of the situation directed Belle's own dealings with the barony's workers. Old people held a special place in her heart.

Belle had a particular interest in making sure that everyone had adequate medical care. If someone became ill on a day when the doctor was not due to visit the dispensary, transportation was arranged to take them into Georgetown or Pawleys Island.

Lois Massey recalled a time when she visited a black man in Friendfield Village. "He had a cancer on his leg," she said, "and Belle was shocked when I told her how he had filled the hole the cancer had eaten with sand. It was an old home remedy, he said." The root doctor who had served the black people of Hobcaw had died. Her remedies were often preferred by the blacks and were often sufficient, but with her passing, people who were reluctant or too poor to visit the white physicians often resorted to old folk medicines. Lois helped the man into the car and took him to a doctor on Pawleys Island for treatment.

Belle stayed mostly on the plantation, contented and self-sufficient. She had a few old friends in Georgetown, like Aileen Donaldson, whose father had been the first superintendent at Hobcaw, and she attended services regularly at the Episcopal Church of Prince George Winyah, but for the most part, few people in Georgetown knew her well.

Dr. Philip Assey was a close friend and often called on Belle for help with an indigent patient or for much-needed hospital equipment. Belle, as always, performed her acts of charity quietly and without fanfare. While Bernard Baruch preferred large, public philanthropies, Belle chose quiet, unobtrusive acts of kindness. Belle's money provided medical care for many poor Georgetown patients in the better-equipped hospitals of Columbia, Charleston, Duke University, or even New York.

Belle was not inclined to mope, but she was lonely, missing Barbara Donohoe desperately. She filled her days and nights with activity and often made flying visits about the United States, the Caribbean, and Mexico. Lois Massey recalled a weekend trip to Nassau and a visit with the Duke and Duchess of Windsor: "They [the Windsors] were staying in a house owned by the British Embassy, and we all used to meet at a small restaurant in Nassau overlooking the ocean." Belle, she recalled, was not particularly fond of the Windsors, considering their political attitudes to be too pro-German. While she felt some sympathy for David, she disliked Wallis, having little respect for a woman who sought power through a man rather than earning it herself. She made no effort to pursue the relationship and did not invite them to the barony.

Belle entertained at Bellefield, hosting Caroline Post and Rear Admiral Earl T. Smith, ambassador to Cuba. Mrs. Wilson, as always, visited three or four times a year, and William C. Bullitt, former ambassador to Russia and France, asked to call.

On December 7, 1941, Belle shared the world's horror at Japan's infamous bombing of Pearl Harbor that would lead to the United States' entry into the war. Bernard Baruch's years of sounding the alarm were over. The nation's denial that it could be sucked into the maelstrom was ended. Belle found little solace in seeing her father's judgment vindicated and grieved over the thought of her country at war.

The winter of 1941–42 was one of those periods when FDR wanted to make use of Baruch's acknowledged expertise on war mobilization and his enormous influence on the American public. He was careful, however, not to bestow power that might rival his own. Baruch always believed, and even his enemies agreed, that if he were not a Jew, he could have been president.

Just before Christmas of that year, Belle and Lois Massey flew to New York with a long Christmas shopping list. Belle was forty-three years old, cut off from her beloved France and many friends, and so crippled with arthritis that she could no longer compete in show jumping. Without the daily rigors of training, she began to gain weight. She still mourned the loss of Barbara Dono-hoe. She was feeling lonely and vulnerable and decided that, while she was in New York, she would visit some of her European friends at the British Canteen. There she met Alison "Dickie" Leyland and invited her and a friend, Helen Lewis, to visit Bellefield over the Christmas holidays.

Belle and Lois flew back to Hobcaw Barony, and a few days later Belle sent her plane back to pick up Dickie and Helen. The attraction between Belle and Dickie was instantaneous and intense—something they could neither hide nor deny. Shortly after the holidays, after an evening of drinking and obvious displays of affection between Dickie and Belle, Helen, who had been Dickie's lover, vented her anger and started what employees described as a "knock-down, drag-out brawl."

The next morning Belle called Lois Massey upstairs to her private study and informed her that she wanted her to go to Helen Lewis and tell her to leave Bellefield immediately.

"Leave?" Lois asked.

"Yes," Belle replied. "I want her out of the house in the next hour."

Lois was dismayed. She did not relish the thought of demanding that anyone leave the barony. The Baruchs were renowned for their hospitality. It was not like Belle to do such a thing or to push anything so unpleasant onto someone else. With trepidation, Lois knocked on Helen's door.

"Good morning," Helen said, opening the door.

"Well," Lois replied, "I don't know if it's a good morning for you and me." She then relayed Belle's message and told her to pack her bags—the car would be ready to take her to the train station at Kingstree within the hour.

"Well," recalled Lois, "she went into a rage. She picked up everything that was loose and threw it at me—lamps, glasses, pillows, anything that wasn't tacked down. She was rude . . . well anyway she left."[8]

Dickie was to remain with Belle for more than a decade, and her influence, beginning with the summary dismissal of Helen from Bellefield, was to change the tenor of life at Hobcaw Barony for years to come.

20

U-Boats and Spies along the Carolina Coast

World War II wrought changes throughout the United States, but the coastal areas, in particular, were affected. Even before the war began, volunteer plane watchers manned lookout towers in Georgetown and Horry counties. Detailed instructions were given to coastal inhabitants as to what action to take in the event of an air raid.

Blackouts were instituted in January 1942, and Belle made certain that no violations took place on Hobcaw Barony. Automobiles must travel at night with only parking lights showing. On the few occasions Belle drove at night, she drove entirely without lights, so well did she know each mile of Hobcaw's roads. Gas rationing, tire rationing, Defense Bond sales, and the general mobilization of U.S. citizens were all implemented to help the war effort.

Young men aged twenty-one to forty-three were already registered for the draft. By March, Selective Service called for the registration of all men ages forty-four to sixty-five, and by June 1942 males from eighteen to twenty were also required to register. Young men from Hobcaw were either drafted or volunteered to enlist in the military.

Belle imposed restrictions on gas use at the barony and organized the women for first aid classes. Everyone pitched in to roll bandages, prepare surgical dressings, and knit sweaters for the army. No one was exempted, including Bellefield guests. Yvette Darthez recalled that "Belle and Mrs. [Edith] Wilson rolled bandages alongside the rest of us. They were very patriotic, real Americans."

To her distress, Belle's planes were confiscated by the army, but she could do little, her father advised, except surrender them graciously. From May through September 1942, Belle's hangar and airstrip were commandeered by the U.S. Army Air Corps as a base for field operations.

In the spring of 1942 Belle was contacted by an old acquaintance from Naval Intelligence. The German submarine menace off American coasts, she was told, was increasingly dangerous. American ships had been blown up all along the eastern coastline. Belle was aware of the flash of explosions on the sea's horizon at night and the oil slicks and debris that washed ashore. There had even been whisperings of bodies, though she had seen none herself. Newspapers had reported the recent torpedoing of an American ship immediately off the coast of Wilmington, North Carolina, not far from Hobcaw's shores.

The United States was defenseless against the U-boats. At the outbreak of World War II, the highest ranking officer of the antisubmarine warfare section was a chief petty officer.[1] Prime Minister Winston Churchill sent the chief of his antisubmarine warfare section and several British-manned trawlers to teach the Americans antisubmarine tactics. Operating almost at will, the German submariners designated American waters as their happy hunting ground. In February 1942 they sank nine ships from Convoy OSN 67 in a single night. In March, German subs sank eighty-four Allied merchant ships with a total tonnage of 446,000.[2]

Undetected and unchallenged, they had not only engaged Allied ships but also ferried spies and saboteurs across the Atlantic. Enemy agents had been sent ashore from German U-boats from the coast of Maine to Florida. Germans had acquired property at Martha's Vineyard, Massachusetts, and enemy submarines had been spotted in the vicinity. J. Edgar Hoover was particularly concerned about "fifth column" activities along the coast. The Coast Guard, an integral part of the U.S. Navy, would be primarily responsible for patrolling the coast, and all information would be coordinated with the FBI and Army and Naval Intelligence.

There were concerns about Hobcaw Barony, its isolation and gasoline storage facilities, its miles of beachfront and access to Winyah Bay. Belle was asked to work for Naval Intelligence and became one of the many volunteer coastal observers who would aid the military from 1942 to 1944.

Belle asked permission for either Lois Massey or Dickie Leyland to accompany her on night patrols until the military was able to organize sufficient manpower to patrol the beaches at night. Permission was given, but Belle was not to discuss certain aspects of her intelligence work or, for that matter, to let anyone know she even worked for Naval Intelligence except as a coastal observer.

Even today, people who knew her for over thirty years were unaware that she had worked for Naval Intelligence or even that she was a coastal observer.

"Not surprising," said Cynthia Taylor, who lived at Bellefield for many years when her husband was superintendent there. "Miss Belle was not interested in talking about herself or the past. She lived in the present . . . wasn't interested in gossip or small talk, especially about other people." Belle carried letters from the army authorizing her access to the beaches and permission to carry binoculars and a sidearm.

Most observations were made from the Baruch-owned portion of DeBordieu Beach. The balance of DeBordieu was owned by Arcadia Plantation and was largely undeveloped except for the Arcadia beach house, sometimes called DeBordieu House. The Baruch beach could be reached only by boat from Clambank or by riding or driving to the main highway, U.S. 17, and heading north a few miles to an access road on Arcadia property that led to the area. Barbara Donohoe had designed a comfortable thatched shelter on the beach that was used for picnics, fishing, and overnight camping on the beach. Belle called it the Grass Shack, but locals referred to it as Belle's Camp.

On night patrol on May 29, Belle saw a blinker light flash for about three seconds each at 10:20, 10:30, 10:45, and again at 10:55 between North Island lighthouse and a wreck off Jones Creek. They saw no responding light on shore but did spot a shadow dodging among the sand dunes. Belle said it could have been man or deer. There was not enough moonlight to see clearly. Much later that night there were flashes of explosions far out at sea.

The next day a Coast Guard officer called at Bellefield and told her that a German submarine was sighted off the coast. That afternoon, when Belle and Dickie checked the beach, they found a ship's rudder, flares, canvas covering, and boards with identification numbers marked "Navy Yard, N.Y." Belle turned them over to Ensign Cram of the Coast Guard. For several days they watched carefully, combing the beaches for debris, noting heavy footprints in the area, but acknowledging they might easily belong to fishermen.

On June 6 Belle and Dickie arrived at the Grass Shack about 9:10 P.M. It was ebb tide, and a slight land breeze stirred the humid, salt-laden air. Low cloud cover blocked the moonlight, and the only sound was the gentle rolling of the surf. Two ship's lights glowed briefly at sea, far beyond the North Island lighthouse. Nothing moved on the long, lonely stretch of beach.

Belle and Dickie settled in for the long night's watch, sitting in the shadows of the Grass Shack. At 10:00 P.M. they saw a light appear from the direction of Jones Creek. It moved closer, then stopped in the vicinity of the inlet, blinking brightly at varied intervals. There was no immediate responding signal.

Anxiously they waited. At 10:40 the signal light went out for a full ten minutes, then began signaling again. It was midnight before an orange light flashed in answer. The boat carrying the orange light approached the brighter signal, but it was too dark to see any identifying marks. Then a much smaller craft, riding lower in the water than the other two, joined them. The small craft remained only a brief time before leaving the scene.

Suddenly it was dark again as the three lights disappeared. Shortly thereafter Belle and Dickie heard one loud seagull cry but could see no gulls in the vicinity. Almost immediately they saw a light glow near the inlet, and the original signal light began flashing again and continued signaling until 1:30 A.M. The numbers 12, 20, 12, 27 were flashed several times.

For nearly two hours there was nothing except the darkness and the sound of the ocean. They had no radio with which to contact authorities, and there was no telephone for miles. At 3:10 A.M. there was another long, loud cry of a single seagull, again with no birds in sight. At 3:20 A.M. they saw a large, bright light in the sky just above the horizon opposite the Grass Shack. The light remained stationary, then seemed to rise. Belle observed that it looked like a lighted balloon. There was a smaller light on the horizon occasionally just below it, indicating that it might have been released from a small boat bobbing up and down in the waves below.

Shortly after the balloon rose into the atmosphere, six vivid flashes were seen at sea. Minutes later a man appeared on the beach walking toward the Grass Shack from North Inlet. Belle's job was to observe and report, not to intercept, but she reached for the pistol at her hip. Seeing the two figures on the beach, the man stopped suddenly and cut across the dunes, running toward some abandoned fishing camps. Belle and Dickie raced after him but lost sight of him in the predawn dark.

After noting the presence of heavy tar on the morning tide, Belle and Dickie left their post at dawn and reported immediately to the Coast Guard. No Coast Guard ships had been operating in the vicinity of North Inlet or Jones Creek. No balloons of any kind had been released by U.S. authorities. Later Belle talked to the Naval Intelligence agent who had recruited her. He knew she was a trained radio telegrapher who would not mistake random flashes for Morse code. Her reports were forwarded to the FBI.

For several weeks thereafter, things were fairly quiet. There had been disturbing activities off the Carolina shores, and reports circulated that a German U-boat captured off Long Island had planned to put agents ashore in South Carolina. At the request of Georgetown chief of police Fred Nobles, Belle used both an outboard and a rowboat to make a thorough search of the creeks and marshes around Clambank with William Kennedy who, Belle said, knew the waters better than anyone. She was asked to be on the lookout for a rubber boat like those that had been found in other areas, a type favored by U-boat landing parties.

On Monday, July 27, Belle and Lois Massey arrived at DeBordieu Beach about 8:50 P.M. The tide was out and the sea calm and still beneath a brilliant moon. A gentle southwest wind blew gently on their skin. They began to patrol along the water's edge and soon discovered the prints of two barefooted men coming from the ocean, headed toward the Grass Shack. They approached the shack cautiously but found it empty.

Half an hour later they saw a light flash a brief signal from somewhere between the Grass Shack and North Inlet, back of the sand dunes. An hour later a twin-engine plane flew low over the beach and headed toward Georgetown. At 11:35 the light behind the dunes began to signal again.

Belle decided to head for Georgetown and report instead of waiting until dawn. Between DeBordieu House and the woods she and Lois were stopped by two men in Coast Guard uniforms. The men carried revolvers and flashlights. Seeing that they were two women, the men lowered their weapons and after a brief conversation asked directions to the highway, saying they were on duty at North Inlet and had run out of cigarettes. They said they had been to Pawleys Inlet but had been unable to get across.

Suspicious, Belle asked for identification. Neither had an identity card but gave their names as H. Aumann and Bredmankamp, both claiming to be from Chicago. Intelligent enough not to draw against two armed men, Belle reluctantly left the two men behind but headed straight for the Georgetown police station. Chief Nobles and Border Patrolman Tueton went with Belle to the beach. Going to the spot where the women had been stopped by the uniformed men, they found footprints leading not to the highway but to the water's edge. Again, the Coast Guard claimed that no men were on duty there at the time Belle and Lois encountered them.

The Coast Guard boats began to patrol North Inlet more frequently and were often seen offshore of DeBordieu Beach. Things were quiet for several days, and Chief Nobles and Patrolman Tueton occasionally came by during night patrol and brought two Coast Guard men in a jeep to exchange information with Belle. On the night of August 5 the Coast Guard patrolled the area for a few hours before heading north to Pawleys Island. About 3:00 A.M. a slight storm with strong winds, thunder, and lightning struck, and Belle and Dickie sought refuge in the Grass Shack. At 5:06 A.M. they heard once again that distinctive single cry of a seagull, again with no birds in sight. Seconds later a red light shone at sea directly facing the Grass Shack. Then all was silent and still. Belle and Dickie were relieved to see daybreak at 5:45.

Two days later, at about 9:30 P.M., Belle and Dickie found tracks of a jeep on the beach, uncertain if they belonged to the Coast Guard. At 10:00 they saw a light at Clambank, and fifteen minutes later bright flashes signaled from the direction of North Inlet. Belle and Dickie raced to Georgetown and reported the signals. The Coast Guard had no jeep assigned to DeBordieu Beach. Georgetown authorities headed for Clambank and enlisted the help of William Kennedy. Chief Nobles asked Belle to come back with him to Georgetown at about 1:00 A.M., where Belle met with an FBI agent named Little who was sent by J. Edgar Hoover in response to her reports.

Varying their routine somewhat, Belle and Lois went to DeBordieu shortly after 2:00 P.M. on August 14. A fishing dory was beached on North Inlet. There were three men in a rowboat just off shore. One waded ashore but on seeing Belle approach, raced for the woods. Belle fired three warning shots into the air but the man kept running. Tracks of the mysterious jeep were found near the Grass Shack and around the first sand dune. The two men still in the rowboat headed back to the fishing dory and scrambled aboard, abandoning the smaller boat in the creek. Again, Belle rushed to Georgetown, but by the time they returned to the beach, the dory was gone.

Belle was increasingly frustrated. In 1942 two-way radios were scarce and reserved for military use. They were not handed out to civilian volunteers. Without telephones, the tardy responses netted few results.

Two days later Lieutenant Commander J. Ceballos, on special duty for the Horse Patrol, came to talk with Belle and survey the area. The Coast Guard increased their patrols, sending boats in at night as well as during the day.

Belle, Dickie, and Lois continued their night patrols into the early fall. There had been little activity and no signal flashes observed for several weeks. Belle began to think that whoever had been sending the encoded messages had abandoned the area due to persistent patrolling and increased Coast Guard activity. Then one night, things came to a head.

Belle and Lois Massey were on night horse patrol, riding near Clambank. The moon was full and the night was quiet with only a gentle, offshore breeze. Then Lois's quick eye saw something move on the water across the inlet. She touched Belle's arm and pointed. Quickly the women dismounted, not wanting to be silhouetted against the sky. Softly they touched their horses, gentling them to silence. Unmoving, they watched as a man in a small rubber boat paddled ashore. He stowed the boat behind some dune grass and paused to get his bearings. There was no way to cross the inlet on horseback. All they could do was try to parallel his movements as he started off, apparently headed for the highway. They kept him in sight as long as possible, finally losing sight of him in the thick brush and trees away from the shore.

After a hurried conference, it was agreed that Belle would ride to Bellefield for a car and drive to Georgetown for help. Leaving Lois to follow, Belle rode hell-for-leather for home and, without stopping to explain, leaped into her car and sped to Georgetown, tearing perilously over the dark, rutted roads. "I tell you, it's a wonder we didn't get ourselves killed out in them woods," Lois said.

This time they caught their man as he followed the road toward Pawleys Island. Lois said that neither she nor Belle was present at his questioning, but Chief Nobles said the man appeared to be a German agent who had come ashore from a German U-boat. He was turned over to the FBI. Security was tight during World War II, and a seal of silence was imposed on all participants. Belle received a letter from FBI director J. Edgar Hoover thanking her for the reports leading to the investigation and subsequent arrest.

In October the Coast Guard announced that they had recruited and trained enough men to take over night patrols along the Carolina beaches and was placing all such areas off-limits to unauthorized personnel after dark. Belle was asked to continue her work during the daylight hours.

In early November 1942 Belle and Lois went on horseback to Clambank at about 3:30 P.M. From there, Alfred Legare took them by boat to DeBordieu Beach. They discovered footprints and jeep tracks in front of the shack and found two-strand insulated wire, presumably for telephone communication, leading along the edge of the sand dunes and grounded at the shack. Belle immediately reported it to Naval Intelligence. Three days later they spotted a small cabin cruiser with no identifying numbers off DeBordieu Beach. They reported it immediately to the Coast Guard at Georgetown, but it was gone by the time the Coast Guard responded.

Belle's hunting companion, James Bessinger Sr., had become suspicious of a man with a heavy European accent who appeared in the area, seemingly from nowhere. He introduced himself as Dr. Gredinger and claimed to be a veterinarian. In fact he treated animals at both Arcadia, where Bessinger worked, and at Hobcaw Barony. Still, Bessinger and others were uneasy about the man.

Several days after Belle and Lois discovered the telephone wire, Bessinger and a companion decided to go fishing off Pawleys Island and, at the same time, keep an eye on the house at Pawleys where the stranger had rented an upstairs apartment. The men stayed for several hours, catching a few fish and watching the house.

The hour grew late, and the two men decided to call it a night. Suddenly they saw what appeared to be ship-to-shore signals flashing from the upstairs window. "We reported what we had seen," said Bessinger, "and the authorities kept watch. He was just ready to move out when they got him. He had a map of everything, from the naval base [at Charleston] to North Carolina . . . everything drawn and mapped out, the airports, all the naval bases."

In February 1943 Hoover asked to meet with Belle in Washington, D.C., but Belle never revealed their conversation. So closemouthed were Belle and those involved with the government during the war that most people who lived in Georgetown and Horry counties were unaware of any espionage activity along their coast.

German submarines were active along the eastern coast of the United States throughout 1942 and 1943. The threat diminished in late 1943 because Hitler, against the advice of his admirals, pulled the U-boats out of American waters. Belle was somewhat relieved to give up the dangerous patrols.

21

❧

Dickie Leyland at Hobcaw Barony

The advent of Dickie Leyland at Hobcaw Barony signaled an era of discord. With a single exception, no one speaks kindly of Dickie. She was considered rude and overbearing, spiteful, jealous, and deceitful. Dickie had two faces, one individual noted, one for Belle and one for everyone else. The relationship was, and remains, a mystery in the minds of everyone who knew Belle. "Dickie," noted Robert Darthez, "was not a good influence on Miss Belle."

Dickie was a British citizen who had been raised in Poona, India, which she pronounced "Inja." Dickie had been in Trinidad when the war broke out and had come to New York to help at British War Relief. She was a tall, attractive woman, almost as big as Belle. She rode reasonably well and liked to fish and hunt, enjoyed music and dancing. She fell in easily with Belle's plans and at first seemed compliant and pleasant if somewhat haughty and aloof.

Christiane Darthez protested that people simply did not understand Dickie's English ways and manner. "She was a very complex person," Christiane said. "She and Belle enjoyed many of the same things, and I believe she loved the plantation every bit as much as Belle did. She had a passion for all animals, was a very good photographer, loved flowers and arranged them beautifully. . . . She was very artistic and quite tenderhearted. Dancing and music were also great passions of hers."

Dickie was kind to the French girl, giving her books and helping her learn English. Perhaps Dickie recognized in Christiane the shared loneliness of being in an alien country. Apparently Christiane saw a kinder, gentler side of Dickie that was hidden from others. Perhaps, too, it was a side that Belle knew well, an aspect of Dickie's personality that offset the darker forces within her.

One cannot doubt that Belle had a deep, abiding affection for Alison "Dickie" Leyland. If, as some thought, she appealed to the darker side of Belle's nature, that cannot have been the sole attraction. Like any newly enamored lover, Belle could see no faults in her friend, at least in the beginning. She was happy to have someone in her life to fill the void created by Barbara Donohoe's defection.

It was a disturbing, tumultuous time for Belle. Her entire life had been turned around. At first she had the distraction of building Bellefield and the companionship of her beloved Barbara. Bellefield and Barbara compensated somewhat for the loss of her life and friends in Europe, a life filled with challenge, pleasure, and compatible friends. Bellefield without Barbara seemed an empty, beautiful shell. She needed someone to fill the well of loneliness.

The early war years were active for Belle with the beach patrols and other war work. In January 1943 she sponsored the launching of the submarine *Pargo*, built by the Electric Boat Company of Groton, Connecticut. When Belle was with her father, Dickie either remained on the plantation or visited friends elsewhere.

Gradually, however, things began to change at Hobcaw. After consolidating her position with Belle, Dickie set out to undermine Belle's relationships with longtime friends and employees. Her methods might be subtle with Belle, but she was often cruel and abusive to others. Dickie was never satisfied with harmony but sought to "stir the pot" with subtle innuendo and sly insinuation. "Dickie could not tell the truth about anything," said Elizabeth Navarro, "she was the biggest liar in the world."

Dickie detested Jim Powell and was jealous of his long, loving relationship with Belle. When Belle was in residence, Captain Jim would come every morning to chat, even after he retired. Bernard Baruch had given him a house and property in Pawleys Island as a retirement gift, but Powell preferred to live at Hobcaw and did so until his death.

If Belle was not down from her study when Powell came in the morning, Dickie would tell him Belle had no time for him that day and rudely slam the door in his face. She would make caustic comments within the old man's hearing about his filthy tobacco-chewing habits and ignorant, hillbilly manners, doing her best to make him feel gauche and unwelcome. Powell was known to have fathered at least one child by a black woman, and Dickie was scathing in her comments about that. Powell was too proud to complain to Belle. Gradually he called less and less often. If Belle suspected the true reasons, she preferred not to face them.

Dickie would be overbearing and rude to Jean Darthez, but the Frenchman simply ignored her and went about his business with his beloved horses. Darthez knew his own worth and had mingled with royalty and the cream of European society during his years with Belle. Dickie was beneath his concern, and she was never able to drive a wedge between Jean and Belle no matter how she tried.

Dickie was clever enough not to criticize Belle's family and recognized that Edith Wilson was as dear to Belle's heart as her own mother had been. But anyone who lived day-to-day with close contacts at Bellefield was a target for her venom. Dickie wanted the sole position of influence in Belle's life. Greed may have been part of it, for Dickie had few financial resources and was economically dependent on Belle. The primary forces driving Dickie, however, were jealousy and possessiveness.

In the early years of Dickie's residency at Hobcaw Barony, Bernard Baruch was there only occasionally, being tied up in New York and Washington on various assignments for President Roosevelt. Although seventy-one, Baruch was deeply involved in the crisis politics of the war years. In 1942 he headed a committee to study the nation's rubber shortage. Roosevelt knew that if Baruch encouraged the American people to conserve rubber and gas and recommended rationing, the public would accept his recommendations. The president gave him special assignments with high press visibility, knowing that the American people believed in the wisdom of Bernard Baruch.

Jordan Schwarz noted that "the war made Baruch one of the most celebrated Americans of his time. . . . By 1944 a Hearst columnist would declare that 'Baruch today is without doubt the most respected individual in the country.'"[1] "Baruch's influence," Schwarz said, "was based upon his hold upon public opinion. It was awesome and even frightening. A Baruch dissent was capable of bringing a torrent of constituent letters and outraged editorials down upon the heads of Washington officials. . . . Baruch's power came from the people. Throughout the war commodity shortages evoked demands for the president to appoint 'a Baruch committee' in the manner of the Rubber Survey Committee."[2]

President Roosevelt resented Baruch's power over American opinion, but he used it. Belle's reactions to her father's awesome influence were mixed. She was enormously proud of him and respected his wisdom, but she was also well aware of his weaknesses, including his childlike vanity and obsessive need to be liked and admired. She also knew that he went to considerable effort to ensure a favorable press and had such power within the journalistic community that his every word and opinion merited immediate and extensive coverage.

Belle knew of his numerous affairs, even as a septuagenarian, and accepted them philosophically. Even when her mother was alive, she was aware of his philandering but never criticized nor commented, even to close friends. She recognized that he basked in the companionship and admiration of beautiful, successful women and had the rare capacity to maintain lifelong friendships with his former mistresses. She also suspected that many of his affairs were more of the mind and the ego than the body. She felt that it was not her place to approve or disapprove. Nor did she suffer the opinions of others, saying curtly that it was no one's business.

Bernard Baruch disliked Dickie Leyland, and it was tacitly understood that invitations for Belle to dine or visit did not include Miss Leyland unless so stated. When her father came to lunch or dinner, Dickie did not appear at the table or join them in their long, intimate conversations in the sunroom.

While preferring simply to ignore most of Belle's previous companions, Baruch's antipathy toward Dickie was exacerbated by her heavy drinking, for he loathed drinking in a woman. He was also aware that Belle's drinking increased proportionately the longer Dickie remained. One also suspects that he found it extremely difficult to deny his daughter's lesbianism when Dickie was present. Dickie, Baruch's friends commented, was extremely "Butch" in both appearance and mannerisms.

Belle's father was genuinely fond of Lois Massey, and her inclusion in luncheons, shooting parties, and social visits did not endear Lois to Dickie. Lois's relationship to Jim Powell was another strike against her, for Dickie knew that Lois resented her treatment of the old man. Lois was firmly entrenched, but Dickie bided her time.

Bernard Baruch was repelled and disgusted when Dickie created a terrible scene at Bellefield, something Baruchs abhorred. Dickie was stricken with acute appendicitis but in a fit of hysterical screaming and cursing refused to be touched by a male physician or taken to the hospital in Georgetown. Belle was frantic, terrified that Dickie would die if not treated immediately, a fear confirmed by the physician who eventually saw her. Bernard Baruch clearly did not understand why the hysterical woman refused treatment until it was explained that she had a pathological fear and hatred of men and refused to have one touch her or look at her body.

Baruch was more concerned about his daughter, who rarely displayed such emotion and, against his inclinations, consented to talk to the doctor Belle had called in from Georgetown. Eventually they concurred that a nurse would sedate Dickie so that she could be transported to Georgetown for surgery, unaware that a hated man was near. It did not take a psychiatrist to realize that at some point in her life, Dickie Leyland had suffered severe trauma at the hands of a man, but Baruch felt more distaste than sympathy at the time.

He did relent occasionally and include Dickie in his invitations. Once he invited her to dine with Belle at a dinner that included Henry and the Honorable Clare Boothe Luce. Clare was one of those ex-mistresses with whom Baruch had maintained close ties, even after her marriage to Henry Luce. The Baruchs and Luces exchanged visits often when both families were in South Carolina.

Baruch had encouraged Luce to buy property in South Carolina, and in 1936 the Luces purchased historic Mepkin Plantation on the Cooper River near Moncks Corner. The 7,200-acre plantation had once belonged to Henry Laurens, a hero of the American Revolution and president of the First Provincial Congress in South Carolina. The Luces eventually would sell all but 3,000 acres of the property in 1949. The 3,000-acre parcel, which included the house and other buildings, was donated to the Trappist monks of the Abbey of Gethsemani in Kentucky. In November 1949, Trappist monks arrived in South Carolina to establish the Monastery of the Immaculate Heart of Mary, now known as the Abbey of Our Lady of Mepkin.

Dickie was seated next to Henry Luce at dinner, and during a lull in the conversation, Dickie loudly and somewhat condescendingly asked the head of the Time-Life publishing empire what he did for a living. Total silence prevailed as a stunned Luce floundered for an answer. Clare Boothe Luce's hearty peals of laughter relieved the silence, and reluctantly Luce and the others joined in. Secretly, it tickled Baruch that someone did not know just who the great Henry Luce was, but pride dictated that a prestigious guest in his household should not be so offended. It was a while before Baruch invited Dickie again.

In 1943 Bernard Baruch deeded all of Hobcaw Barony, except about 1,800 acres surrounding Hobcaw House, to Belle. To celebrate, Belle and Dickie flew off to New York for a round of theater, shopping, and films. War was a popular theme that year in books, theater, and film. Lillian Hellman's *Watch on the Rhine* was playing on Broadway. Gary Cooper was starring in *For Whom the Bell Tolls,* and Humphrey Bogart and Ingrid Bergman were appearing in the now classic *Casablanca.* Browsing among the bookstores for Christmas gifts, Belle found *Guadalcanal Diary,* by Richard Tregaskis, and *Here Is Your War,* by Ernie Pyle.

How long, Belle wondered, would the war continue? The news of Jewish persecution was becoming more and more disturbing. In June, Joseph Goebbels had made his ominous announcement that "Berlin is now free of Jews." The world was beginning to realize how horrific such announcements were.

Belle identified strongly with the Baruch side of the family and felt great inner peace and a sense of rightness when she prayed with her Jewish relatives. Although raised an Episcopalian, Belle occasionally attended synagogue with her devout Jewish grandmother. She especially loved to spend Sabbath eve at her grandparents' home. Her eyes would fill with tears at the lighting of the Sabbath candles, and she loved to hear Grandfather Baruch speak the ritual blessings in Hebrew. He translated part of it for her: "May the Lord bless you and protect you. May the Lord shine His countenance upon you and be gracious to you. May the Lord favor you and grant you peace." Was it so different, she wondered, from her own Christian prayers? At times Belle would join Baruch family mourners as they observed shivah for deceased loved ones.

She could not comprehend the unreasoning hatred of someone simply because he or she was Jewish. Her grandfather had spent a lifetime serving others. Belle remembered her father telling her about the time he had gone to his father to announce that he was worth a million dollars. Simon Baruch had been singularly unimpressed, simply asking his son how he planned to use that money for the good of others. Who could hate such a just, compassionate, and moral man?

Belle began to understand how much her father's power, wealth, and influence had shielded the family from anti-Semitism. She was aware of the subtle and sometimes overt snubs that occurred because of her Jewish heritage and remembered the vitriolic attacks by Henry Ford and others. Her romance with Chita Davila had ended because of her "Jewishness." Still, she could not imagine the pain and terror that European Jews were suffering. She had never felt physically threatened or afraid of the reality of her Jewish blood, until now. She began to appreciate her father's wisdom and foresight in insisting that she leave Europe.

22

FDR's Visit to South Carolina

Spring had always been Belle's favorite season at Hobcaw. As Easter approached in 1944, the woods of the barony were at their loveliest, with purple wisteria cascading from the trees and fragile dogwoods swaying in the soft breeze. Brilliant azaleas were in bud, and crocus and jonquils bloomed in glowing color. Flowing yellow jessamine gleamed amid the newly green trees.

That year alien sights and sounds rang throughout the peaceful acres as the forests teemed with Secret Service men intent on "sanitizing" Hobcaw Barony in preparation for a visit from President Franklin Delano Roosevelt. For weeks his doctors had been advising a sick and weary president to find a place to rest. The war was slowly turning in favor of the Allies. In January the Yanks landed at Anzio. By the end of February, General Douglas MacArthur had begun his campaign to drive the Japanese from the Pacific. U.S. planes had bombed Berlin for the first time on March 4. The president, his physicians urged, must rest.

President Roosevelt first contemplated a visit to Guantánamo Bay, the U.S. naval base in Cuba, but Admiral Ross McIntyre, his physician, reminded him that he did not like flying; moreover, the high altitude was not good for his condition. Roosevelt then decided that he was going to accept Bernard Baruch's oft-repeated invitation to visit Hobcaw Barony.

Eleanor Roosevelt had always felt at home with the Baruchs and encouraged her husband to visit Hobcaw. She might not have been so eager had she realized that one of the traits Baruch and FDR shared was a fondness for pretty women and a cavalier attitude toward discreet dalliances. Baruch, in fact, previously had arranged liaisons between the president and his longtime friend,

Lucy Mercer Rutherfurd, and arranged for Lucy to come to Hobcaw while Roosevelt was in residence.

In any event, Eleanor encouraged Franklin to visit Hobcaw. FDR was curious about the fabulous tales he had heard from the famous and powerful people who had been guests of Baruch and his daughter Belle at their South Carolina plantation. Colonel Edwin "Pa" Watson, Roosevelt's military aide, regaled FDR with tales of the "boys" who joined Baruch at his southern retreat and the memorable hospitality of both Bernard at Hobcaw House and Belle at Bellefield Plantation.

Watson and Roosevelt shared an earthy sense of humor, and Roosevelt laughed long and hard over Pa's mock court-martial at Hobcaw in 1935. In *FDR: A Biography,* Ted Morgan described it:

> Pa was the object of a mock court-martial proceeding for alleging that another member of the party, Admiral Cary Grayson, had shot a turkey tied to a tree. FDR issued humorous memos in the following vein: "Rather than incur the expenses of a Court Martial, it is suggested that General Baruch tie Colonel Watson and Admiral Grayson to convenient trees, distant one hundred paces, that each be armed with a bow and arrow, that each be blindfolded, that each be required to emit turkey calls and that thereafter firing shall begin."[1]

Pa had also described Belle's magnificent horses and those wild, moonlit foxhunts. It all sounded appealing, restful, and lighthearted to Roosevelt after years of war and months of sickness. Emphatically he declared that he was going to Hobcaw!

Preparations began and it was not long before rumors began to fly. Every building, every person, and every acre of Hobcaw was scrutinized. Wooden ramps to accommodate Roosevelt's wheelchair appeared at the entrances to buildings and fishing docks. A canvas chute was attached to the first-floor bedroom the president would use so that he could be evacuated quickly and safely in the event of fire.

Baruch's rule of "no telephones" certainly would not do for the president. Communication lines were brought in connecting the president to the White House and to communications centers in special railroad cars in Georgetown. Squads of armed marine guards appeared, and anyone with eyes and ears knew "something big" was happening. Belle, of course, was taken into her father's confidence and was deep in preparation for the president's arrival. Hobcaw Barony had hosted other illustrious men—such as Prime Minister Winston

Churchill and President Grover Cleveland—but this had to be the most exciting visitor in Hobcaw's history.

Both Baruchs had well-deserved reputations as generous and considerate hosts. Margaret Coit noted that "Senator Joseph Robinson once commented that 'Miss Belle' was simply wonderful because she always said and did the things which made her guests 'comfortable and happy without seeming to make an effort' and never bored them with excessive attention."[2] Both Belle and Bernard were genial hosts who excelled in small, thoughtful acts that made their guests feel welcome, but their styles were reflected in their homes. Hobcaw House, like its owner, was gracious and formal whereas Bellefield was casual and comfortable.

Hobcaw's splendid baronial dining room sparkled with glittering silver, crystal, and imported china. Bellefield guests ate in more casual splendor on Blocaille's exclusive set of magnificent china depicting hunt scenes hand-painted in Belle's official riding colors of hunter green and white with touches of red in some of the hunting jackets. Even the crystal reflected Belle's love of the hunt. Both houses were polished and buffed to a high gloss in preparation for the president's visit.

Roosevelt was scheduled to arrive on Easter Sunday. FDR's biographers always write about the "secret" journey and preparations, but it was no secret to the people in Georgetown and Horry counties. Hobcaw Barony employees were not briefed until the actual day of the president's arrival, but conclusions had been reached long before that. Three well-known White House correspondents had checked into the Prince George Hotel on the Georgetown waterfront. Inez Alford Villafranca, who lived in Conway, recalls: "It was no secret. We [she and her friends] knew about it, and we were just average young people of no special importance or standing in the community."

FDR chuckled over the three-foot-tall Easter Bunny waiting to greet him and announced his intention to rest. "I want to sleep and sleep," he said. "Twelve hours every night."[3] The president, his aide, physician, and close staff members stayed at Hobcaw House while others went to Bellefield. Roosevelt was extremely ill, his skin gray with fatigue and stress. He suffered with arteriosclerosis, hypertension, hypertensive heart disease, cardiac failure (left ventricular), and acute bronchitis.[4]

No one was allowed to leave Hobcaw Barony while the president was there, with the exception of the Baruchs, the schoolchildren, and Belle's secretary, Lois Massey. Lois would go into town for groceries and other articles, always accompanied by a Secret Service agent.

"They had two hundred marines stationed from the front gate to the house and Secret Service men behind every bush," Massey recalled.

> I started out of the house one morning—I was going down to the laundry with some linen—and this man walked up from around the corner of the house and said, "Where do you think you're going?"
>
> "Well," I said, "I thought I was going to the laundry, but if you don't want me to, I'll go back in the house." And he walked me down to the laundry to make sure I wasn't taking anything but clothes.
>
> It was the same way in town. People would come up to me and say, "Well, I hear you've got the president over your way," and before I could answer, the Secret Service man would frown and say, "I beg your pardon?" Of course, it scared them to death and they'd just walk away. But I enjoyed the whole thing, and Mr. Roosevelt was just as nice and down to earth as could be.[5]

Francena McCants, a Baruch employee for over thirty years, spoke of the president's charm and kindness. "I was pregnant then, and Mr. Roosevelt said I should name my baby after him." She laughed happily. "My baby, Franklin, was born a few months later."

No president can ever escape the responsibilities of office completely. Plans for the Allied invasion of Europe were being laid and required the approval of the commander in chief. But insofar as humanly possible, Roosevelt's staff shielded him from all but the most urgent matters. Cabinet members and the chiefs of staff of the various armed services came to Hobcaw to brief the president, and all enjoyed the hospitality of the Baruchs. Unobtrusive and gracious, neither Belle nor Bernard ever impinged on Roosevelt's privacy.

Christiane Darthez recalls meeting one of Roosevelt's top advisers. "One day as I waited by the gate, a black chauffeur-driven car came out and stopped beside me. The door opened, a smiling white-haired gentleman leaned out, offering me a lift. As I took my seat beside him, I suddenly recognized him, even as he introduced himself and the lady sitting beside him. They were Mr. and Mrs. James Byrnes!

"Both were charming to me, putting me at ease by asking about my school activities and about my life. They deposited me in front of my school, making me feel like quite a celebrity for the day!"

Byrnes was then director of war mobilization and later became secretary of state. It was said that Byrnes was elected to more public offices than any other man of his era, serving in the House of Representatives, the Senate, and later as governor of South Carolina. The Byrnes and Baruch families were lifelong friends, and Mr. and Mrs. Byrnes were frequent visitors at Hobcaw Barony, Bellefield, and Little Hobcaw.

Roosevelt slept, basked in the sun, fished in the inlets, rivers, and ocean, hunted ducks with William Kennedy, crabbed with Belle from the Hobcaw docks, and slowly rebuilt his strength.

Occasionally he drove to neighboring Arcadia, owned by the Vanderbilts. James Bessinger Sr. recalled that the president was interested in seeing the watchtower at Arcadia where volunteers watched for enemy planes. He also enjoyed fishing at the well-stocked ponds on Arcadia. Bessinger's father was one of the supervisors at Arcadia and was a state game warden.

Hearing that the Bessingers had sons serving in the military, Roosevelt said to their mother, "You worry about your sons, don't you?" Mrs. Bessinger replied that yes, she did worry, that she didn't know exactly where they were or how they were. The president promised to check on her boys, and Bessinger said that later his parents received a letter from FDR assuring them that their sons were well and "doing a good job for their country."[6]

Roosevelt claimed that he was limiting himself to one and a half cocktails per evening and nothing more, "not one complimentary highball or nightcap" and he had cut his cigarettes down to five or six a day. More often than not, FDR shared his cocktails with Belle, both having a fondness for dry martinis. Roosevelt enjoyed an afternoon drive around the area each day and would stop at Bellefield for a visit. He enjoyed Belle's humor and they shared a love of animals, nature, and horse racing. They sipped their drinks, smoked, swapped tales about fishing and sailing, and discussed the possible candidates for the next Triple Crown champion.

One day he came for lunch, which Belle prepared and served on the brick patio. She served chicken and fresh asparagus and other vegetables grown at Hobcaw. She sat down to start her own lunch when she noted that the president was not eating.

"Is there something wrong, Mr. President?" she asked hesitantly.

FDR flashed his famous smile and drawled, "Well, if I had a fork, I could eat!"

Pa Watson made nightly use of Belle's hospitality. He would arrive at the cocktail hour, walking in the door with his pals, shouting: "Lulu! Lulu! [one of his pet names for Lois Massey]. It's time for a gargle!"

One night a nervous Secret Service agent who was patrolling the woods around Hobcaw House was startled by a sudden rustling in the brush. Freezing in place, he strained to hear as the intruder moved closer and closer. Throwing a light on the bushes, he saw a snorting, drooling beast and, without thinking, let loose a shotgun blast.

Lights popped on all over the house, marine guards, and Secret Service agents came running. Roosevelt's staff came dashing from their rooms in various stages of undress, and the embarrassed agent had to point to his giant pig. Only FDR slept on, undisturbed by the ruckus. He roared with laughter next day when his staff recounted the tale of the "snarling beast."

Life for the marine guards and Secret Service agents was tedious and uncomfortable. Those assigned to communications sweltered for a month in broiling-hot railroad cars parked on a Georgetown siding. Those assigned to guard duty swatted mosquitoes, pried off ticks, and tried to stave off boredom to remain alert.

Some of the staff rigged a temporary movie theater out in the stable, and an agent swore that one of the horses actually watched the movies each night with apparent fascination. While his stable mates largely ignored the screen, this one would stick his head out of his stall the minute the film began and watch until it was over.

One evening the Baruchs invited the plantation staff and their families to watch the latest hit, *Cover Girl,* starring Rita Hayworth and Gene Kelly. President Roosevelt watched too, and the children and parents were torn between watching the movie and staring at FDR.

Intending to stay two weeks, the president remained a month, soaking up sun and tranquility. Both Franklin and Eleanor were grateful for this respite from the rigors of the presidency. Eleanor came once for a brief visit (not the same day as Lucy Mercer Rutherfurd!) but left to pursue her own duties once she was assured that her husband was on the mend.

Tanned and fit looking, the president returned to Washington in May to prepare for his campaign for a fourth term in office. Letters of thanks from the White House arrived at Hobcaw and Bellefield, and Edwin "Pa" Watson was particularly effusive in his note to Belle in her guest book: "I just want you to know how much I appreciate your kindness to all of us, from the great President down, and how much you contributed to the pleasure, comfort and physical well-being of all concerned. That annex to your home built of stone, called The Bar [Belle's sunroom], is indeed a monument. . . . I look forward to again appearing at your front door."[7]

Almost two months later, on June 6, the plans discussed and approved by the president at Hobcaw Barony were implemented, and the Allies landed on the beaches of Normandy. By September 15 General Omar Bradley's First Army breached the Siegfried line just east of Aachen, where Belle used to ride in horse shows. For the first time in World War II, U.S. troops were fighting on German soil. General Douglas MacArthur kept his promise to the Philippine people to return on October 25.

Delighted with the progress of the war, Congress created a new rank and named four five-star generals: the Baruchs' old friend George C. Marshall, Chief of Staff of the Army; Douglas MacArthur, Commander, Southwest Pacific; Dwight D. Eisenhower, Supreme Allied Commander in Europe; and Henry "Hap" Arnold, General of the Army Air Force.

The Allies continued their victorious march. The Russians liberated Auschwitz in January 1945, and the world witnessed the limitless horror of the Nazi's "solution to the Jewish problem." The world would never again be so innocent. In the Pacific the U.S. Marines raised the Stars and Stripes over Iwo Jima. By March, U.S. troops had crossed the Rhine at Remagen.

Bernard Baruch and the president were discussing another visit to South Carolina in the spring. "Hobcaw," Baruch assured the president, "is more beautiful than ever with all the spring flowers about to come out. You would be very welcome to take the place. Belle assures you of good fishing, good mixings and her own good cooking."

The president, however, needed Baruch in London to discuss with Prime Minister Winston Churchill various problems relating to the impending peace —a peace he did not live to see. On April 12, 1945, President Franklin Delano Roosevelt died. The president had insisted that Baruch take his own plane, the "Sacred Cow," on his mission to Europe, and when word came of the president's death, Baruch immediately contacted the president's son Elliott, who was serving in Europe, and returned with him to Washington. Once again, the Baruch family joined a nation in mourning.

A few years passed before Eleanor Roosevelt could find it in her heart to forgive Bernard Baruch for the Lucy Mercer Rutherfurd affair. Time, however, mellowed her attitude, and she came once more to Hobcaw Barony to visit both Belle and Bernard. In time the bonds were reestablished, and James Roosevelt commented: "Despite his advanced age, Bernie always liked the ladies. He was close to mother, father's mother and father's former lady friend, which was quite a parlay. . . . One of the funniest scenes I ever witnessed was a banquet Bernie attended with mother. Bernie kept falling asleep, and mother kept nudging him so he would awaken and applaud at the right time. After a while it was mother's turn, and she grabbed a few winks while Bernie nudged her at appropriate times. Obviously they had worked out an agreement and it was successful."[8]

Belle was relieved and happy for her father because she knew how much Eleanor's friendship meant to him. He was getting on in years, approaching eighty, though still vigorous and hearty, still hunting and fishing. She wished him peace in his late years, and the reunion with Eleanor Roosevelt at Hobcaw delighted him.

In Washington and New York, he frequently escorted Mrs. Roosevelt to various functions. They maintained an extensive correspondence and affectionate Victorian-style affair until her death in November 1962. His press statement summed up his regard for his old friend: "Mrs. Roosevelt's death is a blow to me; we were friends for almost fifty years. I will miss her greatly as will all her friends and the millions of men and women in every country to whom she was the First Lady of the World. She was a rare combination of wisdom and goodness." Baruch had made it a policy not to accept positions on any boards of directors, but when asked by Adlai Stevenson to serve on the board of the Eleanor Roosevelt Foundation, Baruch said, "I feel I cannot refuse this."[9]

23

War's End and
the End of an Era

The Allied armies continued their thrust in both theaters of war. The world knew the end was coming when Benito Mussolini was shot on April 28, 1945, and Adolph Hitler committed suicide just two days later. By May 7, Germany had surrendered unconditionally.

On August 6, Paul W. Tibbets Jr., flew the *Enola Gay*, the plane that dropped the first atomic bomb on Hiroshima, stunning the world. Still Japan did not bow to Allied might. Three days later, on August 9, 1945, a second atomic bomb was dropped on the city of Nagasaki. Six days later Japan signaled surrender, signing the official unconditional surrender papers on September 2. Stunned by the unleashed fury of the atom, the Baruchs had no way of knowing that Bernard Baruch would play a major role in determining the future of atomic weapons control.

Belle was in New York when word of peace came and joined the cheering throng in the streets as horns honked, whistles blew, and Americans celebrated victory. Belle had experienced her own small war at Bellefield over the past few months and was feeling dissatisfied and guilty about the outcome.

Dickie's resentment of Lois Massey had grown to unmanageable proportions by the spring of 1945. She considered Lois to be an uneducated, southern hillbilly and hated the ease with which Lois responded to the many dignitaries who visited Hobcaw. Lois, she felt, was nothing more than a servant and had no right to presume to extend the hospitality of the barony to anyone, let alone the president of the United States. Yet Lois Massey had welcomed guests to Hobcaw Barony for over twenty-five years, often representing the Baruchs in their absence. She was loved and respected for her unassuming charm and concern for the comfort of Hobcaw guests. It was the obvious affection Lois garnered so easily that galled Dickie most. Dickie stepped up the campaign to get rid of Lois Massey.

More often than not, Lois stayed at Bellefield day and night when Belle was in residence. Belle liked to have her available to ensure that the household ran smoothly, to act as liaison with the many Hobcaw workers who had known and respected Lois and her uncle, Jim Powell, for decades. She was treated as a friend as well as employee, joining the family and guests at cocktails and meals, often accompanying them on shopping trips and outings. Usually it was Lois who coordinated schedules and transportation, often escorting guests on sightseeing and shopping tours in lieu of Belle, who had little liking for such ventures.

Lois admittedly resented Dickie as well. When Barbara Donohoe left, Belle relied heavily on Lois for both assistance and companionship. Lois had enjoyed their close friendship and resented Dickie's barbed reminders that she was, after all, nothing more than an employee who did not know her proper place.

One night, according to Lois Massey, everyone had gathered in the sunroom around the French bar. Dickie was pouring the drinks and, so Lois believed, slipped something into Lois's cocktail.

"Everything became distorted," Lois recalled. "I didn't know what was happening. I just knew I had to get out of there." At two o'clock in the morning, Lois got in her car and somehow managed the drive up the dirt road to her mother's home at Pawleys Island.

"What in the world's happened to you?" her mother exclaimed when Lois staggered into the house.

"I don't know," she said, "but I'm going to find out."

The next morning, Lois returned to Hobcaw and went looking for Dickie. She found her in the pantry, mixing an early-morning drink. Dickie's cocktail hour had been starting earlier and earlier, commencing with breakfast.

In a rare loss of temper, Lois grabbed the lapels of Dickie's robe and slammed her against the sink. "You dirty son-of-a-bitch," she said, "I want to tell you something. If you ever put anything in my drink again, I'm going to beat the hell out of you, and I mean it!"

Dickie opened her mouth to deny Lois's allegations, but Lois shook her violently and said, "Now don't say you didn't do it, because I know you did!" Lois was as tall and strong as Dickie and in much better shape since she limited her alcohol consumption. "I was so mad that morning," she recalled, "I could have throttled her. She steered clear of me for the next few days."[1]

But Lois had played into Dickie's hands. The British woman went sobbing to Belle to complain of Lois's attack, exaggerating her terror and fear that Lois meant to harm her. Belle was torn between her love and her longtime employee. Belle had been drinking heavily in those days as well. Dickie was well on the road to alcoholism and did not want to make the journey alone. She would appear in Belle's room early in the morning, drinks in hand. Belle's morning libation usually went untouched, but throughout the day Dickie was pouring, usually doubles and triples.

Nolan "Red" Taylor, Belle's employee for nearly twenty years, insists: "I know folks said Miss Belle drank a lot when Miss Leyland was there, but I saw her pour many a glass of liquor down the sink when Dickie wasn't looking."

"I know Dickie was spiking Belle's drinks," said Elizabeth Navarro, "but I blame Belle too. She didn't have to drink them."

Taylor stoutly insisted that he never saw Belle obviously drunk. "She never drank more than she could handle." Others agreed but acknowledged that Belle could handle a great deal.

Belle's abstemious father was thoroughly disgusted and appalled at the amount of liquor flowing at Bellefield. He could not bear to see his daughter, or anyone else for that matter, under the influence, and Belle made an effort to stem the flow when her father came to visit. When his car pulled up, all visible evidence was pushed out of sight. To appease the elder Baruch, Dickie was often pushed out of sight as well, smoldering with jealousy as Lois joined the Baruchs for lunch or dinner.

Dickie finally won. She cried and nagged and badgered Belle for months to get rid of Lois. Belle flew off to New York and on July 12, 1945, mailed a curt letter of dismissal to Lois:

> For some time past, things have been unsatisfactory at Bellefield. Therefore, I think a change is in order. There has been considerable friction on the place causing me a great deal of unhappiness.
>
> I am enclosing a check for $1625.00—one year's salary—to take care of you until you find another position.
>
> Please leave the keys with Jean and place my papers in order in my files.
>
> I trust you will be able to arrange your departure within the week.[2]

Bernard Baruch was embarrassed and disgusted but counseled Lois that it would be better if she were not involved in "that mess" at Bellefield. Thus ended over a quarter century of service to the Baruchs. Lois never saw Belle again, but when she became postmaster at Pawleys Island, Mr. Baruch would stop by for an occasional chat.

"She [Dickie Leyland] spoiled things for all of us," Lois Massey reflected in later years. To her surprise, Belle left Lois a small legacy (five thousand dollars) in her will. "I know she didn't really like what happened," Lois said. "I don't hold any malice against Miss Belle."

Hobcaw without Lois Massey was never the same. While there was a general superintendent, it was Lois who had seen to the minutiae of managing a property the size of Hobcaw. Lois knew every person on the property, their skills, strengths, and weaknesses. The black residents liked and respected her. People looked to her for leadership and knew she spoke for Belle. She knew the tradesmen and craftsmen of Georgetown and had always dealt with them on behalf of the Baruchs, reviewing performance, bills, payments, and the like, assuring a smooth, uninterrupted function of the domestic aspects of the vast property.

Lois had maintained a log on Hobcaw Barony's guests, listing their preferences in food, drink, and recreation so that each visitor could be assured faultless hospitality tailored to his or her personal needs and interests. Belle dealt with the major decisions, leaving hundreds of details to Lois. Now they all tumbled down upon her. Dickie wanted to fill the void but lacked the empathy and communication skills to deal with the employees, particularly the blacks for whom she had little tolerance. Sensing her disdain, they retreated behind the time-honored custom of cleverly feigned ignorance when Dickie attempted to issue orders. Darthez and Belle's other supervisors simply ignored her, taking orders only from Belle.

24

Winds of Change in Postwar America

In 1946 Belle made her first trip to Europe since the end of the war. She held a tempestuous reunion in London with Varvara Hasselbalch, then married to Guy Ingram. For some reason, Belle was spoiling for an argument, probably resentment at Varvara's last-minute refusal to leave Paris during the German occupation. It had also been one of the rare times that she had asked her father for a favor. Her feelings toward Varvara those first few minutes were much like those of a parent who experiences relief that a child has survived a perilous situation, followed by extreme anger because the child got herself into such a predicament in the first place.

"I had a check for her," Varvara recalled, "and Belle claimed it wasn't the correct sum. I was flabbergasted! I knew it was correct." Both women got angry, then pushing and shoving deteriorated into a wrestling match, with neither the victor. Finally, tempers cooled. Belle tore up the check and peace was restored.

They caught up on each other's lives and the whereabouts of old friends. Many were dead, swept from life by the Nazi madness. Belle was shocked and saddened at the condition of her beloved France and shattered London. If she had nursed any dreams that the old life might be restored, they died in the realities of postwar Europe.

When Varvara told her the fate of the magnificent thoroughbreds who had jumped against Souriant, Belle was grateful that she had persuaded Jean Darthez to move the entire stable to America. Most of the gallant horses had been impressed by the French army and used as dray horses or cavalry mounts. Petted, pampered, and bred for a different life, the poor animals did not long survive their duties in wartime France. However gallantly they struggled to obey, their delicate legs were not genetically strong enough for the heavy loads of ammunition and supplies some were forced to haul. They ended their lives with broken limbs and shattered lungs . . . if the solders were merciful, a bullet in the brain.

The Nuremberg trials were underway, and the world was just beginning to learn the extent of Nazi atrocities. Haunted by visions of postwar Europe, Belle returned home, doubly grateful for the peace and security of Hobcaw Barony. Belle was delighted the following year when her good friend General George C. Marshall was named secretary of state. When he proposed the Marshall Plan to finance the reconstruction of Europe's economy, Bernard Baruch testified in favor of it before a Senate Committee.

The postwar social changes taking place throughout the United States filtered down to Hobcaw Barony as well. The young black men returning to Hobcaw from military service had experienced a different world, acquired new visions, longed for broader horizons. Only a few were content to return to the barony and economic dependence upon the Baruchs.

Belle's view of the plantation blacks had altered since she had returned to Hobcaw as a permanent resident rather than an occasional visitor. Formerly nameless black faces had become individuals, each with a unique personality. Before she had known only those few who were employed as household help at Hobcaw House or in the stables.

She was brusque and demanding and often aloof, but those blacks that knew her well saw behind the mask to the kindness she tried to hide. They knew also that she had a roguish sense of humor and could sometimes be jollied out of her bad humor. They respected her shrewdness and knew better than to take advantage of her good nature too often. Like many wealthy people, Belle had a horror of being taken advantage of. This was particularly true of the Baruch children, who had been lectured on the subject often by their father. Belle was never known for her racial tolerance or liberal attitudes, but she dealt fairly with her employees by her own standards.

African Americans were still a long way from economic parity or even the beginnings of social change in the South, but inchoate longings began to stir in the minds of southern blacks. Slowly, the young blacks began to leave Hobcaw, first the young singles, later whole families, as they sought broader opportunities for themselves and better education for their children.

International Paper Company in Georgetown was offering tempting wages, and more and more young black men from Hobcaw were seeking employment there. In hopes of stemming the flow, Bernard Baruch decreed that no black family that left Hobcaw could return to the property to live. The decision to move would be irrevocable. Such a decree was heartbreaking for families who had lived on the barony for generations. They were leaving relatives behind, and their ancestors were buried on the plantation. Several members of the Kennedy family had been buried at Hobcaw the same year as the result of a tragic accident.

William Kennedy had taken several young people, including Roland Mc-Cants, his nephew Arthur Kennedy, a visiting schoolteacher named Alma, and his son Edwin to Georgetown on Baruch's boat, *Sea Dog.* The young people were going to a movie, but William Kennedy said he had to return to Hobcaw before the movie would end. The young people told him to go on, they would find a way back.

At the movie's end, they set out for Hobcaw in a small rowboat. A sudden storm blew up and capsized the boat, drowning all four. The next day, the grieving family and neighbors searched the water for the bodies. They found Roland, then Arthur, but did not find Alma or Edwin.

That night Nettie Kennedy had a dream about her brother Edwin. "Edwin," she told her mother, "was at the foot of the stairs calling to me."

"How come you're here?" Nettie said to Edwin. "You're supposed to be drowned. They're all out looking for you."

"They're out there having a good time," Edwin answered, "they're not looking for me." He went on to tell her to look for his body near a fallen tree around a bend in the river (near Fraser's Point). The high tide, he said, had trapped his body between the tree and the shore, but the water had not been high enough since to float his body back out into the river.

The searchers looked along the riverbank as Edwin had said in the dream and found the young man's body cradled in the branches of a fallen tree. Edwin and his cousins are buried in the Friendfield Cemetery.[1]

Baruch's decree slowed the exodus, but freedom and opportunity beckoned until the last family moved to Georgetown in the early 1950s, less than a decade after the war's end. In his own satisfaction with the status quo, it had not occurred to Baruch that his black workers wanted homes with electricity, running water, and indoor toilets. Since the magnanimous doubling of their one-room living quarters at the turn of the century, no effort had been made to upgrade the living conditions of the Hobcaw blacks. Some still earned a mere fifty cents an hour, plus their two-room-cabin living quarters. An era that had ended nearly one hundred years earlier in most of America lingered on at Hobcaw Barony.

Belle did not view the exodus of the black population with the same dismay as her father. While there were valued friends among them, she viewed the majority as so much additional responsibility. She was also concerned about certain activities among them. On May 16, 1949, she wrote to her father:

Dear Father,

I should like to bring a matter to your attention and trust that you will see fit to take some action, namely to give the negroes some instructions promptly.

About this time last year George [Shubrick] came to me and asked about having what they call a "prayer band" meeting at the church in Friendfield. Thinking it was a special church meeting with a few added starters from Arcadia I gave my o.k. to go ahead. To my horror I was told the next day by William that over *50 cars,* truck, buses, etc. and *several hundred* people had appeared from all over. You can well imagine that included people that have moved off the place, people we have fired and those high yellow dudes and bums with fancy ideas.

I hear rumors of another jamboree about to take place (June 5, I believe) and think William has not the courage to ask permission until about one hour before the time. Won't you please advise both George and William [Kennedy] that you approve of their local regular church meetings held on the place even with their Georgetown preachers coming over to address the Friendfield congregation (a pretty big word for about 20) but on no account will you allow any big get to gether [*sic*] admitting outsiders and strangers on the property.

There is too much lawlessness going on with house breaking, assault and battery and Taylor could not possibly keep track of that crowd going back and forth and tearing up the roads. If you notify them promptly they can arrange to meet at any one of the churches around G'town.

The last "prayer band" meeting was held at Arcadia [the plantation owned by the Vanderbilts] and resulted in five cases of assault & battery to put it politely. The man is still at large, blood hounds and the main high-way watched and patrol failed [*sic*]. Now negroes are not permitted to enter or leave Arcadia at will.[2]

Bernard Baruch immediately wrote to George Shubrick, advising him that no outsiders were to come onto the property. He said that the people who lived there were welcome to have all the meetings they wanted at the Friendfield Church, including guest preachers from the surrounding area. "Remember," he cautioned, "what I told you about not permitting anybody to come back onto the place who once leaves it."[3]

Living at Hobcaw year 'round, Belle felt that she knew the Hobcaw residents better than did her father. She knew the reliable workers and the laggards, the good folks and the not-so-good. She might grumble about them but was committed to their welfare. Even though she was overseeing the barony, Bernard Baruch still signed the paychecks of those employed directly by him, and Belle once interceded on behalf of an elderly woman:

> Would you mind checking your Hobcaw payroll cheque? Vickie Fraser (Bopig's wife) has come to see me twice saying that she was to work in your yard if there was no work for her in the laundry but when payday came around was told there was no money for her but all the others had been paid.
>
> I told her I had no authority to do anything but bring it to your attention as I know nothing about the arrangements you had made. I did tell her to continue going regularly to work in your yard and I would see that she got paid eventually as the small pension that Bo-pig gets from the government is not enough for both and I don't think you want to let the old people down completely.[4]

The exodus of the Hobcaw blacks coincided with the waning of Baruch's political power. He did not get along well with President Harry S. Truman. Truman, wary of Baruch's power and influence, maintained an uneasy cordiality with him but privately referred to him as a "meddler." In 1946 he appointed the seventy-five-year-old Baruch as the U.S. representative to the United Nations Atomic Energy Commission. Baruch performed other high-visibility tasks at the beginning of the Truman administration, mostly because Truman needed Baruch's public-relations value, but the relationship was tense. Nearing eighty and disinclined to earlier diplomatic niceties, Baruch testily criticized Truman's decisions publicly, something no president would tolerate for long. The final break came when Baruch refused to serve on the Democratic financial committee for Truman's reelection in 1948 and expressed the opinion that the Republican candidate, Thomas E. Dewey, had a good chance of defeating Truman.

For the first time since the election of Woodrow Wilson, Bernard Baruch was not invited to the White House for intimate luncheons and asked for counsel and advice. The aging Baruch felt keenly his banishment from presidential circles, but their mutual pride precluded a healing of the rift between the two men. Baruch still wielded diplomatic and financial power, but that special cachet of adviser to the current president of the United States was sorely missed.

The public and the media were still fascinated by anything Bernard Baruch had to say, and it was Baruch, in a speech written for him by Herbert Bayard Swope, who introduced the term "cold war" to the American people.

Hobcaw House was still opened for the hunting season in November, and Baruch maintained a full staff, some of whom still lived on the property or came in from nearby Georgetown or Pawleys Island. The rich and famous still came to shoot and recreate, but the great deer drives were long over, and with the stricter gaming laws, duck hunting was not the great joy it had been. Besides, at eighty-plus years, Bernard Baruch took less pleasure in getting up before dawn to wade through the mud and water to a chilly duck blind. For years he had rented acreage in Kingstree, South Carolina, to hunt quail. It was more open country than duck territory and much more comfortable for an octogenarian.

Baruch purchased one thousand acres near Kingstree as a preretirement gift for his longtime nurse/companion, Elizabeth Navarro. Later he built a house on the land and would stay there often, hunting quail, entertaining friends. Then they would make the forty-five-mile drive back to Hobcaw for the night or weekend. As the years passed, he stayed more and more at Little Hobcaw in Kingstree than at the barony.

Belle steadily assumed more responsibility for the vast acreage and in late 1947 hired Nolan "Red" Taylor as superintendent. In Taylor she found a man of diverse abilities who had both the skills and the desire to devote himself to the maintenance of Hobcaw Barony. Taylor dedicated twenty-eight years of his life to Hobcaw Barony and loved the land almost as much as Belle.

When he first arrived at Hobcaw House with his wife, Cynthia, and two children, Charlotte and Eric, the family lived in the house at the entrance to Hobcaw Barony. Later they moved to a small house near Bellefield Plantation. There were still many black workers at Strawberry and Friendfield Villages, and at Baruch's instruction, Taylor kept them all employed. As they gradually left the property, however, Taylor maintained the entire barony with the help of seven men, some of whom lived on the property with their families.

Taylor's father had been caretaker of a 53,000-acre estate near Cherry Point, North Carolina, and Taylor apprenticed at his father's side. He also had been trained in forestry and tree surgery, an asset in Hobcaw's diverse woods. Outside workers seldom had to visit Hobcaw Barony. Nolan Taylor and his crew could meet every demand, whether it was for carpentry, plumbing, electricity, painting, road repairs, or general maintenance.

Taylor also doubled as game warden and, with the help of Belle's air patrols, kept a close eye on poachers. To Belle's delight, the army had returned her airplanes, and after consultation with the Smithsonian Institution's Bureau of American Ethnology, she selected the names *Wamdi* and *Wamdida,* Lakota Sioux words meaning "eagle" and "eaglet," for her aircraft. During the Christmas holidays in 1947, Edith Wilson wrote in the Bellefield guest book: "May all the winds be fair for 'Wamdi' and 'Wamdida' and all the skies be bright for Belle; As the tender wish of one who loves her much, much more than she can tell."[5] Mrs. Wilson returned the following spring to officially christen the two airplanes.

Nolan Taylor shouldered a lot of the burden at Hobcaw for Belle, and his wife provided warm, loving friendship. Belle liked the young woman, and Cynthia looked on Belle as a second mother. The two women shared an earthy humor and sense of fun.

In July 1948 Belle was saddened to receive a wire from the secretary of the army advising her of the death of General John J. Pershing on July 15 and inviting her to his funeral at Arlington National Cemetery. She telegraphed her acceptance and sorrowfully attended the burial services for her old friend.

Belle thought of the time they had inaugurated the cemetery in France for the U.S. soldiers who had died in the First World War defending Europe. How many more had died in the Second World War? Already there were ominous rumblings around the world. The Russian blockade of Berlin had begun in June, and Jews and Arabs were fighting in Palestine. Continued peace seemed unlikely.

In the summer of 1949 Belle received an urgent message from Varvara seeking counsel and comfort. "My Ingram marriage was on the verge of breaking up," Varvara said. "Who would be my lifesaver? Belle, of course."

Belle wired that she was welcome at Bellefield, but before Varvara could make the trip, she began having medical problems and discovered that she was pregnant, threatening to abort. A long trip to America was out of the question. Guy Rurik Ingram was born several months later but, alas, his birth did not patch up his parents' marital problems. It would be 1954 before Varvara would again join the Baruchs in America.

Charles "Chita" Davila, 1930.
Courtesy of the Belle W.
Baruch Foundation

Belle on Souriant III, Italy, 1931. Courtesy of the Belle W. Baruch Foundation

Belle and Jean Darthez, France, ca. 1931. Courtesy of the Belle W. Baruch Foundation

Fathers and daughters: Belle and Bernard Baruch, Diana and Winston Churchill on the dock at Hobcaw Barony, ca. 1932. Courtesy of the Belle W. Baruch Foundation

Annie Griffen Baruch and Belle, crabbing at Clambank, ca. 1932. Courtesy of the Belle W. Baruch Foundation

Cartoon of Belle by Maurice Taquoy, 1933. Courtesy of the Belle W. Baruch Foundation

Baroness Louise Hasselbalch, Belle, Varvara Hasselbalch, and Barbara Donohoe, France, 1936. Courtesy of the Belle W. Baruch Foundation

Belle hunting at Hobcaw Barony, ca. 1937. Courtesy of the Belle W. Baruch Foundation

Renee, Bernard, and Belle Baruch at Belle-field, ca. 1936. Courtesy of the Belle W. Baruch Foundation

Bobbie Hamilton helping Belle corral an alligator at the Bellefield pond, ca. 1937. Courtesy of the Belle W. Baruch Foundation

Belle in Rapallo, Italy, 1937.
Courtesy of the Belle W. Baruch
Foundation

Barbara Donohoe at Bellefield stables, ca. 1938. Courtesy of the Belle W. Baruch
Foundation

*Varvara Hasselbalch at Clambank with a wheelbarrow filled with ducks, 1938.
Courtesy of the Belle W. Baruch Foundation*

*Jean Darthez near the Bellefield stables, 1939. Courtesy of the Belle W. Baruch
Foundation*

Lois Massey, Belle, and Alison "Dickie" Leyland, ca. 1940. Courtesy of the Belle W. Baruch Foundation

Ken Unger and Belle in the cockpit of her Beechcraft, ca. 1946. Courtesy of the Belle W. Baruch Foundation

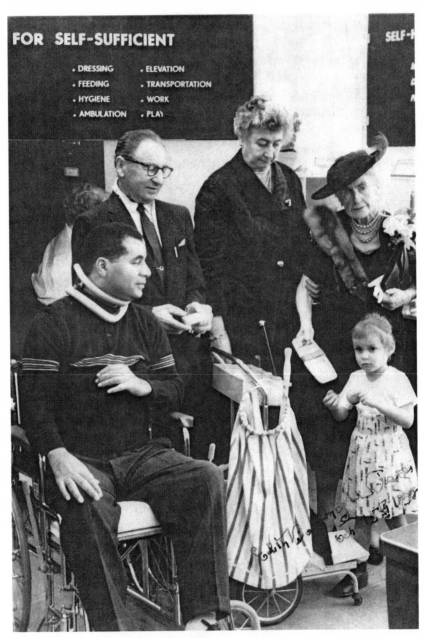

FOR SELF-SUFFICIENT

- DRESSING   - ELEVATION
- FEEDING   - TRANSPORTATION
- HYGIENE   - WORK
- AMBULATION   - PLAY

SELF-H

Roy Campanella, Dr. Howard Rusk, Belle, Edith Wilson, and an unknown child at the opening of a rehabilitation room at the Institute of Physical Medicine and Rehabilitation of New York University's Bellevue Medical Center. Belle donated the room and equipment to honor Mrs. Wilson's eighty-sixth birthday on October 15, 1958. Courtesy of the Belle W. Baruch Foundation

Christmas at Bellefield, 1962. Row 1 (kneeling): Mrs. Broder, Heflin daughter, Bernard Taylor, Ella Severin. Row 2 (kneeling): Heflin daughters, Frances Milam (wheelchair), Belle. Row 3 (standing): Mrs. Heflin, Dr. and Mrs. Charles Jones, Cynthia and Nolan Taylor. Back row: Eric Taylor and Ben Milam

Belle and Ella Severin with Deary-Deer, Christmas 1963. Courtesy of the Belle W. Baruch Foundation

Bernard and Belle Baruch, Bellefield, ca. 1963. Courtesy of the Belle W. Baruch Foundation

25

Philanthropy and Ecology

As the years passed and development increased in Horry and Georgetown counties, Belle was alarmed by the destruction of natural habitat and the diminishing wildlife. The wild turkeys were seldom seen anymore and the number of ducks dwindled each year. Awareness grew within her that the land and creatures she had taken for granted since childhood would not necessarily always be there.

Until she became active in the management of the property, it had not occurred to her that the land had to be replenished and nourished if it was to continue to give its bounty. Habitat had to be maintained for the birds and animals and varieties of vegetation planted to feed the deer, ducks, and other wildlife.

A major problem was the proliferation of feral hogs, domestic animals gone wild. The woods and rice fields were full of them. They would root up the young pine seedlings, raid the eggs of those birds that nested on the ground, and generally destroy the vegetation in parts of the woods. Taylor trapped them year 'round, often catching as many as ten to fifteen in a single trap. Belle hunted them almost daily, usually from late afternoon until sundown.

James Bessinger Jr., only a boy of eight or nine at the time, recalls seeing Belle out in her jeep hunting. "Nolan Taylor, Ms. Baruch, and a black fella named Chappie [Chappel Green] came over to ride on the beach [DeBordieu]. They had a four-wheel drive jeep with kind of a wooden back at the rear. The jeep had a headlight on each fender. If you sat on a pillow on the light, the light would hold you on the jeep. Chappie would drive and Taylor and Belle would each sit on a headlight, riding up and down the roads, shooting pigs."

"She always had a hat on," Bessinger recalled. "She reminded me of a man to be quite honest with you. I remember her as just an outspoken person. She didn't mind a minute tellin' you what she thought. The way I feel now that I've grown some, it was either her way or no way. The kids all knew who she was. She'd always come by the school and blow the horn, waving at the children."[1]

Few people in Georgetown knew her well. She would attend church, go to a movie, or dine in a restaurant, but she was content to live quietly on the plantation and seldom socialized. Debby Baruch Adams, a distant cousin of Belle and a friend of Aileen Donaldson, said, "In the twenty years I knew Belle, I never saw her in a dress but one time—at a ceremony in Camden honoring her father. She made a great impression on people, had quite an air of command about her. She was the kind of person that when she came into a room people would say, 'Who is that?' Our mutual friendship with Aileen was my only contact with Belle, but I found she had a great sense of humor and was very kind."

Belle always preferred pants and usually wore jodhpurs, riding boots, tweed hacking jacket, and a black beret. Occasionally a wide-brimmed hat that offered more protection from the weather replaced the French beret. When fishing she favored a man's green brimmed hat festooned with fishing lures. In the hot summers she wore beautifully tailored slacks with a shirt outside the waistband.

Pants were eminently more suited to riding, hunting, and exploring the woods. They offered protection from the ubiquitous ticks and mosquitoes, just as riding boots were practical in the saddle and thick, high-topped rubber hunting boots were ideal for wading through mud, snake-infested swamps, and vegetation.

Belle was sophisticated and "dressed to the nines" in New York and Europe but saw no reason to bother with formality at home at Bellefield. Designer dresses and furs would be ridiculous in the Hobcaw woods. It was well known among the Hobcaw residents that Bernard Baruch hated pants on women except when riding or hunting and had been known to append a postscript to his invitations for Belle to dine that read "Please wear a skirt."

Belle would snort and grumble to Nolan Taylor: "Pa expects me to come and host those people and I haven't got a damn thing in common with them. I'd rather go shoot coons and hogs with you." Then she would peer over her glasses at Cynthia and say: "Well, I've got to go get my mothballs out and I must remember not to pick my nose or scratch my butt."

"She did love her dad, though," said Cynthia Taylor, "and would do anything to please him. I loved her because she was just 'plain Jane,' she never put on airs."

Nolan Taylor laughed in agreement. "One time her friend Aileen Donaldson wanted a load of manure for her garden. Miss Belle had the men load the truck, then drove it over there herself."

"Some people in Georgetown didn't like Miss Belle,' said Cynthia, "because she didn't go over and associate with them. She was happy just like she was. She started at first letting them come over [hunting], but next thing you know they'd come and bring others and she didn't know who was in there [Hobcaw]. If anybody'd been hurt over there, she'd have been sued to the hilt."

James Bessinger Sr. remembers Belle best as a hunting companion.

I had a pack of foxhounds and I'd hunt sometimes at night when the moon was shining and then on dark nights, I would hunt early every morning. If Belle heard the dogs running she would get Jean [Darthez] to saddle up the horses and here they come. I could hear them coming up the road you know and, of course, I had my horse that I rode and one of the darkies to drive the pickup.

The Frenchman would always be way behind her 'cause she had this tremendous, large horse. She was a big lady, and we'd sit down and listen to the hounds, talk foxhuntin', fishin', you know. . . .

When we went over on the beach (DeBordieu) we'd go by Belle's camp and if they were there, they'd wave us down, you know, ask us to have a sandwich. Sometimes we'd hunt wild hogs. She was a very likeable person . . . had a mind of her own.

Old Captain Jim [Powell], he was the law over there [Hobcaw]. He had this old truck and he would ride with that hand hanging out that truck and the whole side of that truck was brown from tobacco juice where he spit it out. He was a good old man, though. Folks around here had a lot of respect for him.

He'd come huntin' sometimes with Miss Belle. Sometimes she'd want to do something over on the property he didn't approve of and he'd call her down if he thought she was doing something wrong. "Now, Belle," he'd drawl, "you cain't do that now." Usually she listened to him. She sure cared a lot about him.

I thought the world of her and I think she'd do just about anything for you. I don't know of anybody, except outlaws [poachers], that didn't like her. And that's because she would take her plane and buzz them, take pictures of them too. Folks just didn't know her.[2]

Quietly and without fanfare, Belle donated land, money, and assistance to the Georgetown community. "She gave the land for the hospital," Cynthia Taylor said.

In Belle's files is a voluminous record of an effort by her and Renee Baruch Samstag to build a hospital for Georgetown in memory of their mother. The two sisters would provide the money for the initial building and equipment, but the city of Georgetown must provide the annual operating capital. At that time, the citizens appeared to be unable to guarantee the operation of the hospital, so the project died.

Belle continued to help Philip Assey and other physicians, donating the use of her plane and pilot to transport patients to distant hospitals, paying for the care of a child with a brain tumor, absorbing the medical costs of a child born without arms or legs, supporting another who had leukemia. Her philanthropies were endless and usually anonymous.

Taylor and Belle discussed the practicality of cultivating oysters. There were many fine beds on barony land, and in 1951 Belle leased an additional seventy acres at seventy dollars per year from the South Carolina Board of Fisheries. She wrote to her father that the state inspector had come to okay the work of replanting Hobcaw's quota of seven thousand bushels of shell. Belle, who loved oysters, was unhappy to learn that she had to share them, writing indignantly to her father:

> It seems that although I hold the lease on the oyster rights of those 70 acres any individual can gather two bushels, twice a week for his own consumption from that ground according to the law. To me it does not make sense if I have to keep up the beds.
>
> The inspector . . . was very impressed with the quality and amount of oysters we had. He comes from Conway and I only hope that he does not broadcast the good tidings.[3]

Life at Hobcaw was relatively quiet. Belle supervised both Bellefield and Hobcaw House, making sure that the latter was kept in shining order for her father's visits. Later that year she and Dickie traveled to Europe, where Belle renewed her acquaintance with Ella Severin. Impulsively, she invited Ella to visit Bellefield.

When the Germans had occupied Paris, Ella was in Vichy. As the German army moved closer, she went to Bordeaux and from there headed for the French Pyrenees. The roads were clogged with refugees, horse carts with people lying in the straw, bicycles and cars moving slowly through the throngs. Eventually she arrived at Malineau, not far from Belle's beloved Pau in what was then free France. She stayed there throughout the war.

At war's end she returned to Paris and went to work for the French branch of the RKO film studios, working as an interpreter and escort for visiting film stars and dignitaries from the American branch of RKO. Ella enjoyed her job, accompanying stars like Jane Russell around Paris. She had no thought of staying in America when she accepted Belle's invitation to visit.

When she arrived in the States, Belle asked where her mother was living. When Ella told her she was in Mexico, Belle suggested they fly down for a visit. Flying in Belle's twin-engine Beechcraft, they flew first to Houston and then to Mexico.

Kenneth Unger was Belle's pilot at the time and lived with his family on the plantation. "He was so nice," said Ella. "Belle always said she didn't know whether he was a better flyer or bartender. Nobody made a drink to more perfection than Ken Unger." When they returned from the trip to Mexico, Belle asked Ella to stay on. She had grown close to Ella and enjoyed her spirit, humor, and intelligence. Ella was competent, well organized, and a superb cook.

Ella hesitated, saying that she had to return to Paris to resign. Belle insisted that she cable instead, and Ella's bosses at RKO responded with a long cablegram wishing her success in America. A friend shipped her belongings and Ella settled into Bellefield.

Dickie Leyland was furious and bitterly resented Ella's presence. She was drinking heavily, and Belle was deeply concerned and discouraged. Dickie would have driven Ella away as she had so many others, but Ella was made of sterner stuff. One morning Dickie came to Ella's room before breakfast, a glass of whiskey in hand. When Ella declined the drink, Dickie sneered. "What's the matter? Are you a teetotaler?"

"No," Ella replied with quiet dignity. "But I don't start drinking in the morning."

The scales of her infatuation with Dickie had fallen from Belle's eyes long before, but she still loved the memory of Dickie as she had first known her and felt a deep loyalty and commitment to her. She was saddened and weary and suffered the guilt that the loved ones of chronic drinkers endure, wondering if she were the cause, if she had contributed to it, if she could have done something to prevent it. In the beginning the shared drinks and parties had been gay, carefree, and fun. Now the drinking dominated their lives. Belle was well aware that she often drank more than she should.

Ella brought some peace and order to the household, at least insofar as Dickie would allow. Eventually the atmosphere became strained and unpleasant. When Ella would enter a room, Dickie often would get up and stomp away. Ella tried to avoid unpleasantness by leaving herself if Dickie joined them and appeared belligerent. It was uncomfortable for everyone.

Belle was torn. She felt intense loyalty to Dickie but enjoyed and needed Ella's soothing presence, her humor and good sense. For some time Dickie had been having a clandestine affair with the underage daughter of one of Belle's employees. Dickie could be charming when she wished, and on the isolated plantation where one had limited contact with the outside world, the naive young woman found Dickie exciting and sophisticated. She was thrilled when the Englishwoman began to pay attention to her. In a final act of betrayal and anger, Dickie seduced the girl into running away with her.

Belle was deeply hurt and bitterly humiliated. For Dickie to have seduced a young girl was contrary to every moral precept Belle held dear, and to seduce the child of one of her respected employees was a cruel insult to both the parents and to Belle.

Dickie contacted Belle several months later, but for Belle the hurt had been too great. Out of pity she arranged a job for her with a friend in New York, but the relationship ended. She always felt guilt and a great sense of responsibility toward Dickie and on her death left her a lifetime income from a $250,000 trust. Once the initial pain and humiliation subsided, Belle felt great relief, albeit tinged with guilt. Another era had ended at Hobcaw.

26

*From Constable
to Baroness*

Belle and Ella were to share many happy years at Hobcaw. They did not always agree but deferred to each other. Ella, for instance, was an animal-rights activist and deplored hunting in any form. Belle, of course, was an avid hunter, though she never shot deer or turkey once she took over the plantation and rarely shot ducks in order to protect their diminishing numbers.

Ella did not enjoy riding but for Belle's sake made an attempt. It caused her great pain in her hip, however, and after dismounting one afternoon she said to Belle: "I love you very much but I'm not going to get on that horse anymore."

It wasn't long after that Belle came home from riding and said, "Well, I really think it's over for me." The arthritic pain in her back and knee was so severe that it was almost crippling.

"Thank God she had her airplane," said Ella. "She was so happy when she was in the cockpit, a big smile on her face."

Ella would rather fish than fly. Belle would take the plane up for its daily spin, often flying low over the lake where Ella fished. "You should have come flying," Belle would say, "you didn't catch anything anyway."

"True," Ella would answer, "but I enjoyed just standing there fishing."

Belle would coax Prince Jenkins and Francena McCants to come for a ride, but both refused. Prince would shake his head and say, "No, Ma'am." Laughing, Belle would say, "Stay, you big sissy," and climb aboard.

Francena was even more determined not to go than Prince. When Belle pointed out that a plane was safer than a car, Francena said, "Yeah, but I'm not goin' up there. They may be able to find me in a car wreck, but if you come down [in a plane wreck], they can't find you."

Besides the simple joy of flying, Belle used the plane to search for poachers. They were a constant worry, and she consulted attorneys on trespass laws and precedents. Except by air, it was impossible to effectively patrol the woods, marshes, and inlets of the barony.

Research showed that as far back as 1897, the courts had found that hunters could use only navigable streams (those that had two termini). If a stream ended in a marsh or land, then the stream was unnavigable and the public had no right to be in it except with the owner's permission. Even if a stream was navigable, a hunter could use it and the immediate banks but could not go onto private land through which it passed or into the marshes at which it ended.

Belle and Taylor enforced those rulings to their limit. Hunters soon found that if they hunted on Hobcaw property, Belle Baruch was ruthless in pursuit and prosecution. She wanted no poachers in her beloved Hobcaw. If she spotted violators from the air, she would buzz them whether they were on foot or in a boat, often creating turbulence that rocked their boats precariously. She would snap photographs as she dove, and it wasn't uncommon to find Belle and the sheriff waiting when disgruntled hunters pulled up to the dock in Georgetown.

In 1953 Belle was appointed South Carolina's only woman constable, without pay but with the right to carry a gun and make arrests. She later became an investigator for SLED (State Law Enforcement Division) under the same circumstances because of statewide concern for both poaching and smuggling.

Belle's relentless war against poachers did not earn her many friends among the avid hunters in Georgetown County, but it earned her respect. Those who had the temerity to hunt on Hobcaw Barony much preferred to encounter Taylor than Belle. Taylor would give at least one warning; with Belle there was no warning, only prosecution. Nor were the guilty inclined to argue. One look at Belle's implacable brown eyes, towering height, and unwavering shotgun barrels would convince even the most courageous man that it would be wise to admit defeat.

Once when she was up for her afternoon flight, she flew low over Ranger Island and saw a herd of goats on the property. Landing her plane, she immediately contacted Taylor to find out how the goats got onto her land. They discovered that an enterprising farmer from Georgetown had decided the island would make ideal free grazing. The goats were removed immediately.

Bernard Baruch was pleased with his daughter's handling of the property. They drew closer, sharing many interests. Baruch had taken a hand in the development of Saratoga Springs and liked to go both for the waters and the horse racing. Belle sometimes joined him there, or they would go to Belmont or the

Carolina Cup in his native Camden. Both were thrilled when Citation became the first horse to win one million dollars.

Bernard Baruch called a press conference in June 1951 to announce that he would soon disassociate himself completely from Wall Street. "I don't want anyone to think I'm getting rusty and am going to retire. I'm not, positively. I'm going to be as active as I've always been. But it will be a different kind of activity." He went on to say that, among other things, he would be writing his memoirs.[1]

Baruch was vigorous for a man of eighty-one years and still deeply interested and involved in world politics. His good friend Sir Winston Churchill was re-elected Britain's prime minister that year, and the two old friends corresponded faithfully.

Baruch was still very much his own man and publicly supported Dwight D. Eisenhower on the Republican ticket in 1952, only the third time in his life that he had voted Republican. He had enjoyed a close relationship with Eisenhower for many years, having met him when Ike was still a major in the army. Eisenhower had often appealed to Baruch for advice over the years and listened carefully to the financier's counseling on economics.

Baruch had no intention of surrendering the reins of power entirely, particularly now that he once again had access to the White House and one of his closest allies was prime minister of Great Britain. His old paramour Clare Boothe Luce was appointed ambassador to Italy in 1953, so once again Bernard Baruch had close friends in positions of great influence.

Still, the years had taken their toll and he cut back his working hours, spending more time in South Carolina writing his memoirs. He found the summers too hot, however, and retreated to New York or traveled abroad. Belle and Ella spent the early summer of 1953 on the plantation. On June 26 Belle wrote to her father:

Dear Chick,

I have insisted that Jean and his family take a vacation so a short motor trip has been planned, so I am guardian of the menagerie and jack of all trades. Luckily the grass is good in the yard so at dawn can turn Souriant and the others out to graze although I have over 15 acres in Sweet Sudan. The hounds, chickens and pheasants are a less familiar occupation but I enjoy puttering about. The pool and Debidue [DeBordieu Beach] have been joys. Not a nibble at Clambank.

Never have I seen so many quail, even to being in the camellia bushes around the pool.[2]

Belle and Ella went to New York later that summer, and on August 19 Belle was asked to unveil a bust of her father at the dedication ceremonies for a civic housing project on New York City's Lower East Side named in honor of her paternal grandfather, Dr. Simon Baruch. With her on the platform were President Dwight D. Eisenhower; Francis Cardinal Spellman, archbishop of New York; Herbert Bayard Swope; and her father, who was celebrating his eighty-third birthday.

Belatedly, Belle and Ella sailed to Europe, and in October Belle wrote to her father from her favorite hotel, the Lancaster:

> . . . have seen some of the big clothes collections. One would have to be a bit daft to wear them and a bit cracked to pay the prices, but it is fun to look.
>
> The big jewelers still have gorgeous shop window displays and I often think of you making them extraordinary offers as I peer in at their baubles.[3]

By November Belle was back at Hobcaw Barony, happily walking the woods, preparing for Thanksgiving and Christmas celebrations.

In the early summer of 1954 Belle and Ella went to New York to prepare for a trip to Europe. Varvara Hasselbalch flew in to visit the Baruchs. She was in love with a man with no money, which horrified Belle. She was also being pursued by a Cuban sugar king named Julio Lobo who was at least twenty years older than Varvara.

Bernard Baruch expressed his disapproval. "If you want to marry for money," he said, "I have a whole list of more suitable bachelors and friends than that Cuban!" Beautiful Varvara laughingly declined the list of eligible suitors and teased her hosts into better humor.

Belle and Ella left for Europe and were there when Hurricane Hazel blasted the South Carolina coast in October. The buildings on Hobcaw stood fast, but the forests were decimated. Her father cabled her at the Lancaster Hotel about the timber damage, telling her that he was selling the fallen trees on his remaining acres before they became valueless and recommended that she do the same.

Early in 1955 Belle signed her first timber contract and from that experience became interested in forest management. She and Taylor would select the areas to be cut and began a systematic logging program known as the seed tree or shelterwood method, designed to remove old-growth timber and regenerate the forest.

Taylor laughed about the time Belle had decided maybe she wouldn't log one year, then lost considerable money in the stock market. She had "taken a flyer" without consulting her father and was anxious to cover the loss before he found out. "We better sell that timber, Taylor," she said, "before Pa finds out what I did."

Once Belle became involved in a project, she wanted to know everything about it. While she relied on Taylor and respected his judgment, if she was going to log, her perfectionism demanded that she do it wisely and well. It was unthinkable that she do anything that might jeopardize the future of her beloved land. She insisted that Taylor personally mark each piece of timber that was to be cut. She usually included a clause in the logging contracts that allowed her to stop the cutting or move the logging site at her or Taylor's discretion. She preferred that they log in the summer so as not to disturb the game in the winter. Belle personally decided which roads on the property were to be used by the logging company.

Belle was autocratic when it came to Hobcaw. When she gave an order, it was to be obeyed. Once she encountered a logging truck on a road other than those designated for its use. When she demanded of Taylor who authorized the use of that particular road, Taylor replied that since it was raining, he had decided on his own that that was the better road to use. Furious, Belle said, "You don't make decisions like that. . . . I make decisions as to what road the logging trucks will use. Is that clear?"

Belle and Taylor clashed occasionally. As usual, Belle had not hired a "yes" man. Belle would be gone for several months at a time, and Taylor had full responsibility for maintaining Hobcaw. They would sometimes quarrel over decisions Taylor had made in her absence, but Taylor stoutly defended his choices, asserting that if he had the responsibility he must also have the authority to act in her absence. One bitter quarrel flared over the way in which Taylor was building a new causeway. When she complained to her father, however, he said, "Daughter, that [Taylor's method] is the only way to build a causeway."

Another time, following a major power outage, Taylor had gone to considerable effort to bring in two experienced power experts, beginning at daylight. Lightning had struck a major power source, and the fault lay underground. Taylor and the men labored to repair the break, and when the strenuous job was finished, Taylor brought the bill (eighty dollars including parts and labor) and Belle wrote out a check.

Dickie Leyland, who had long been trying to undermine Taylor, saw an opportunity and implied to Belle that Taylor had padded the bill. She knew Belle had what amounted to a phobia about being cheated. They were on their way out of town, so Belle penned a hasty note to Taylor implying that he had taken advantage of her. Furious, Taylor quit and left the plantation.

Belle hired a replacement but was disgruntled and dissatisfied. The new man was competent, but he lacked that special feeling for Hobcaw that Taylor shared with Belle. Taylor loved the land and, in his way, could be as possessive about it as Belle. She missed Taylor and Cynthia and the children. She even missed their arguments. Hearing he was in the vicinity, Belle sought him out, apologized, and asked him to come back. They made peace, at least for the moment, and Taylor returned.

Until the Taylors moved to Hobcaw, Belle had little contact with children. Taylor used to joke that Belle liked children "a long way off." The Darthez children were extremely shy of Belle, but not so the Taylor children. The older two, Eric and Charlotte, had been raised with old-fashioned, southern manners that Belle appreciated. They were polite and respectful but full of spirit.

When Cynthia had a baby boy in 1954, Bernard Baruch had insisted that the Taylors name the boy Bernard Baruch Taylor after him. Belle called Cynthia aside and said, "You name that baby Bernard Wilcox so he's named after me too. Let Pa think his middle name is Baruch but you and I will know better." And so little Bernie was named Bernard Wilcox Taylor and was a delight to Belle, whose experience with infants had been limited to newborn colts.

When he was first learning to talk, Bernie would toddle up to Belle, wrap his arms around her shiny boots, and laugh up at the tall woman, saying, "Mister Belle!" Belle would laugh, lean down from her great height and say, "You're the only one who could get away with calling me *Mister* Belle."

When the child developed lobar pneumonia, Belle and Ella kept vigil with Cynthia at the Georgetown hospital. So high was the boy's fever that he had been packed in ice, and the prognosis was guarded. As they worried and prayed for the child, a nurse entered the room, looking with disapproval at the non-family members. Apparently Belle thought she and Ella would be asked to leave.

"She unwound her big frame," Cynthia Taylor recalled, "towering over that nurse. She said, 'I hope you haven't come in here to ask me to leave because if you did, I think you'd better take a look at me and maybe you'll change your mind. I have no intentions of leaving that boy and I don't want anybody else bothering him.'

"That nurse looked up at Miss Belle's size, smiled, and said she was welcome to stay."[4]

As Bernie grew older, Belle liked to come for the boy and stand him on the front seat of the truck between her and Ella or, sometimes, just by herself. She loved to tell about the time the curly-haired tyke had scolded her for wasting gas. As sometimes happened at Hobcaw, Belle and Bernie came upon a tree across the middle of the road. Belle climbed down from the truck, leaving the engine running, and reached into the back of the truck for the axe.

"She could swing an axe as good as any man," Nolan Taylor recalled.

As she strode past the window toward the downed tree, Bernie called out, "You're not s'posed to leave the motor running. It wastes gas."

"Who says so?" demanded Belle.

"My daddy," Bernie answered.

"Huh!" Belle grunted and walked on to the fallen tree. Bernie watched for a moment, then leaned over and switched off the motor, much to Belle's amusement. "Just like his old man," she would say.

The Taylors had the first television set on Hobcaw, and Belle and Ella would walk down from time to time to watch. Belle so loved all the westerns, such as *Gunsmoke, The Rifleman, Bonanza, High Chaparral, Have Gun, Will Travel,* and so forth, that she decided to buy a TV herself.

These were among the happiest and most contented times of Belle's mature years. Ella loved the plantation and was devoted to Belle. Cynthia Taylor recalled the happy times together. The "in" place to eat at that time was the Clipper Ship in nearby Garden City, about twenty-two miles north of Hobcaw. The counties of Georgetown and Horry were "dry," and if you wanted a drink before dinner, you had to "brown-bag." Customers would bring their own bottle in a small brown paper bag and order "setups," pouring their liquor into the mix from bottles concealed in the brown bag.

"Miss Belle's 'brown bag' was a fitted, round case," said Cynthia Taylor, "and she'd usually carry some scotch, bourbon, and vodka. One night we were all going to the Clipper Ship and got as far as the gate when she said, 'Oh my gosh, we've left the booze at home.'

"So we turned around and went flying back to the house. She made the mistake of letting Nolan go in for it [Nolan was a teetotaler]. 'Lord, I shouldn't have done that,' Belle said, 'he's liable to empty the things and pour water into them.'"

There was a lot of "girl-talk" and fun and laughter. Belle would tell Taylor, "Now you get out of here, we've got business to tend to." Then the women would sit around the kitchen table telling risqué stories and jokes. One of Cynthia's fondest memories of Belle is seeing her slap the table with her hand, laughing until tears filled her eyes.

At Christmas, the Taylors would always go up to the big house for a while, and each year Belle would send Nolan ahead with the children to have a private moment with Cynthia. "Well, Miss Belle," Cynthia would say shyly, "I guess it's about that time." She would stand on tiptoe to hug the big woman she looked on as a second mother and say, "I love you." Belle would turn away to hide her tears and say gruffly, "Well go on now, and get the hell outta here. . . . Merry Christmas."

Sometimes Elizabeth Navarro would come and join in the fun. Elizabeth's presence was due to Ella's gentle influence. All the Baruch children had been suspicious of the new woman in their father's life. They resented her closeness to him and the way she sometimes monitored their access to him. Belle especially resented her presence at Hobcaw House when her father came there to hunt and host his many guests. Navarro was always with him, supervising his diet, entertaining his guests, hunting and riding with him.

Knowing she was unreasonable did not stop Belle from feeling that Navarro was usurping her mother's rightful place. Belle made little effort to hide her dislike of her father's nurse/companion. When her father moved permanently to Little Hobcaw near Kingstree, he would sometimes come to Hobcaw for lunch or a visit, and Navarro would wait patiently outside in the car, aware that Belle would not welcome her to Bellefield.

Finally, Ella took Belle to task. "She is your father's hostess, Belle," she said, "and she takes excellent care of your father. Would you like to have the daily responsibility for his care?"

Belle, knowing that Ella spoke the truth, and knowing how demanding her father could be, conceded that perhaps Ella was right. As her father aged, he slept intermittently, and the patient Navarro would answer his knock at her door, getting up two or sometimes three times a night to play canasta or read to him. She gave him his medications, saw that he rested properly, ate only what was good for him, and ensured that guests did not overtire him by staying too long.

Frowning, Belle stalked out to the car and invited Navarro to join them inside. "No sense in your sitting out here in this car," she said gruffly.

Though they had a somewhat guarded relationship in the beginning, Belle and Elizabeth eventually became friends. Belle took great pleasure in teasing her about the outcome of Cynthia's efforts to dye Elizabeth's hair a particular shade of gray. "We had this big Weimaraner named Old Smokey who was a beautiful shade of velvety gray," recalled Cynthia.

Elizabeth was at the house getting ready for a big party that night. She looked at Smokey and said, "That's just the color I want my hair."

Well, I liked to mess around with hair and said I'd do it for her. I drove into Georgetown and got all the stuff from this friend of mine who was a hairdresser, and she told me what to do. Well, something went wrong and the color was just awful. Miss Belle was standing there laughing and said, "It looks awful green to me, Navarro."

I rushed back to Georgetown and told my friend what happened and we talked about how to fix it. I went back and worked on it some more and Miss Belle would look in every once in a while and tell Elizabeth that it looked worse than ever to her . . . then laugh and go away.

Well, we finally got it finished and it was the most beautiful color! Elizabeth loved it, but I never could duplicate that color again.[5]

Belle also laughed uproariously when Elizabeth came back from hunting marsh hens cussing, soaking wet from a tumble from the boat. "Prince [Jenkins]," said Nolan Taylor "had turned the boat over and dumped her overboard. Fortunately, they were up in the grass where the tide wasn't so high. If it had happened in the big creek, they could have drowned."

Prince was defensive and said to Taylor: "Captain, that wasn't my fault. She got too close beside the boat and I couldn't straighten it up fast enough." Taylor grinned a little and soon both men were laughing. Once she dried off, Elizabeth laughed too. Belle appreciated a good sport, and Elizabeth went up a notch in Belle's estimation.

Elizabeth was a raconteur with an endless fund of stories and jokes. Many of them she heard from the newspapermen who surrounded Baruch, and she had a retentive memory. General George C. Marshall, who visited Baruch often, loved a good story and would pull Elizabeth off into a corner and exchange jokes. Baruch would see them laughing and later ask Elizabeth what they were talking about. "You always bring out the best in General Marshall," he would say.

Elizabeth, knowing how straitlaced Baruch could be, would smile and remind him that the general was a great gardener and they were discussing putting manure on the asparagus. Marshall would often call Elizabeth from Washington to ask if she had heard any good jokes lately.

To Belle's amusement, the mischievous Elizabeth once asked Churchill if she could tell him a story she had heard about him. Churchill drew on his cigar, nodded, and said, "Go right ahead."

"Well," said Elizabeth,

it seems that when Mr. Churchill became prime minister, he needed to enlarge his staff and was interviewing a gardener. "I think you'll be all right," he told the man. "By the way, are you married?"

"Oh, yes, sir," the man replied, and when Churchill asked if he had children, he answered, "Yes, sir, thirteen."

Astounded, Churchill said, "That's a bloody lot!"

"But, Sir Winston," the man said, "I love my wife!"

"I love my cigars," Churchill said, "but I take them out of my mouth once in a while!"

Elizabeth and Belle went off into gales of laugher. Churchill blushed, took his cigar out of his mouth, and said, "Elizabeth, I didn't say anything of the kind."[6] On his next trip to visit Baruch, Churchill honored Elizabeth with the gift of one of his paintings that hung in her home until her death.

Friends and family came often to Hobcaw. Renee and Bob Samstag came once or twice a year, pleased to see how much happier affairs were at Bellefield. "Thank God for Ella Severin," Renee Samstag often said.

Renee loved duck, and the one time each year Belle hunted them was when Renee was due for a visit. Sometimes Renee liked to go alone. On one occasion she heard Taylor talking about the plentitude of ducks and that he would be going out at the crack of dawn patrolling for poachers.

"Well," Renee said, "if you see any ducks close in, tie them down and come get me."

Taylor agreed and when he went out at dawn the next morning, he spotted dozens on the water and turned back to the house to call Renee. She was still in bed but told him to wait and was down in five minutes, gun in hand. As plainspoken as Belle, Renee said to Taylor, "Now if you're fooling me, I'm going to shoot you!"

"Well, they *were* there," said Taylor.

Stopping the truck far enough from the water so as not to frighten the ducks, Taylor led Renee to the boat and pushed it into the water, turning it so she would be facing the ducks. Suddenly the ducks took alarm and soared into the air, their wings beating frantically. Renee shot twice, hitting seven ducks.

"Boy, she was thrilled to death," Taylor said. "We picked up the ducks and she said, 'Now you can call me any morning you want if I can do that same thing again.'"

Ella loved flowers and added to those at Bellefield, planting some prize camellias. Belle became interested, and they began to enter Bellefield camellias in flower shows throughout the area, rising at daybreak to supervise as Taylor helped pack the delicate blooms in damp moss to preserve their freshness for the competitions. Together, Ella and Belle won numerous silver bowls and prizes.

At one point they decided it would be nice to have some peacocks strolling the grounds of Bellefield and bought a pair. Ella especially enjoyed them, and they would soon come when she called them to eat.

Belle also bought turkeys, hoping they would breed in the wild and expand the wild turkey population at Hobcaw. Ella, however, was inclined to make pets of them and soon they, too, came running when Ella would call the peacocks. Before long they had taken over the grounds from the peacocks, claiming it as their territory. Bernard Baruch was fascinated and was as eager as a child to help in the feeding when Ella would call them. The peacocks wandered around the periphery of Bellefield's grounds, and the male was especially raucous in his morning calls.

"Can't you do something about that damn bird?" Belle would ask Taylor, "he wakes me up every morning."

"Well," Taylor said judiciously, "I could shoot him."

"Hell," Belle growled, "I could do that myself." She tolerated the morning disturbance, however, until the birds aged and fell prey to predators.

And so the peaceful years passed, with Belle falling more in love with Hobcaw each passing year. In December 1956 Bernard Baruch signed over the last parcel of Hobcaw Barony to his daughter Belle. The following August, Belle wrote to Mrs. Wilson: "Father has now transferred to me all of his remaining holdings of Hobcaw including the house and furnishings. So I am now really a Baroness."[7]

27

Paul Dollfus and Frances Milam

Next to Hobcaw and her beloved horses, Belle's greatest pleasure was doing for others, giving not only money but her time and attention. Her philanthropies were extensive and included organized charities such as the Seeing Eye of Morristown, New Jersey; the Eye Bank for Sight Restoration of New York; the Visiting Nurse program of New York; and the Catholic Guild for the Blind of Newton, Massachusetts. All but one were legatees in her will.

Belle did not just donate money. She personally visited and investigated the work of the organizations to which she contributed and often became friendly with their staffs. Father Thomas J. Carroll, director of the Catholic Guild for the Blind, became a close friend and visited Bellefield often. Father Carroll had written what was then the definitive book on blindness, including the psychological and emotional trauma involved. Belle had enormous respect and affection for him, and the two had many long discussions on theology and philosophy.

Another good friend was Dr. Howard Rusk, director and founder of the Institute of Physical Medicine and Rehabilitation of New York University Bellevue Medical Center. Bernard Baruch was a cofounder, and the Baruchs were active supporters of the institute, donating funds for buildings and equipment.

For Edith Bolling Wilson's eighty-sixth birthday, Belle donated a rehabilitation room at the institute in Mrs. Wilson's name. The new room was equipped with self-help devices designed to give the disabled more independence and mobility in their daily living. Former Dodger catcher Roy Campanella, who was paralyzed in an automobile accident, joined the Baruchs, Jean and Robert Darthez, and Mrs. Wilson for the dedication.

Belle was especially fond of Dr. Rusk, who visited Bellefield several times. Rusk liked French wines, and Belle sent him a case every year for Christmas, a practice Ella Severin continued after Belle's death. Rusk would call Belle from time to time, confident of receiving help as he needed it. She always saw Rusk when in New York each year, and he would often introduce her to some of his more interesting patients.

Once Rusk called Belle and said he wanted to introduce her to a young Frenchman named Paul Dollfus. Rendered a paraplegic by polio in 1953, Paul had been sent by his father to Dr. Rusk to see if anything further could be done for him. Rusk was impressed with the young man's courage and attitude. Dollfus had been an accomplished athlete and flyer and was a fourth-year medical student. Although confined to a wheelchair, he was determined to complete his studies. Dr. Rusk offered him an internship at Bellevue, and Dollfus accepted.

"I was very grateful," Dollfus said, "because it allowed me to know a little bit more about what was, in fact, going to be my medical future. One evening, he [Dr. Rusk] told me that he would like to introduce me to a very nice person who likes France and speaks French."

Dollfus still remembers what a wonderful first evening he spent with Belle and Elsa (many of Ella Severin's European friends called her "Elsa," as did Belle on occasion). "We became very good friends," Dollfus recalled, "and I can still remember a telephone call asking me if I wanted to come to Bellefield in South Carolina for Christmas.

"Naturally, I accepted with great enthusiasm, and I still remember the day when we flew from an airport outside of New York to Bellefield. It was a twin-propelled aircraft, if I remember, a Beechcraft, which was piloted by one of the most famous pilots who had been a pioneer during the first days of the airmail in the United States [Kenneth Unger]. . . . I can remember how struck I was by the smallness of the airfield amongst the forest of Bellefield, but we managed to land quite safely thanks to this excellent pilot."

At that time Belle had one black servant and a French couple who were in charge of housekeeping. Dollfus remembers the pond near the house and, being a fisherman, asked Belle if he could try his hand. Belle teased him, saying, "If you can, but instead of a fish, you might get an alligator, and then you will be in real trouble. You won't even have time to ask for help."

"Yes," Dollfus replied, "perhaps, but the alligator will have to eat other than me, also my wheelchair, and after such a meal, it will have indigestion!"

Dollfus remembers Belle's kindness, her intelligence, her great generosity, and her air of command. Once when Belle had snapped out instructions in her usual brusque style, he teasingly called her "Mon Colonel" (my colonel), a sobriquet Belle accepted good-naturedly, and Belle in turn called him "Mon Lieutenant."

"If memory serves me," Dollfus said, "Elsa was declared 'Officer in Charge of Foreign Affairs and Lieutenants,' all in one."

Bernard Baruch was in residence at Hobcaw House and came often to Bellefield. "What an extraordinary man!" said Dollfus. "He was very kind to me and also was an excellent bridge player."

Baruch invited everyone for Christmas lunch, and when they arrived, he asked Paul to sit in the armchair that had been specially made for President Franklin D. Roosevelt. "As you can see," said Baruch, "this house is completely accessible [to a wheelchair]."

"I must say," Dollfus said, "I was very honored to be able to sit down in this special armchair."

Dollfus asked Belle's permission to shoot a deer. She frowned at first, not liking to kill one, but also wanting to grant any request from Paul. She turned to Ella Severin. "What do you think, should I let him shoot a deer?"

"Well, I don't know," she replied. She turned to Paul. "If you shoot the deer, will you eat it?"

"Oh, yes, I love venison," he answered.

"Well, if Paul promises to eat the deer, let him shoot it," said Ella.

Dollfus borrowed Belle's rifle, and Taylor took him in the jeep to hunt. They spotted a buck and Taylor halted the jeep about two hundred feet away. Taking aim, Dollfus dropped the deer with a single shot. "I was surprised what an excellent shot he was with a rifle," Taylor commented.

"Well, in fact," Dollfus said, "the poor animal was very friendly. . . . When I came back with the deer, Elsa said, 'Now you have to eat it.'

"I was put on a deer regimen for quite a long time during the holiday and, in fact, at the end, was quite fed up with deer meat."

"Yes," Ella Severin laughingly recalled, "Belle and I would have fish and Paul would have venison—venison stew, venison fried, venison this way and that way, even ground venison. He'd say, 'Oh, what are you having?'

"'Oh, shrimp . . . or oysters . . . or whatever,' I'd say, 'but don't forget you said you'd eat the deer, you know. There's a lot of it left.' Poor Paul, he had venison for about a week until he said, 'Elsa, please, can I have something else?'

"No," I said, "you've got to have one more meal."

"I promise you," Dollfus said fervently, "I'll never shoot another deer." Finally Ella and Belle relented, and Paul enjoyed the bounty of Hobcaw's inlets and woods.

Knowing Paul had qualified for his pilot's license prior to being stricken with polio, Belle allowed him to fly the Beechcraft with help from Ken Unger. "It was something extraordinary to be able to pilot again," Dollfus said. "The only thing I could not manage was the rudder, but then I was helped, as I say, by one of the kindest men I have met."

Dollfus's visit to Bellefield was the beginning of a lifelong friendship with Belle and Ella Severin. After Christmas they met often in the States, and when Paul returned to France, Belle and Ella would see him when they went to Europe.[1]

One Christmas after he had returned to France, Dollfus had a real French colonel's hat, or *képi,* made up by a military tailor and sent to Bellefield. According to Ella Severin, Belle was thrilled and wore the hat frequently. Belle was always "Mon Colonel" to her "Lieutenant" Dollfus.

Dr. Rusk also introduced Belle to another Frenchman, Dr. Dennis Leroy, of Rennes in Brittany. He, too, became a Bellefield guest and told Belle of the innovative work he was doing in physical rehabilitation at his institute in France. On what was to be her last trip to France, Belle attended the Conference on Handicapped Children as a guest of Dr. Leroy. Belle and Ella were amazed at what Dr. Leroy had accomplished at his institute with very little money and few resources. Leroy was indefatigable in his efforts to help his patients.

"He was the most practical man I have ever seen," said Ella Severin. "He would go to junkyards and get bearings and things like that to use in his work. He had this little child that had polio and could move only her arm. He made her a little board, mounted on wheels, so she could lay flat, and attached a set of ball bearings to another small board attached to her arm so that she could propel herself around by moving that one good arm."

At the conference, Belle and Ella were amazed to see a man without legs riding horseback, patients in wheelchairs engaged in fencing, and other severely handicapped persons engaged in various sports. The courage and spirit displayed were both heartwarming and humbling. Belle contributed generously to Leroy's institute.

Another favorite friend of Belle's was Frances Milam of Georgetown. This beautiful child had been stricken by polio in 1950 and left totally paralyzed except for some movement in the left hand. She could not even hold her head up without a brace to support her neck. The family had taken her to Warm

Springs, Georgia, where they tried to equip her with braces, but they could not seem to fit her properly.

For the next six years, her world had narrowed to the bed in her room and the couch in the living room. Dr. Assey spoke to Belle about Frances, and immediately Belle swung into action.

Calling Dr. Rusk, Belle scheduled Frances for a complete checkup at the institute at Bellevue. Belle bought a motorized wheelchair for Frances, opening a new world for the young teenager and giving her a small degree of independence.

While they were in New York, Belle delighted in providing new experiences for Frances. Hiring a van to accommodate the wheelchair, Belle took her to the theater, toured New York City, and even took her aboard the Staten Island ferry. Nothing was too much trouble, no obstacle insurmountable to a determined Belle. When the Milams returned to Georgetown, the new experiences continued. In her wheelchair, Frances was able to go back to school for a while. "She wanted an education so badly," Louise Milam, Frances's mother, recalled. Frances went to school until all the classes that the teenager needed for credit were taught upstairs; since there were no accommodations for handicapped at that time, no way to carry her and her wheelchair upstairs. Frances had to drop out of school but was philosophical. "Our other daughter, Janet, cried when Frances couldn't go to school," Louise Milam said.

With the maneuverability of her motorized wheelchair, Frances's world continued to expand. She planned a concrete walk for the yard of their house in Georgetown. Instead of the traditional circle around the house, Frances's walk extended into the center of the backyard, beneath the shade trees, so that for the first time in nearly seven years, she could venture beyond the house alone.

Once again, Frances could go to one of her favorite places, Brookgreen Gardens, the world-famous statuary gardens built by Archer M. Huntington just north of Pawleys Island, South Carolina.

"Frances never wanted to wear pajamas during the day," her mother recalled, "she wanted to dress." Belle would send her small gifts from time to time, a pretty sweater or blouse. When she was home, she would send Taylor with the car to bring Frances to Bellefield, where she could swim in Belle's pool. Often Frances's brother, Ben, would come to help move her in and out of the pool and car. Belle offered to build a pool in Frances's backyard, but the Milams regretfully declined, concerned about the safety of neighborhood children and liability.

When Belle was away, she and Frances would correspond or Belle would call her long-distance. Belle would send the girl little mementos from her travels.

When she came back from her journeys, Frances would come to Bellefield once more to visit with Belle and Ella and whoever was there at the time. Belle liked to introduce her to some of her celebrity guests, and Frances was thrilled to meet Mrs. Wilson.

During one visit Dr. Leroy was there, and he devised a set of heavy boots for Frances's feet so she could actually stand erect in the pool, the first time she had been able to stand since being stricken with polio. Belle included Frances in Christmas parties and other celebrations at Hobcaw Barony.

Frances was deeply moved when Belle founded the Frances Milam Fellowship for postgraduate training in physical education and rehabilitation. With the advice of Dr. Rusk, the first award was given to Dr. Claire Schiller, a graduate of the University of Witwatersrand in Johannesburg, South Africa. Dr. Schiller, like Frances a victim of polio, was dedicating her life to the field of rehabilitation.

Most of all, Frances was grateful for Belle's continued friendship. "It made such a difference for me also," Louise Milam said, "to know that there were people interested enough to do things for her."

28

The Passing of Jean Darthez and Souriant III

In 1956 Belle's friends joined her in mourning the death of her beloved Toto, Souriant III. Toto had passed thirty years of his life with Belle and Jean Darthez, loved and pampered, but all the affection they lavished on him could not stave off the ravages of age. Toto had reached the point where he could hardly stand, and on a few occasions, Jean had rigged a harness to lift the great jumper to an upright position to prevent pneumonia. Finally, a heartbroken Jean put down the beautiful animal while Belle was in Europe. Belle came home to commiserate with Jean and arrange Toto's final resting place.

Souriant III is buried beneath the spreading live oaks of Bellefield, between the stables and the house where Belle could look out the windows of the sun-room and see his resting place. On the oak tree shading his grave is a plaque that reads:

SOURIANT III

TOTO

ANGLO-ARAB

FRANCE 1923–JUNE 25, 1956

MY GALLANT HORSE AND

FAITHFUL FRIEND——ADIEU

Still mourning Souriant's death, Belle left for New York with Ella. She joined her father on a trip to Saratoga and returned with him to celebrate his birthday at his New York home on Fifth Avenue. Her brother also attended and expressed his sympathy at Souriant's death. Because of their strained relations, Belle was surprised and touched that Junior would sympathize. Writing to Edith Wilson about her father's birthday luncheon, she wrote: "Jr. appeared too and I don't suppose you heard any resounding noise in Washington when he kissed me."[1]

Belle was concerned about her father's health early in 1957 and wrote to entice him for a visit:

Dear Chick,

You have been often in my thoughts as I thought it would not be long before you would be enjoying this ideal weather. Not a drop of rain and yesterday and today 65–70 degrees.

George [Belle's golden retriever, "Gorgeous George"] has retrieved ducks four or five times now in the salt water pond near the fording at Clambank.

I am making the feathers fly at Hobcaw as I want it to look as well burnished and cared for as Bellefield.

The hogs are plentiful everywhere—big as I am but they can run faster.

Get feeling tops real soon and come enjoy this beautiful land and sunshine.

Much love, devotedly,
Belle[2]

Bernard Baruch was still active, articulate, and brilliant, but he had small illnesses and the ailments of an octogenarian. Belle worried about him, and Ella Severin said that Belle would never travel without first calling to talk to her father. If he was ill, she would postpone any trip, sometimes flying to New York to be available should he need her.

She was also deeply concerned about the health of Edith Wilson, who was also in her eighties. In January, Belle was deeply touched when Mrs. Wilson sent her a set of President Woodrow Wilson's cuff links. She wrote in reply:

Dear Mam,

We returned here yesterday after a lovely flight and found your wonderful gift awaiting me. I think your sweet message on your card meant more to me than anything. I am deeply grateful and honored that you should want me to have Mr. Wilson's cuff links and I shall keep them as a very special memento. I am deeply grateful and very appreciative that you want me to have them.[3]

Later that year, the first volume of Bernard Baruch's memoirs, *Baruch: My Own Story*, which dealt with his career as a financier, was published and immediately jumped to the top of the best-seller list. At almost the same time Pulitzer Prize–winner Margaret Coit published her biography, *Mr. Baruch*, which was a Book-of-the-Month-Club selection. The eighty-seven-year-old Baruch was more popular than ever.

Ella and Belle attended a summer-stock performance of *The Solid Gold Cadillac* at the Ocean Forest Hotel in Myrtle Beach, South Carolina. They went backstage afterward to meet one of the stars, ZaSu Pitts. Belle had long admired the actress, who had made over three hundred films. Belle and Ella took an immediate liking to Miss Pitts and spontaneously invited her to Bellefield to see a "real southern plantation." The three women became close friends. ZaSu visited at least once a year until her death in 1963.

The contented years with Ella continued as Belle lovingly tended the land and waters of Hobcaw Barony. There were flying visits to New York and Europe and frequent visitors at Bellefield. It was an idyllic life, disturbed only by the effects of development on the wildlife. Conservation efforts were pursued at Hobcaw, but Belle could not control the destruction of wetlands and the destruction of waterfowl nesting grounds at either end of the Atlantic flyway through which the migratory ducks and geese passed. Their numbers continued to dwindle. Domestic birds that lived at Hobcaw all year fared somewhat better because of curtailed hunting and pursuit of poachers. But even Belle and Taylor could not be everywhere at once. Belle often told Ella that she wanted to preserve Hobcaw Barony forever, to keep it as she remembered it as a little girl.

Time did not stand still, however, and the world was changing. Pan Am World Airways established its first transatlantic service, and Belle was soon flying to Europe rather than sailing. The National Advisory Committee on Aeronautics (now called the National Aeronautics and Space Administration) was established in 1958. Charles de Gaulle was recalled to power in France. The following year, Fidel Castro came to power in Cuba.

Then tragedy ripped the peaceful fabric of life at Hobcaw. Jean Darthez was diagnosed with advanced throat cancer in 1958, and the long, futile battle for his life began. Belle spared no expense, flying him and family members to New York for treatment. Ella and Belle gave Jean's wife, Lucie, all the loving support of which they were capable. Both were fluent in French and able to interpret for her the findings of the specialists Belle consulted. The Hobcaw community gathered to offer support. Elizabeth Navarro would come from Little Hobcaw to administer shots and enemas, give medications, and use her nursing skills to ease Jean's discomfort.

The temperatures at Hobcaw that year were sweltering, and Nolan Taylor found a window air conditioner and brought in the power lines for it. The cool air made Jean a little more comfortable and eased his breathing. The Taylors, like everyone at Hobcaw, took turns sitting with Jean in the final months of his illness as he struggled valiantly against the pain and debilitating sickness. At that time cancer treatment was more limited, but Belle explored every possibility for her good friend before accepting Jean's inevitable death.

Robert Darthez said, "I shall go to my grave being eternally grateful to Miss Belle for her kindness to my father and mother. . . . Many times she and Ella Severin got our spirits back up after we would get some bad news. No expense was spared to try to cure my father and, when the situation became hopeless, to make his last days comfortable. It is still difficult to talk about it, but I feel that it should be known that Miss Belle could be as kind as anyone I know. Miss Ella was also wonderful. She is one of my favorite people."

Yvette Darthez Bozigian recalls: "She [Belle] was there for our mother, and she took care of all the medical expenses, visited him constantly during his final three-month stay at the Georgetown hospital."

Belle and Jean had shared so much through the years—fun and excitement, the thrill of international show jumping and steeplechase, hours of practice and training the horses, their great love for Souriant, their sorrow at his death, jokes and stories and a thousand memories. Jean was the only one left who could reminisce and dream with Belle of the "old days" in Europe. Without Jean, Belle felt that an important part of her past was gone forever.

Seeing her old friend suffer so horribly was almost more than she could bear, but Belle's humor and demeanor never faltered in his presence. No matter how their own spirits flagged, both Belle and Ella did everything they could to cheer and encourage Jean's family.

When at last Jean died, Belle could only weep and pray for her old companion, grateful that his suffering had ended. When Taylor suggested that Jean should be buried on the property to which he had devoted his life, Belle made the arrangements for the funeral. Jean is buried at Bellefield near his beloved garden.

Lucie Darthez wanted to live with her daughter in California, so Belle asked the Taylors to arrange the transfer of Lucie's belongings to Yvette's home. When Mrs. Darthez died in 1961, Belle offered to bring her body to Hobcaw for burial next to Jean, but the family declined, wanting to keep her remains in California.

Belle brightened a little when Mrs. Wilson wrote inviting her to attend her eighty-seventh birthday party, to be celebrated at the annual meeting of the trustees of the Woodrow Wilson Birthplace Foundation at Staunton, Virginia. Wilson had been born there while his father was rector of an Episcopal church. The manse had been turned into a national shrine, and Belle was nominated and duly elected to serve on the board. And so the rich, full years, marred only by Jean Darthez's death, flowed peacefully into the 1960s.

29

~~~~

Into the Twilight

Bernard Baruch ushered in the new decade with the publication of volume 2 of his autobiography, *Baruch: The Public Years,* creating quite a stir among his political contemporaries. He still had enough clout that the young Senator John F. Kennedy from Massachusetts came to pay his respects as he sought the presidency.

Friends and family celebrated his ninetieth birthday in August with an enormous tiered birthday cake. At Christmas he sent photographs of himself swimming at Little Hobcaw to intimate friends and relatives.

The following year, shortly after Christmas, Edith Bolling Wilson died, leaving Belle bereft. Her relationship with her beloved "Mam" was among the most important and enduring of her life. Edith Wilson had given Belle unconditional love and acceptance. She felt as though she had once again lost a beloved mother. She would miss Mrs. Wilson's wise counsel, humor, and undemanding affection.

Varvara Hasselbalch Ingram flew to American with her son, Guy Rurik, nicknamed Eggy, for a visit with the Baruchs. Belle met them in New York and transported them to Bellefield in her twin-engine Beechcraft, much to Varvara's distress. "The Baruch Cadillac was emptied, and as it stood on the airfield next to Belle's plane, it seemed to be the same size as the plane. . . . Either the plane was small or the Cadillac large!"

Varvara's twelve-year-old son wanted to get out of his seat to look at New York from the sky but was ordered back. "Otherwise we tilt," said Belle. Her message did not reassure a nervous Varvara. Part way through the journey, the plane's engines suddenly stopped. "Our stomachs hit our mouths," Varvara said, "I thought our last second had arrived." Then the plane settled as the pilot restarted the engines. Belle explained nonchalantly, "The pilot forgot to change the fuel tanks over . . . that can happen."

Three and a half hours later, Varvara was delighted to recognize the approach to the plantation. "The landing was somewhat bumpy," Varvara recalled. "Never again, I said to myself. And that is why we took the Greyhound bus back to New York, which caused a major drama!"

The changes at Hobcaw Barony were startling to Varvara, whose memories were of the busy, bustling community of thirty years earlier. All the blacks had left the plantation. Their cabins stood empty, the church was silent and musty. No smoke came from the chimneys, no chickens scratched in the overgrown yards. There was not even an echo of children's laughter at the Friendfield School.

"On one of the porches, an old broken rocking chair was not inviting anybody to sit in it," Varvara recalled. "It was just gaping into nothingness. I remembered the old Negro woman, Venus, who would sit there and rock and puff on her pipe. The wild boars seemed to be the masters of the paths now."

The weather added to Varvara's gloom. In the verdant South, the trees had quickly overtaken the grounds and seemed to close in on the small wooden cabins. "The moss knitted itself together more tightly than ever," said Varvara, "and swept softly across your face, cold and damp, when you tried to make your way through the overgrown paths."

Hobcaw House had an abandoned air, its blank windows filmed with dust. "The buds of the camellia bushes were brown from an early frost," said Varvara. "Hobcaw lawn was covered in dead leaves. One never saw a lonely leaf in the old days because it was picked up by the Negro gardener."

Varvara missed the glamor and excitement of the past, but Belle seemed to prefer the peace and tranquility, content to let nature take its course throughout the barony. Perhaps it was the other guests, but the atmosphere seemed depressed and gloomy. ZaSu Pitts, suffering from terminal cancer, had made her final pilgrimage to Hobcaw. Belle had also opened her home to a tragic couple trying to deal with the husband's impending blindness. Father Tom Carroll was there to counsel them, but the wife seemed unable to cope with her husband's affliction.

Other things had changed, too. When Varvara made a nostalgic trip to formerly sleepy Georgetown, she found a thriving little community. "As I stood on the sidewalk trying to bring back old memories of the shops, a group of Negro kids passed us and shouted: 'You white stinkers!' Then they stuck out their tongues! I was shocked."

Most of all, Varvara was distressed by the changes in Belle. She had gained a great deal of weight, and her face was puffy and swollen from the cortisone she was taking for her arthritis. There were personality changes as well. Belle experienced mood swings and lacked her usual patience and humor. She was apt to fly into a temper or suddenly become unreasonable over small things. At times she showed her old gaiety and zest, but at others the old vigor and joie de vivre seemed sadly diminished. Later, Varvara realized that these changes were symptomatic of Belle's as yet undisclosed illness.

Varvara's son, Guy, recalls Hobcaw as "not a happy place. There was an image of decay, a claustrophobic feeling. I quickly learned to avoid Miss Belle, sensing that she felt only a mild impatience or irritation with me, or any child for that matter. Miss Pitts was funny and kind, and I had more contact with Elsa [Miss Severin] and Miss Navarro. Miss Belle and I avoided each other."

Belle's lifestyle had changed dramatically. The French couple was gone, unable to tolerate the isolation and summer heat at Bellefield. Ella and Belle did their own cooking, although they did have a housekeeper and the house was immaculate, as always.

"We took all our meals in the kitchen with pewter plates and paper napkins, and did the washing up," Varvara recalled. "Where, I wondered, were all the beautifully decorated Blocaille plates. There was plenty of fresh fruit and oysters, and caviar twice a day! That someone with such a colossal fortune could live like that was difficult for a European to grasp—six fridges stuffed with food, two planes and a pilot at her disposal, four cars, two TVs—we seemed to be jumping from canteen level to caviar level with nothing in between."

Belle, however, seemed quite content with the casual, unpretentious lifestyle, though Varvara noted that many of the responsibilities seemed to fall on Ella Severin's shoulders.

Belle did, however, break out the good china and silver for a New Year's luncheon that included Governor and Mrs. James Byrnes, Carroll Godwin, Lucille (Lulu) Vanderbilt, ZaSu Pitts, Mr. and Mrs. Buist Rivers, Father Tom Carroll, Nolan and Cynthia Taylor, Bernard Baruch, Elizabeth Navarro, and others. Belle entertained with style when the occasion warranted.

Bernard Baruch was delighted to see Feather (Varvara) and invited them to lunch at Little Hobcaw. He received them at the door, standing tall and straight, in excellent spirits. He was dressed jauntily in a black-and-white wool sports jacket with a red-and-white flannel striped shirt and discreet (by comparison) tie. "Chick," said Belle, somewhat awed by his sartorial splendor, "that is the busiest suit I have ever seen on you."

He hugged Feather and ushered them into the living room. Varvara soon found his mind as quick and keen as ever. When he discovered she was then living in Portugal, he announced that he admired Salazar and talked knowledgeably for half an hour on Portuguese politics.

"The Portuguese," he informed Varvara, "should buy us out cheap [referring to the U.S. air base in the Azores], let's say $12 million—no, tell them $15 million. Salazar doesn't like the U.S. and their money." With that Baruch reached for *Baruch: The Public Years* and read pages 409–10 aloud. "Read that to Salazar," he instructed.

"I said, 'yes, sir,' as if I had access to Salazar!"

During lunch, which included turkey stuffed with walnuts and all the trimmings, plus Pol Roger champagne, Baruch shut off his hearing aid, something he frequently did when he was tired, bored, or simply did not want to listen to what was being said. "Papa is off the air," Belle quipped, "so we can talk." The party grew very gay with much laughter, so Baruch switched his hearing aid back on so he would not miss the fun.

Varvara was delighted to find Mr. Baruch in such excellent spirits and health. Elizabeth Navarro, with great good humor, confided some of his idiosyncrasies to Varvara. Mr. Baruch, it seemed, had an excellent appetite, eating as often as six times a day, twice at night, and always carried cookies in his pockets, to Navarro's despair.

He took frequent naps and his bed was made five times daily. He talked to his stockbroker at least twice a day and liked to swim late at night in the heated pool, sometimes after midnight. He left everything on the floor, Navarro said, which was all right when they had kept lots of servants, but now there were only two at the smaller Kingstree house.

Baruch never opened a parcel himself, Navarro said, because he was afraid of bombs. He never wrote a check or carried cash, leaving all such transactions to Navarro. The night before Varvara's arrival, Baruch had been unable to sleep, so they had played cards until 4:30 in the morning. But the worst part, Navarro said, laughing, was the cookie crumbs in his pockets.

Varvara had purchased a copy of *Baruch: The Public Years*, intending to bring it for his autograph. She had left it at Bellefield but Navarro said never mind, there were some in the attic and she would fetch one. But Mr. Baruch heard and at first refused to sign it, saying that his was a first edition and Varvara's no doubt was a second edition. Finally, he gave in and autographed a first edition, addressing it to "my pretty Feather."

Varvara told him a story going around Portugal about his brother Herman Baruch, who had been ambassador to The Hague and was at that time accredited to Portugal. Like his famous brother, Herman enjoyed beautiful ladies. When invited to a cocktail party or reception, he would accept "with pleasure." When he arrived at the event and was received by his host, he would point to the pretty blonde or brunette on his arm and say, ". . . and this is *pleasure!*"

Carroll Godwin, a well-known television personality in Charleston, South Carolina, was often a visitor at Bellefield, and after meeting Varvara, he insisted on interviewing her for his program. Belle was opposed to the idea, jealous of her privacy. She eventually agreed, but only on condition that Feather not mention Bellefield or the Baruch name. Varvara talked mostly about the war and her experiences as an ambulance driver. "I think it went off all right," Varvara said, "at least I wasn't given hell by Belle, and she had watched it."

Varvara was determined that she would not return to New York aboard what was, to her, a tiny airplane. "I decided Eggy and I would take the more secure Greyhound bus back to Washington and, from there, go on by train to New York. It meant also that my son could see some of the countryside." Belle and Varvara argued about it for twenty-four hours.

"You are mad," Belle shouted, "you might have to sit beside a Negro and that would be out of the question."

"To me," said Varvara, "the danger of falling down from heaven seemed greater than having to sit beside a Negro."

Belle's final argument, amusing since Belle never cared what anyone thought of her, was: "What will they say in town if guests from Bellefield travel on a Greyhound bus. You have to think of my reputation!" Belle was truly hurt, however, mostly because of Varvara's lack of confidence in her beloved airplane.

Feather was determined to have her way and in due course was driven to the bus station in Georgetown. Unfortunately, the bus did not arrive, having been delayed by an unexpected and unseasonable snowstorm. The kindly agent asked his daughter to drive the Ingrams to a nearby town where they could make a connection. "I must admit," said Varvara, "that she was quite amused that we came from Bellefield.

"The fun part of the story is that Belle's intuition was right—I sat between two well-behaved Negroes all the way. His name was Tim and she by a charming coincidence was called Belle!"

Belle had flown ahead to New York and was over her pique by the time the Ingrams arrived. "When I was to leave New York, Belle, with tears in her eyes, gave me a pair of gold earclips. It was as if she felt it was the last time we were to meet.

"It was my last impression of Belle, the tears. I was never to see her again, much to my despair. I dearly loved and respected her. She had meant so much to me. A chapter of my life closed with her death. She remembered me in her will, which deeply touched me."

Later that year Belle lost another dear friend, Dr. Philip Assey. When she was paid $750 by the state for the new highway right-of-way at the edge of her property, she endorsed it over to the Georgetown Memorial Hospital "in memory of my friend, Dr. Philip Assey, for any purpose that you believe would have met his approval."

For some time Belle had felt considerably below par and checked into the New York Hospital of the Cornell University Medical Center in New York in late 1962. Her father was a patient there also, having some minor procedures performed. He checked out shortly after Belle was admitted.

Anne Johnston was the private nurse assigned to Mr. Baruch and came often to the hospital with him to visit Belle. "I had met her briefly when her father was ill another time," she said.

> She always came in to speak to the nurses. She always sat down, always had time to talk. She would bring up large baskets of camellias [from Hobcaw]. She just made you feel completely at ease. She was very witty, very bright, very fast . . . able to catch any little thing in a conversation and make fun out of it.
>
> We were all amused because she was so tall, they had to bring in a special bed. When she came in the first time, her diagnosis was, of course, questionable, but she was not, I think, aware of the gravity of the situation. She was reconciled to all the tests, joking about them, saying, "Let's see what they are going to come up with. Maybe I am built different or made different." Sometimes I think she shocked the doctors a little with her comments.
>
> She was so much her own person. She fell in with everybody, no matter if they were aides, cleaning people, or professors at Cornell. She was the same for all—a unique personality.
>
> She had a lot of friends who came to see her, a lot of political people, they were coming back and forth all the time. There was a lot of laughter down there in that room. She immediately got the stiffest person in a good mood.
>
> Her eyes were bright and her smile! . . . I'm sure she was the type that could think herself out of any situation. There was always something going on with her, something happening.[1]

Dr. Charles Jones was Belle's physician, and after consultation, exploratory abdominal surgery was recommended. Dr. Francis Glenn, chief of surgical services at Cornell University, performed the surgery with Drs. Jones and Howard Rusk in attendance. Elizabeth Navarro was also in the operating room. They discovered cancer and removed a part of the large intestine. They also realized that the cancer had already spread and there was little to be done.

"I had said to Charlie Jones," recalled Ella Severin, "that if there was something seriously wrong with Belle, please ask Dr. Glenn not to say anything. Belle has seen too much cancer, watching poor Jean suffer as he did. If she was told she had cancer, she'd go to Bellefield, go out in the woods, and blow her brains out."

"I think you're right," Dr. Jones said.

"I know it, that's what she would do," said Ella.

Dr. Glenn at first did not agree, saying, "I've got to tell Miss Baruch."

"I said to Charlie Jones," Ella said, "you tell Dr. Glenn that if he wants to have a suicide on his hands, all right, go ahead and tell her."

Dr. Glenn reluctantly agreed and Belle went home to Hobcaw, only Ella and Elizabeth Navarro aware that she had cancer.[2] "When I came out of the operating room, all the family was waiting," said Navarro. "I said everything was fine, worst lying I ever did because it was awful."[3]

Some of those close to Belle felt that she should have been told, that she had a right to know that she was dying. "Miss Belle was a stronger woman than they gave her credit for," said Cynthia Taylor. "She might have done things a lot differently if she had known that she was dying. At least she should have been given that choice. God knows I would have helped take care of her with my dying breath. I loved her like a mother."

Belle had been thinking of buying one of the small private jets newly on the market. Her father was opposed to the purchase, calling it a needless extravagance. "We'll talk about it when you come to New York," he said. When Belle flew in to do some shopping about a month after her surgery, they made a date.

Just before Belle was to come, Navarro and Baruch went out for their daily walk. Navarro knew of the contretemps and did not want the aging man left with the memory of having denied his beloved daughter's last request. "I didn't want them to have any hard feelings," she said. As they walked, Navarro said, "Mr. Baruch, don't fight with Belle, go on and let her have an airplane."

"Well, what's this all about?" he asked.

"I'll tell you when we get to the house," Navarro replied. But Baruch insisted that she answer him.

Reluctantly, Navarro told him, "She's dying of cancer. . . . She won't be here . . . so what difference does it make?"

Baruch paused, deeply affected. Finally he said, "Navarro you never told me a story in your life. I believe you."

"Belle came all dressed up," Navarro said, "she looked lovely. Her father said, 'Daughter, go on and buy the airplane. I was only joking . . . do what you want with your money.'

"Belle kissed his cheek and said, 'Father, I decided I don't need it.'"[4]

Belle seemed to recover well from her surgery and was soon flying and hunting. "She had some trouble getting in and out of a boat because of her arthritis," said Taylor, "but she'd had that problem for a while."

She would still go to the Taylors' house in the afternoon and pick up their older son, Eric, to hunt. If he had friends present, Belle would simply say, "It's time for you boys to go on home, Eric and I are going hunting."

Eric recalled that usually Belle shot first if they saw a feral hog, but one day she stopped the jeep in the road, nudged Eric, and said, "Look, there's one right over there." Eric nodded but did not get out of the jeep. Belle turned to the boy and said, "Aren't you going to get out and shoot?"

Surprised that Belle was not taking the first shot, Eric jumped out with his gun and cautiously approached the hog. As he slowly moved forward, Belle shouted, "Shoot the damn thing!"

Eric raised his gun and fired, bringing down the hog. When he returned to the jeep to load the animal in the back, Belle growled: "What were you trying to do, stick the gun up his ass?"

Eric laughed. "No, ma'am," he said, and Belle looked over and began to laugh too.

On Easter Sunday 1963, to Belle's great delight, Taylor brought home a tiny fawn that had apparently been abandoned by its mother. "It was precious," Ella Severin said, "its tiny hooves no bigger than your fingernail." A baby bottle was fetched from Georgetown, and Ella and Belle took turns nursing the little buck. They named him Deary-Deer, and he was the favored pet of the household.

Francena McCants laughed happily talking about Deary-Deer. "He'd follow Miss Belle around like a child, right on through the house. Usually, she'd be in the sunroom and he'd be right in there with her. He didn't dirty the house."

Belle lavished love on the little deer and spoiled him like she had spoiled no pet since Toto, who had been far too large to bring into the house. Deary-Deer loved flowers, and once when the florist delivered a dozen long-stemmed roses to Bellefield, Deary-Deer ate the blossoms before they even opened.

"Miss Belle" said Francena, "she didn't ever get mad at him . . . no, no. One year he just tore up everything under the Christmas tree, but Miss Belle, she just laughed."

Nolan Taylor said she would even send him into Georgetown to buy carnations for the deer. "He liked candy, too," Taylor said. "He'd get into a box of Stouffer's and eat what he wanted. And cigarettes—he loved them. He loved to chew the tender leaves off the poinsettias, too. There would be four or five big poinsettias in the house, some with ten or twelve large blooms. He'd walk by and eat what he wanted."

"Yeah," said Cynthia Taylor, "Miss Belle would have these great bare stems with big red poinsettias on the top but not a single leaf."

Belle would look at the little buck and say to Ella, "I really do love that deer."

"We made him a green bow with bells on it that Christmas, and he really made the holiday special," said Ella. He slept in a little cage some nights, and they would entice him into it with a fresh carnation to nibble. Deary-Deer brought great joy and affection into their lives, and they cherished the little animal.

When the New Year rolled around, Belle held her annual party but was complaining about abdominal cramps and not feeling well. In March she picked up Nolan Taylor to go hunting and drove while Taylor sat on the front fender with his rifle. "I noticed she seemed to be looking off to the left side all the time," Taylor said, "and she would get too close to the ditch. She nearly brushed me off up against a tree . . . like to scared me to death. When I asked her to stop and let me drive, she hadn't even realized it."

One evening Belle said, "Elsa, I'm having trouble balancing my checkbook. I can't make the figures come out right or something." Ella noticed that Belle's handwriting was slanted and almost illegible and that she was slurring her words slightly. She suggested an immediate trip to New York to see Charlie Jones.

"I didn't even know Miss Belle was sick," said Francena McCants. "She didn't change. She leave one night and I was away. . . . They take her and she never did come back.

"I miss her always a-comin' and a-goin', always walking through. She'd smile and say good morning, off to the stable or her garden, or down to Clambank for fish or oysters, or up in her plane or out huntin' with Taylor—always comin' and goin' and always smilin' when she come through. . . . There never was enough hours in the day for her to do all she wanted to do."

"The weather forecast for the next day was bad," Taylor recalled, "so she decided not to fly. We loaded up the car to catch the train out of Kingstree. Getting in I had to pick up her feet because she couldn't seem to do it. I knew then that if she ever came back, it would be a surprise."

When they arrived at the station, Cynthia reached over and said, "Listen, Miss Belle, when you get to New York, I want you to behave yourself and do what the doctor tells you to do."

"You're talking to me just like you talk to your children," Belle growled.

"Well, you need it," Cynthia answered.

Before she left, Belle insisted on giving Cynthia the cash she had in her pocket because she knew Cynthia was going to have extensive dental work done and she wanted to pay for it.

"Now call me every night," she told Cynthia, "because you can get me better than I can get you."

"But I never talked to her again," said Cynthia Taylor sadly, "because I was taken ill with pneumonia and was in the Georgetown hospital. Nolan didn't tell her I was in the hospital because he didn't want to worry her. I just wish I could have talked to her again. I know she didn't understand why I didn't call."

Nolan Taylor did, however, speak to Belle, and she asked him to come to New York. Cynthia's condition was serious and Nolan was reluctant to leave South Carolina at first, but when Cynthia improved and Belle asked him again to come, he agreed, teasing her a little at first.

"What do you think I can do for you up there that the doctors can't?"

"Well, you can turn me over," Belle joked.

When Taylor arrived Belle was semi-comatose and mostly unaware that he was there. He sat by her side, however, holding her hand, tears in his eyes. Twice she seemed aware of his presence and squeezed his hand.

Sometime during the early stages of her final illness, Belle had been alert enough to call Frances Milam in Georgetown and talk to the teenager at length. Louise Milam said that Frances did not reveal their conversation but had tears in her eyes when she hung up the telephone. It would appear that Belle was not as unaware of the possibility of death as everyone thought. She remembered Frances in her will, but the fragile girl died of pneumonia just three years after Belle's death.

Certainly Belle had faced her own mortality in providing for the future of Hobcaw Barony. For over two years prior to her illness, Belle had been talking to her attorneys about the preservation of Hobcaw. She repeated the wish that she had often made to Ella that Hobcaw could be as it was when she was a child. She briefly considered turning Bellefield into a home for the aged but then laughed and said, "The old ladies would probably get snake-bit and fall into the swamp."

Long before ecology became fashionable, Belle Baruch was seeking ways to preserve the environment. Finally, after much consultation, she decided to establish the Bernard Baruch Foundation Trust, preserving Hobcaw Barony, to be changed only by nature, and to be used for research by South Carolina universities "for the purpose of teaching and/or research in forestry, marine biology, and the care and propagation of wild life and flora and fauna in South Carolina."[5]

It was typical of Belle not to give the property outright to the state but rather to establish a private trust, with parameters set by herself for the protection of her beloved Hobcaw Barony. Belle always wanted to be in control, and her will assured that she would guide the future of Hobcaw Barony for generations to come. Belle signed the will a few days after entering the hospital.

Anne Johnston was asked by the Baruchs to be one of Belle's private-duty nurses. She is confident that Belle was unaware that she was dying when she checked into the hospital. In fact, no one but the doctors and nurses knew the true situation, although by then the Baruch family knew that Belle had cancer. No one realized, however, that death was imminent.

Ella was there each day, staying long into the night. Renee came often, and Mr. Baruch came every day. The cancer had metastasized into the brain, forming three tumors. Belle was semi-comatose within a few days and in a coma toward the end. She did rouse long enough to say, "I want to become a Catholic."

Ella was startled at first and hesitant about what to do. She knew that Belle and Father Tom Carroll had many long discussions but was not aware that Belle had decided to join the Catholic Church. She decided that she could not refuse such a request and sent for Father Carroll. Belle was baptized into the Catholic faith, much to Bernard Baruch's dismay and anger. He was furious, but Ella stood her ground, convinced that such a decision was Belle's to make.

"I have never known anyone in my whole life," said Anne Johnston, "who was so faithful as Ella, and who helped so much with the care of a patient. There was nothing she wouldn't do for Belle. We had to turn her [Belle] quite often, and Ella was always the one to help. She rubbed her back, cradled her head, talked to her."

The doctors recommended cobalt treatments, saying that Belle had had a stroke and that a couple of blood vessels in the brain could be dried out with cobalt. "Oh, Charlie," Ella said "what do you mean, cobalt? I think you're telling me a story."

"Oh, no," he said, "it's absolutely true."

"When we got home to the apartment that night," Ella said, "Renee asked what I thought. He had told her the same thing. I said, 'Well, to tell you the truth, I don't believe it, but Charlie says it's absolutely true.' Renee didn't believe it either."

It was not until a few days before her death that Ella realized that Belle was dying. For several days Belle had been comatose. Ella was sitting beside her, holding her hand, when the hospital neurologist came into the room and asked to see Miss Severin in the hall.

When Ella joined him, he said, "I have seen you sitting here. You're here at six o'clock in the morning, you're here at midnight, you're here at two o'clock in the afternoon." He paused, then continued. "I have to tell you something."

"Well, what is it?" Ella said.

Drawing a determined breath, he said, "Belle is dying."

"What?" Ella gasped. "What do you mean she's dying?"

"She has three small tumors in her head." And thus Ella learned that the cancer had metastasized into the brain. When later she confronted Charlie Jones and demanded to know why they were not told, Charlie said, "If we had told you, you would have shown it."

"No," said Ella, "God would have given me that strength. I never would have shown it." Ella never left Belle's side again.

Belle, who thankfully had suffered no pain, died peacefully on April 24, 1964. Ella was at one side, her father at the other. Bernard Baruch, then ninety-three years of age, stood with his hands folded, the tears running silently down his face.

Even in death, Belle's last deed was one of generosity. Anne Johnston accompanied her body to the operating room, where her corneas were harvested for transplant. It was Belle's final and most personal gift to the blind.

Epilogue

As often happens when someone of great wealth dies, there was dissension and controversy following Belle Baruch's death. Belle had often expressed the wish to be buried at her beloved Hobcaw Barony but had not so designated in her will. Bernard Baruch insisted that she be interred in the family burial plot at Flushing Cemetery in Queens. Disregarding her Catholic baptism, Baruch held the funeral services at the Chapel of the Beloved Disciple, Heavenly Rest Church, where Belle had worshiped since childhood.

Bernard Baruch refused to have the foundation named in his honor. Some felt he was annoyed that Belle had not consulted him about her plans, but then she thought she had time. Certainly she did not expect to predecease her father. He was also ninety-three years old and perhaps thought he had garnered sufficient honors for a lifetime. In the end all agreed to call it the Belle W. Baruch Foundation, which was considered even more appropriate because of Belle's reverence for the "land between the waters."

Belle bequeathed lifetime residency at Hobcaw House to her sister, Renee Baruch Samstag, as well as the income from a generous trust. Renee, stating that there were too many sad memories at Hobcaw, relinquished her life interest in the property to the trustees of the foundation.

Ella Severin was named a trustee of the foundation and was given lifetime residency at Bellefield Plantation in Belle's will. She was also given the income from a large trust, Belle's New York apartment, and other personal belongings.

Belle left numerous bequests totaling $153,000 to private individuals as well as to charitable and religious organizations in both New York and Georgetown, South Carolina. Belle's greatest legacy, Hobcaw Barony, was left to future generations of Americans.

APPENDIX

Hobcaw Barony Today

Hobcaw Barony today is much as Belle left it. The sandy, dusty roads wind through the forests and marshes, and much of the land that had been cultivated when she was a child has reverted to its natural state. White-tailed deer wander the woods, secure in their protected environment. Alligators snooze in the sun and squirrels perch in the trees, scolding the feral hogs that root below. Birdsong echoes through the woods, and the mystique of Hobcaw Barony is preserved for the ages.

Only remnants remain of the black villages—a few houses at Strawberry, more at Friendfield. The little church Bernard Baruch renovated at Friendfield is there, the pews silent and empty. Pa Moses's house, across the road from where Prince Jenkins grew up, is intact, its tin roof gleaming in the Carolina sun, its front porch sagging. Layers of fine dust coat the floor of the dispensary where the residents gathered each week for the doctor to treat their ailments.

Bellefield Plantation's stables are used infrequently, yet a few carriages and leather harnesses remind visitors of Belle's lifelong fascination with the equestrian world. The silver horseshoe engraved with the legend of Belle and Souriant's triumph at the Paris Horse Show is mounted at the entrance to Souriant's empty stall. The stable walls are lined with 171 of Belle's riding trophies.

Bellefield house itself seems to be waiting silently in the midst of its green carpet of grass. Belle's beloved wild turkeys strut across the lawn on the way to the pond. Most of the furnishings have been moved to Hobcaw House. The sunroom remains the heart of Belle's home, the scent of hundreds of winter fires lingering on the ballast bricks.

Ella Severin is gone now, having died in 2000 at the age of ninety-five. A trustee and director of long-range planning for the foundation, Severin shared Belle's love of the land and sense of commitment to future generations. It was Ella Severin who said to the other trustees in the 1960s: "Believe it or not, within twenty years Hobcaw Barony and Brookgreen Gardens will be like oases on the Waccamaw Neck." Severin's words were prophetic. Only those lands of the Waccamaw Neck in Georgetown County that were set aside by Belle Baruch and Archer M. Huntington are preserved for future generations.

Hobcaw House welcomes visitors with mementos of its historic past when presidents, prime ministers, film stars, and royalty enjoyed the legendary hospitality of Bernard Baruch. The vistas overlooking the bay and woods with their peace and quietude are unchanging.

As provided by Belle's will, the Belle W. Baruch Foundation makes the property available to researchers from all colleges and universities located in South Carolina and has formed long-term agreements with the University of South Carolina and Clemson University to carry out research and teaching programs. Two institutes have been formed: Clemson University's Belle W. Baruch Institute of Coastal Ecology and Forest Science was established in 1968 to conduct teaching and research in forestry, wildlife biology, and related sciences, and the University of South Carolina's Belle W. Baruch Institute of Marine and Coastal Sciences was established in 1969 to conduct teaching and research in the marine sciences and related fields.

As a natural laboratory, Hobcaw Barony is unsurpassed. There are maritime and upland forests, two miles of undeveloped beachfront, abandoned rice fields, cypress swamps, freshwater ponds, and nearly five thousand acres of salt marsh, all with different types of vegetation, supporting a variety of wildlife.

Thanks to the foresight and protection provided by Belle Baruch, the North Inlet estuary at Hobcaw Barony is considered one of the least disturbed and most understood estuaries in the world today. It was selected by the National Science Foundation as a long-term ecological research site and has been named a National Estuarine Research Reserve by NOAA.

The foundation has had to battle land developers to keep it so. With spirit Belle would have admired, the foundation has fought long, expensive, legal battles to prevent land developers from emptying drainage canals into the North Inlet estuary and to settle boundary disputes that encroach on the pristine property.

In 1978 the Kimbel Living and Learning Center was built just south of the main entrance and includes a conference center, three cottages, and three dormitories. Hurricane Hugo destroyed the USC Baruch Marine Field Laboratory in 1989. Undaunted, the marine scientists were back at work within days after the storm. After the initial shock of the devastation, Dennis Allen, resident director for the marine field laboratory, realized that the institute now had a rare opportunity to study the effects of a hurricane on the ecosystem of the North Inlet salt-marsh estuary. The laboratory was rebuilt and dedicated in 1993.

The researchers of the forests and wildlife are with the Institute of Coastal Ecology and Forest Science at Clemson University. Originally housed on the second floor of Hobcaw House, the institute inaugurated a new, independent facility near the entrance to the barony in 1990. Clemson is involved in research and teaching in the areas of forestry, wildlife, and the flora and fauna of the coastal region. They are deeply involved in land and forestry management and serve as consultants to area landowners, golf-course managers, and developers. Clemson has also established a long-term research program on the ecology and natural productivity of the forests of Hobcaw Barony.

Professor Gene Wood of Clemson, who did wildlife research at Hobcaw Barony for fifteen years and is now on the Clemson campus, said: "Hobcaw is the best area to do wildlife research that I have seen in North America. Its locale, protected environment, etc., are totally unique in terms of wildlife study."[1]

An overview by Wood of Hobcaw's forest wildlife estimates that 163 species of birds can be found in Hobcaw Barony's woods sometime during the year. Some live there year 'round, others winter there, still others stop to rest a brief time during their winter and spring migrations or come only for the mating season. Some, like the red-cockaded woodpecker, are on the federally endangered species list.

The ducks that made Hobcaw Barony one of the most famous hunting retreats in the world are no longer so abundant. Other than the placement of some wood-duck boxes, there is currently no extensive duck management program at Hobcaw Barony, but there is extensive waterfowl habitat management at nearby preserves. The Tom Yawkey Wildlife Center and the Santee Coastal Reserve are two state facilities that concentrate on attracting waterfowl.

Belle would be delighted at the success of the efforts to reintroduce her beloved wild turkeys to Hobcaw Barony. In 1976 five turkey hens and four gobblers were trapped in the Francis Marion National Forest by the South Carolina Wildlife and Marine Resources Department (now the S.C. Department of Natural Resources) and stocked on Hobcaw Barony. The foundation stocked more turkeys in the 1990s. By 2004 the turkey population was estimated at one thousand.

The feral hogs Belle hunted so assiduously continue to be a nuisance. A nonnative species, they were introduced to North America in the sixteenth century. They are prolific, have a negative impact on timber regeneration, and devour the eggs and offspring of ground-nesting birds and mammals. The foundation currently traps the feral swine to reduce the population on the Waccamaw Neck.

The deer herd has increased due to the pressure of development in the area. The numbers vary according to weather, disease, and habitat. If the population becomes too dense, the deer, like the hogs, undergo population management for the health of the herds. The shy, gentle creatures are used to humans now and seldom run far when people or their vehicles approach. Unfortunately this makes them vulnerable to the occasional poacher who manages to sneak onto the property through the inlets and marshes. The greatest threat to the wildlife is still man, just as pressures from nearby industry and development inflict the greatest damage to marine life in Hobcaw Barony's waters.

There are still foxes, raccoons, opossum, otter, and beaver as well as bobcats. A coyote population is now confirmed by staff, and a few black bears have been sighted as well.

The ubiquitous snakes of Hobcaw are as plentiful as ever. Canebrake and pygmy rattlers, cottonmouths and copperheads can be found as well as their nonvenomous counterparts, such as corn snakes, rat and king snakes.

Exhibits featuring Hobcaw Barony's history and ecology are available at the Hobcaw Barony Visitor Center, which opened in 1982. It is the primary contact for the general public since Hobcaw Barony is only open to the public through guided tours and special programs that require reservations. A variety of educational programs include classes in oystering and clamming, fishing, and lowcountry history. Field studies for schoolchildren focus on slavery, archaeology, and wildlife.

Hobcaw Barony, the directors of the foundation say, is unique in that it incorporates "all of the major temperate coastal habitats—tidal salt marsh, creeks, beaches, maritime forest, swamps, brackish marshes, old rice fields, and various upland habitats, creating the perfect outdoor laboratory."[2]

Visiting scientists come from all over the world, some to stay as long as a year, some to join in cooperative ecological studies between countries, others from throughout the United States who want the opportunity to work in the rare, natural "classrooms" of Hobcaw Barony. In 2004 the foundation celebrated forty years of conservation, research, and preservation.

The trustees and staff of the Belle W. Baruch Foundation and the researchers of the two Baruch institutes are grateful that Belle Baruch understood the true value of Hobcaw Barony. Because of her passionate love of the land, the lessons learned from the natural textbooks of the barony will guide us in protecting the environment and natural resources throughout the world for future generations.

NOTES

Although these notes reference some of the sources I have used, this biography would not have been possible without the generous cooperation of those, mentioned in the acknowledgments, who shared their memories, letters, memorabilia, and insights with me in numerous interviews. The text makes clear the value of their contribution to this volume.

Chapter 1—Paternal Pride and Future Hope

1. Barnett A. Elzas, *The Jews of South Carolina* (Philadelphia: J. B. Lippincott, 1905), 268–69.

2. Scrapbook, Belle W. Baruch Papers, Belle W. Baruch Foundation, Georgetown, S.C. (hereafter cited as BWB Papers).

3. Scrapbook, BWB Papers.

4. Scrapbook, BWB Papers.

5. Margaret Coit, *Mr. Baruch* (Cambridge: Riverside Press, 1957), 104.

Chapter 2—The Only Real Place on Earth

1. Suzanne Cameron Linder and Marta Leslie Thacker, *Historical Atlas of the Rice Plantations of Georgetown County and the Santee River* (Columbia: South Carolina Department of Archives and History for the Historic Ricefields Association, [2001?]), 3.

2. Ibid., 11.

3. Ibid.

4. Hobcaw guest book, Bernard M. Baruch Papers, Seeley G. Mudd Manuscript Library, Princeton, N.J. Used with permission of Princeton University Library. Hereafter cited as BMB Papers.

Chapter 3—Life Lessons at Hobcaw

1. *Georgetown Daily Item,* December 14, 1911.

2. *New York Herald,* December 30, 1911.

Chapter 4—A Study in Determination

1. Langdon Post to Bernard M. Baruch, May 4, 1964, BMB Papers.

2. Undated essay by Belle W. Baruch, BWB papers.

Chapter 5—From Debutante to the World Stage

1. Undated clipping in scrapbook, BWB Papers.

2. Oliver Daniel, *Stokowski: A Counterpoint of View* (New York: Dodd, Mead, 1981), 201.

3. Hobcaw guest book, BMB Papers.

4. Edith Bolling Wilson, *My Memoirs* (Indianapolis: Bobbs-Merrill, 1938), 353.

5. Gene Smith, *When the Cheering Stopped* (New York: William Morrow, 1964), 228–29.

6. Woodrow Wilson to Mrs. William Gorham Rice, November 18, 1923, Woodrow Wilson Papers, Library of Congress, Washington, D.C. (hereafter cited as Wilson Papers).

7. Belle W. Baurch to Bernard M. Baurch, September 1924, BMB Papers.

Chapter 6—Henry Ford and Anti-Semitism

1. Coit, *Mr. Baruch,* 361.

2. William C. Richards, *The Last Billionaire* (New York: Charles Scribner's Sons, 1948), 897.

Chapter 7—Resolution and Independence

1. November 24, 1919, entry, Hobcaw guest book, BMB Papers.

Chapter 8—Lois Massey

1. This chapter is largely based on the following interviews: Lois Massey, interview by author, tape recordings, Pawleys Island, S.C., November 27, 1987, and September 10, 1988, and oral-history interview, Belle W. Baruch Foundation, undated.

2. Alden Hatch, *Edith Bolling Wilson: First Lady Extraordinary* (New York: Dodd, Mead, 1961), 267.

Chapter 9—Travels with Edith Bolling Wilson

1. Kitty Carlisle Hart, *Kitty: An Autobiography* (New York: Doubleday, 1988), 85–86.

2. Hatch, *Edith Bolling Wilson,* 267.

Chapter 10—An Awakening

1. Abraham Chasins, *Leopold Stokowski: A Profile* (New York: Elsevier-Dutton, 1979), 154.

2. Evangeline Brewster Johnson to Edith Bolling Wilson, January 6, 1926, Wilson Papers.

3. Ibid.

Chapter 11—La Belle Équitation

1. Sir Alfred Munnings, *The Second Burst* (London: Museum Press, 1951), 105.

2. Katharine Dunlap, "'Trick' Jumping," *Horse and Horseman,* March 1938, 34–36.

3. Belle W. Baruch to Edith Wilson, October 1931, Wilson Papers.

Chapter 12—Success and Romance at Home and Abroad

1. Bernard M. Baruch, *Baruch: My Own Story* (New York: Henry Holt, 1948), 219.

2. Helen Lawrenson, *Stranger at the Party: A Memoir* (New York: Random House, 1975), 142.

3. William Manchester, *The Last Lion, Winston Spencer Churchill: Visions of Glory, 1874–1932* (Boston: Little, Brown, 1983), 826.

4. Baruch, *Baruch: My Own Story,* 246–47.

5. Edith Wilson to Bernard M. Baruch, February 9, 1931, Wilson Papers.

6. Clipping from unidentified New York newspaper, dated February 26, 1931, scrapbook, BWB Papers.

7. "High Intrigue Enmeshes Departing Envoy and Wife in International Drama," unidentified and undated newspaper clipping, scrapbook, BWB Papers.

8. Elizabeth Henney, "Former Minister of Rumania Back in Capital Setting Feminine Hearts Aflutter," *Washington Post,* September 29, 1941.

9. "Pau Fox Hunting Kept at High Level, Gives Fine Runs," *New York Herald* (Paris), March 11, 1931.

10. Belle W. Baruch to Bernard M. and Annie Baruch, April 16, 1931, BWB Papers.

11. "Belle Baruch of New York, Rides Souriant III to Victory over 118," *New York Herald* (Paris), April 12, 1931.

12. Belle W. Baruch to Bernard M. and Annie Baruch, April 12, 1931, BWB Papers.

13. Max E. Ammann, *Geschichte des Pferde-Sports* (Ittigen, Switzerland: C. J. Bucher, 1983).

14. Isabel Ross, *Power with Grace: The Life Story of Mrs. Woodrow Wilson* (New York: G. P. Putnam's Sons, 1938), 265.

Chapter 13—Triumphs with Souriant and Rumors of War

1. Ella Severin, interview by author, tape recording, Bellefield Plantation, S.C., February 10, 1988.

2. Munnings, *The Second Burst,* 331.

Chapter 14—European Friends and a Fleeting Betrothal

1. Belle W. Baruch to Bernard M. Baruch, August 7, 1934, BMB Papers.

2. Belle W. Baruch to Edith Bolling Wilson, August 14, 1934, Wilson Papers.

3. Munro Cuthbertson to Bernard M. Baruch, April 23, 1964, BMB Papers.

4. Belle W. Baruch to Bernard M. Baruch, August 24, 1934, BMB Papers.

Chapter 15—Bargaining for Bellefield

1. Belle W. Baruch to Lois Massey, May 27, 1935, copies of this and other letters to Lois Massey quoted in this book are in the author's collection.

2. Belle W. Baruch to Lois Massey, June 21, 1935.

3. Belle W. Baruch to Lois Massey, December 9, 1935.

4. Belle W. Baruch to Lois Massey, December 14, 1935.

5. Vincent J. Esposito, *A Concise History of World War II* (New York: Frederick A. Praeger, 1964), 9.

6. Jordan A. Schwarz, *The Speculator: Bernard M. Baruch in Washington, 1917–1965* (Chapel Hill: University of North Carolina Press, 1981), 342.

7. Bernard M. Baruch to Mary Boyle, December 1935, BMB Papers.

8. Undated newspaper clipping from the *Georgetown Times,* scrapbook, BWB Papers.

9. Julian Stevenson Bolick, *Ghosts from the Coast* (n.p., 1966), 76–81.

10. Bolick, *Ghosts from the Coast,* 82–83.

Chapter 16—Lois Massey and Prewar Europe

1. Esposito, *Concise History,* 20.

2. Lois Massey diary, April 24, 1937, copy in author's collection.

3. Lois Massey to her family, May 3, 1937.

4. Lois Massey to her sister, May 10, 1937.

5. Hart, *Kitty: An Autobiography,* 8.

Chapter 17—Varvara Hasselbalch's American Sojourn

1. Varvara Hasselbalch Heyd to Mary E. Miller, September 29, 1988, author's collection, Surfside Beach, S.C.

2. Ibid.

3. Ibid.

4. Ibid.

5. Ibid.

6. Francena McCants, interview by author, June 13, 1988.

7. Coit, *Mr. Baruch,* 457.

8. Heyd to Miller, September 29, 1988, author's collection.

Chapter 18—Life Stateside and War Abroad

1. Coit, *Mr. Baruch,* 469.

2. Schwarz, *The Speculator,* 9.

3. Christiane Darthez Daoudi to Mary E. Miller, October 26, 1988.

4. Belle W. Baruch Papers, Baruch Foundation.

5. Schwarz, *The Speculator,* 366.

6. Varvara Hasselbalch to Belle W. Baruch, April 18, 1940, BWB Papers.

Chapter 19—Personal and National Turmoil in 1941

1. Jim Bishop, *FDR's Last Year* (New York: William Morrow, 1974), 26.

2. Schwarz, *The Speculator,* 472.

3. Lillian Rogers Parks and Frances Spatz Leighton, *The Roosevelts: A Family in Turmoil* (Englewood Cliffs, N.J.: Prentice-Hall, 1981), 117.

4. Eleanor Roosevelt, "My Day," United Features Syndicate, March 26, 1941.

5. Schwarz, *The Speculator,* 422.

6. James Roosevelt, *My Parents: A Differing View* (Chicago: Playboy Press, 1976), 178.

7. Baruch, *Baruch: My Own Story,* 263–64.

8. Lois Massey, interview by author, tape recording, Pawleys Island, S.C., November 21, 1987.

Chapter 20—U-Boats and Spies along the Carolina Coast

1. Edwin P. Hoyt, *U-Boats: A Pictorial History* (New York: McGraw-Hill, 1987), 136.
2. Ibid.

Chapter 21—Dickie Leyland at Hobcaw Barony

1. Schwarz, *The Speculator,* 422.
2. Ibid., 473.

Chapter 22—FDR's Visit to South Carolina

1. Ted Morgan, *F.D.R.: A Biography* (New York: Simon and Schuster, 1985), 444.
2. Coit, *Mr. Baruch,* 642.
3. Baruch, *Baruch: My Own Story,* 244.
4. Bishop, *FDR's Last Year,* 26.
5. Lois Massey, interview by author, tape recording, Pawleys Island, S.C., November 21, 1987.
6. James Bessinger Sr., interview by author, tape recording, Georgetown, S.C., June 12, 1989.
7. Edwin M. Watson to Belle W. Baruch, May 24, 1944, Bellefield guest book, BWB Papers.
8. Roosevelt, *My Parents,* 178.
9. Schwarz, *The Speculator,* 569.

Chapter 23—War's End and the End of an Era

1. Lois Massey, interview by author, tape recording, Pawleys Island, S.C., March 26, 1989.
2. Belle W. Baruch to Lois Massey, July 12, 1945, Personal Papers of Lois Massey, Pawleys Island, S.C.

Chapter 24—Winds of Change in Postwar America

1. Minnie Kennedy, interview by author, May 9, 1991, Georgetown, S.C.
2. Belle W. Baruch to Bernard M. Baruch, May 16, 1949, BMB Papers.
3. Bernard M. Baruch to George Shubrick, May 18, 1949, BMB Papers.
4. Belle W. Baruch to Bernard M. Baruch, May 16, 1951, BMB Papers.
5. December 9, 1947, entry, Bellefield guest book, BWB Papers.

Chapter 25—Philanthropy and Ecology

1. James Bessinger Jr., interview by author, tape recording, Georgetown, S.C., April 17, 1989.
2. James Bessinger Sr., interview by author, tape recording, Georgetown, S.C., June 12, 1989.
3. Belle W. Baruch to Bernard M. Baruch, June 24, 1951, BMB Papers.

Chapter 26—From Constable to Baroness

1. Associated Press Release, June 21, 1951, New York, scrapbook, BWB Papers.
2. Belle W. Baruch to Bernard M. Baruch, June 26, 1953, BMB Papers.
3. Belle W. Baruch to Bernard M. Baruch, October 19, 1953, BMB Papers.

4. Cynthia Taylor, interview by author, tape recording, August 10, 1989, Murrells Inlet, S.C.

5. Cynthia Taylor, interview by author, tape recording, January 24, 1989, Murrells Inlet, S.C.

6. Elizabeth Navarro, interview by author, tape recording, August 22, 1988, Kingstree, S.C.

7. Belle W. Baruch to Edith Wilson, August 23, 1956, Wilson Papers.

Chapter 27—Paul Dollfus and Frances Milam

1. Paul Dollfus, Ella Severin, and Nolan Taylor, personal narrative and interviews by author, tape recordings, September 25, 1988, Millhouse France; June 1, 1988, Bellefield Plantation, S.C.; and June 24, 1989, Murrells Inlet, S.C., respectively.

Chapter 28—The Passing of Jean Darthez and Souriant III

1. Belle W. Baruch to Edith Bolling Wilson, August 23, 1956, Wilson Papers.

2. Belle W. Baruch to Bernard M. Baruch, January 10, 1957, BMB Papers.

3. Belle W. Baruch to Edith Bolling Wilson, January 3, 1957, Wilson Papers.

Chapter 29—Into the Twilight

1. Anne Johnston, interview by author, March 3, 1990, Hobcaw Barony.

2. Ella Severin, interview by author, tape recording, February 6, 1989, Bellefield Plantation, S.C.

3. Elizabeth Navarro, interview by author, tape recording, November 11, 1988, Kingstree, S.C.

4. Navarro interview, November 11, 1988.

5. Last Will and Testament of Belle W. Baruch, March 23, 1964, New York, N.Y.

Appendix

1. Gene Wood, interview by author, June 1, 1988, Hobcaw Barony.

2. Lee Brockington (senior interpreter), interview by author, October 19, 2004, Belle W. Baruch Foundation.

BIBLIOGRAPHY

Archival Resources

Belle W. Baruch Papers. Belle W. Baruch Foundation, Georgetown, S.C.

Bernard M. Baruch Papers. Seeley G. Mudd Manuscript Library, Princeton University, Princeton, N.J.

Woodrow Wilson Papers. Library of Congress, Washington, D.C.

Books and Articles

Ammann, Max E. *Geschichte des Pferde-Sports.* Ittigen, Switzerland: C. J. Bucher, 1983.

Baruch, Bernard M. *Baruch: My Own Story.* New York: Henry Holt, 1948.

———. *Baruch: The Public Years.* New York: Holt, Rinehart and Winston, 1960.

Bishop, Jim. "Dr. Simon Baruch Hailed as Rare Alien Jewel," King Features, 1959.

———. *FDR's Last Year: April 1944–April 1945.* New York: William Morrow, 1974.

Bolick, Julian Stevenson. *Ghosts from the Coast.* N.p., 1966.

Burns, James MacGregory. *Roosevelt: The Soldier of Freedom.* New York: Harcourt Brace Jovanovich, 1970.

Chasins, Abram. *Leopold Stokowski: A Profile.* New York: Elsevier-Dutton, 1979.

Coit, Margaret L. *Mr. Baruch.* Cambridge, Mass.: Riverside Press, 1957.

Colville, John. *Winston Churchill and His Inner Circle.* New York: Wyndham, 1981.

Cornaz, O., and P. Larregain. "Belle Baruch." *L'Année Hippique* 22 (1964): 42–43.

Daniel, Oliver. *Stokowski: A Counterpoint of View.* New York: Dodd, Mead, 1982.

Dunlap, Katharine. "'Trick' Jumping." *Horse and Horseman,* March 1938, 34–36.

Elzas, Barnett A. *The Jews of South Carolina.* Philadelphia: J. B. Lippincott, 1905.

Esposito, Vincent J. *A Concise History of World War II.* New York: Frederick A. Praeger, 1964.

Gilbert, Martin. *The Prophet of Truth, 1922–1939.* Vol. 5 of *The Official Biography of Winston Spencer Churchill.* Boston: Houghton Mifflin / William Heinemann, 1977.

Hart, Kitty Carlisle. *Kitty: An Autobiography.* New York: Doubleday, 1988.

Hatch, Alden. *Edith Bolling Wilson: First Lady Extraordinary.* New York: Dodd, Mead, 1961.

Hook, Lu. "A Quarter Century with the Baruchs." *Coastal Observer,* September 3, 1987.

Hoyt, Edwin P. *U-Boats: A Pictorial History.* New York: McGraw-Hill, 1987.

Lash, Joseph P. *Love, Eleanor: Eleanor Roosevelt and Her Friends.* Garden City, N.Y.: Doubleday, 1982.

Lawrenson, Helen. *Stranger at the Party: A Memoir.* New York: Random House, 1975.

Lee, Albert. *Henry Ford and the Jews.* New York: Stein and Day, 1945.

Manchester, William. *The Last Lion, Winston Spencer Churchill: Visions of Glory, 1874–1932.* Boston: Little, Brown, 1983.

Martin, Ralph G. *Henry and Clare: An Intimate Portrait of the Luces.* New York: G. P. Putnam's Sons, 1991.

Miller, Nathan. *F.D.R.: An Intimate History.* Garden City, N.Y.: Doubleday & Company, 1983.

Morgan, Ted. *F.D.R.: A Biography.* New York: Simon & Schuster, 1985.

Munnings, Sir Alfred. *The Second Burst.* London: Museum Press, 1951.

Nye, David E. *Henry Ford: "Ignorant Idealist."* Port Washington, N.Y. / London: National University Publications / Kennikat Press, 1979.

Parks, Lillian Rogers, and Frances Spatz Leighton. *The Roosevelts: A Family in Turmoil.* Englewood Cliffs, N.J.: Prentice Hall, 1981.

Richards, William C. *The Last Billionaire.* New York: Charles Scribner's Sons, 1948.

Rogers, George C., Jr. *The History of Georgetown County, South Carolina.* Columbia: University of South Carolina Press, 1970.

Roosevelt, Eleanor. *The Autobiography of Eleanor Roosevelt.* New York: Harper & Brothers, 1958.

———. "My Day." United Features Syndicate, March 26, 1941.

———. *This I Remember.* New York: Harper & Brothers, 1949.

Roosevelt, Elliott, and James Brough. *Mother R: Eleanor Roosevelt's Untold Story.* New York: G. P. Putnam's Sons, 1977.

Roosevelt, James, with Bill Libby. *My Parents: A Differing View.* Chicago: Playboy Press, 1976.

Ross, Isabel. *Power with Grace: The Life Story of Mrs. Woodrow Wilson.* New York: G. P. Putnam's Sons, 1975.

Schwarz, Jordan A. *The Speculator: Bernard M. Baruch in Washington, 1917–1965.* Chapel Hill: University of North Carolina Press, 1981.

Sheed, Wilfrid. *Clare Boothe Luce.* New York: E. P. Dutton, 1982.

Smith, Gene. *When the Cheering Stopped.* New York: William Morrow, 1964.

Sprague, Kurt. *The National Horse Show: A Centennial History.* New York: National Horse Show Foundation, 1985.

Wilson, Edith Bolling. *My Memoirs.* Indianapolis: Bobbs-Merrill, 1938.

INDEX

CPSIA information can be obtained
at www.ICGtesting.com
Printed in the USA
LVOW12s0350300317
529024LV00001B/9/P